Praise for *Crazy Time* by Abigail Trafford ...

"A witty and wise guide to surviving divorce. The people in this book—the hurt and the angry, the stunned and the disillusioned—come alive in such skillful brush strokes that you [come to] know them better than your own friends. This is a survival guide to put the rest of the genus to shame, a book not just for people divorcing but for people interested in marriage."

—*Washington Post*

"If divorce is the process of rebirthing ourselves, *Crazy Time* should be the kindly doctor's bedside manual. What Abigail Trafford has given us with *Crazy Time* is nothing less than a survival kit."

—*Los Angeles Herald Examiner*

"It is wonderful that such a badly needed book should be so well-written."

—M. Scott Peck, M.D., author of *The Road Less Traveled*

"Abigail Trafford conveys the absolutely accurate notion that ... the more we understand the 'crazy times,' the more likely we are to recover. Those who read this book will feel they came upon a wonderful friend and guide."

—Eda J. LeShan, author of *What's Going to Happen to Me?*
When Parents Separate and Divorce

Crazy Time

Crazy Time

SURVIVING DIVORCE
AND BUILDING A NEW LIFE

REVISED EDITION

Abigail Trafford

HarperPerennial
A Division of HarperCollinsPublishers

HarperCollins books may be purchased for educational, business, or sales promotional
use. For information please write: Special Markets Department, HarperCollins Pub-
lishers, Inc., 10 East 53rd Street, New York, NY 10022.

FIRST EDITION

Designed by George J. McKeon

Library of Congress Cataloging-in-Publication Data

Trafford, Abigail.
Crazy time : surviving divorce and building a new life / Abigail Trafford.—Rev. ed.
    p.   cm.
Includes bibliographical references (p.   ) and index.
ISBN 0-06-092309-1 (paper)
1. Divorce—United States—Psychological aspects. 2. Remarriage—United States—
Psychological aspects. I. Title.
HQ834. T7   1993
306.8'9—dc20   92-22252

95 96 ❖/RRD 10 9 8 7

For my two grandmothers:

ABIGAIL INGALLS SARD

ELIZABETH MEEKER TRAFFORD

one who was divorced and one who wasn't;

both knew much of life

and generously passed it on.

CONTENTS

Acknowledgments   xiii

Prologue   1

PART ONE CRISIS

1   Deadlock   17

2   Confrontation   36

3   Separation   50

PART TWO CRAZY TIME

4   On the Edge   63

5   Relief/Disbelief   81

6   Deep Shock   99

CONTENTS

7 Anger   112

8 Ambivalence   128

9 Depression   139

PART THREE RECOVERY

10 Emergence of Self   155

11 Public Divorce   167

12 Sex   187

13 Love   206

14 Remarriage/Redivorce   224

15 Married for Good   241

   Epilogue   265

   Selected Bibliography   273

   Index   277

ACKNOWLEDGMENTS

This book began on a damp March weekend more than ten years ago when my editor-to-be Robbin Reynolds unexpectedly arrived at the door. We had friends and family in common but it was soon clear that we shared something else more binding: the experience of divorce. In the end Robbin Reynolds was the godmother of *Crazy Time* as well as its editor. For this new edition, Peternelle van Arsdale picked up the editing reins and helped shape the revisions. My thanks go to them both and my agent Carl D. Brandt.

I also want to thank the many psychologists, psychiatrists, social workers and family counselors who have given their time and insight on the subject of marriage and divorce. I am especially grateful to the following therapists: B. Bradshaw Minturn, founding director of the Marriage and Family Institute in Washington, D.C.; Robert Kirsch of Bethesda, Maryland; Joan Berlin Kelly, co-director of the California Children of Divorce Project; Andrew J. Cherlin, professor of sociology, Johns Hopkins University; Jungian analyst Lawrence H. Staples, psychologist Martha Gross and social worker Irene Pollin of Washington, D.C. I would also like to thank Dr. Edward W. Beal, director of the Georgetown University School of Medicine Seminars on Divorce.

Many friends, relatives and colleagues have cheered me on and helped in different ways: Patricia Avery, Katrina McCormick Barnes, Candace Boyden, Annie Boyden, Perry Trafford Boyden, Elizabeth Reynolds Colt, Mary D. Edsall, Thomas Byrne Edsall, Murray Gart, Jean Gart, Janet Barnes Lawrence, Rebecca Lescaze, Delia Mares, Dennis Mullin, Gertrude M. Neff, Zipporah Raymond, Heddy Fairbank Reid, Thorburn Reid, Christian Robertson, Frances E. Storey, Bayard T. Storey, Mark Trafford Terry, James L. Terry, Maude Terry, Elizabeth Trafford, Perry Davis Trafford, Polly Trafford, Stella M. Trafford, William Bradford Trafford, Ann Waldron, Clare Whitfield.

Most of all, my thanks go to my daughters Abigail Trafford Brett and Victoria Trafford Brett, and to my husband, Donald L. Neff, whom I married after the book was published. (Abbie and Toria, adults now, belong to that first generation of children who grew up in the divorce revolution when the rate of marriage breakups in the U.S. hit an all-time high. They read chapters and made suggestions in the original text and reviewed revisions for this new edition. From the beginning, Don Neff was the mainstay of the project. He read every word of each draft and significantly improved the final product.)

Finally, I want to thank the men and women who shared their stories for the book, who talked honestly and bravely about their lives, laying bare the most painful secrets. It is through these men and women that the stages of divorce take shape on the following pages. Although they remain nameless to preserve their privacy, each one has my respect and profound appreciation.

Crazy Time

PROLOGUE

It's been nearly twenty years since my marriage cracked open on a gray Christmas afternoon. The confrontation scene began, typically, over something inconsequential—in this case, a case of grapefruit, a present from friends in Texas, where we had been living before moving to Washington, D.C. That night, we raged at each other like tormented animals, filled our glasses again and bellowed into the dawn, stripping away a past of deception and pain. The next morning, the house was quiet. My husband had left early for work. The children were upstairs in their room, playing with new toys. I was downstairs, so devastated that I could only whisper to myself. That afternoon I decided to visit my parents in Boston—just a weekend to think things over, I said. In retrospect the marriage was finished. I was on my way to divorce.

There is nothing easy about divorce. It is a savage emotional journey. You don't know where it ends for a long time. You ricochet between the failure of the past and the uncertainty of the future. You struggle to understand what went wrong with your marriage,

1

to apportion the blame and inventory your emotional resources. There's one thing you are sure of almost immediately: You know that life will never be the same again. "Divorce is a death," says counselor Sharon Baker of the Los Angeles Divorce Warm Line. "Divorce is the death of a relationship. It is the death of your dreams. You have to start all over."

Which means divorce is also a beginning. From the moment you confront your spouse—or are confronted—with the breakdown of the marriage, you reset the clock of your life. Whatever the circumstances, you start a new era for yourself, your children, your friends and your colleagues.

Most people go a little crazy when their marriage cracks open. You are rarely prepared for the practical or emotional turmoil that lies ahead. You swing between euphoria, violent rage and depression. You may search frenetically for a new mate or you go the other way and withdraw from people and not answer the phone. Health statistics tell you that you're prone to getting sick and having car accidents. Reports of triangle assaults and murders of estranged spouses make regular newspaper headlines. In the dark hours of loneliness, you think about suicide. At some point, almost everyone coming out of a marriage mutters to what was once the other half: "I could kill you."

You soon discover that cutting the legal bond with your ex-spouse is a relatively small part of the whole divorce experience. Even though the law says your marriage is finished and you've divided up the pots and pans, the memories and the friends ... still it's not over.

You get frightened. What if you never pull out of this?

It's been ten years since America woke up to the startling statistic that nearly one out of two marriages will ultimately break up. Divorce rates have been rising steadily throughout this century but went into a temporary retreat during the post–World War II era that produced the baby boom generation. Then in the mid-sixties, the divorce rate started to rise again; by 1980, the rate had doubled. Since then, it has stabilized, even declined slightly—but still remains high as the nation heads into the twenty-first century. Of the roughly 2.5 million couples who get married every year, half are expected to break up at some point in their lives.

The culture of divorce has changed, too. Ten years ago, it was almost trendy to break up. From what you saw on television and read in newspapers, you'd have thought that getting a divorce was some yellow brick road to personal growth and happiness; all those stories of personal freedom, the joys of being single, the good sex out there. Remember the Me messages of the eighties: If it feels good, do it—if it doesn't feel good, dump it.

But ask anyone who's been through a divorce. When the first edition of *Crazy Time* came out in 1982, it splashed cold water over the comfortable idea that breaking up a marriage is just a blip on the radar screen of personal growth and self-fulfillment.

Now the public pendulum on divorce is swinging the other way. From what you see on television and read in the papers, you'd think that getting a divorce is a one-way ticket to an unmarried wasteland of poverty, broken dreams and loneliness. You don't have to watch *The War of the Roses* to know, as the lawyer in the film says: "There's no such thing as a civilized divorce."

But this bleak, negative image of divorce is just as misleading as the earlier feel-good view. As Jungian analyst Lawrence H. Staples of Washington, D.C., explains: "Divorce is always experienced as a failure. It threatens a person's self-image of being good, being loved, being valued." But, he adds, it is out of failure that a person often finds the inner strength to attain major achievements in life. "A lot of people make a big contribution to society out of their own suffering," he says. "A crisis forces change." Often that is for the better.

You gather up your kids to watch a rerun of the movie *E.T.* There's Single Mom, with three kids, an extraterrestrial tenant, an ex-husband in Mexico vacationing with a girlfriend. But divorce is not the focus of this tender science fiction fantasy. For scriptwriters and moviegoers alike, a single parent in the divorce-extended family is simply no big deal.

Divorce, it seems, is all around you. Even in the White House. Former president Ronald Reagan had been divorced, with a set of children from each marriage. For the electorate, his divorce from actress Jane Wyman years before was also no big deal.

You turn on the radio and hear the country music classic "D-I-V-O-R-C-E." Whatever happened to the traditional love songs like "I Can't Give You Anything But Love" and "Someone to Watch Over Me"? Now the themes of love have changed from the sixties' "Chains, My Baby's Got Me Locked Up in Chains" to Madonna's dictum of "Express Yourself" for the nineties: "Don't go for second best, baby/Put your love to the test."

Divorce, of course, has always been a prerogative of the very rich—and a phenomenon of the very poor. As a childhood friend of my mother's once explained: "People your age think that divorce is something new. Virtually all my school friends' parents had been divorced. True, my schoolmates were mostly affluent. Divorce hadn't hit the small towns in my childhood, I'm sure, but I know it has now."

What's significant today is that everybody can play Rockefeller and get divorced. It is no longer an aberration for the mainstream middle class to break up a marriage. Divorce has entered the realm of normalcy, taking its place next to birth, marriage and death as a basic cultural milestone. The redistribution of wealth and class in the last forty years that has given middle America microwave ovens, compact disks and heart transplants has also given middle America the moral and economic sanction of divorce.

As a result, the old myths and manners of marriage are gone. In their place are new rules for coupling and uncoupling. Interestingly, the option of divorce has led to higher expectations for marriage. In recent years, family therapists have become more sophisticated in recognizing early danger signs and in helping couples through certain kinds of crises. Americans seem to be more willing to work on a troubled relationship and more likely to get counseling than they were a decade ago. Then too, economic hardship and the spreading AIDS epidemic have undermined the appeal of singlehood. This in turn has helped strengthen people's commitment to marriage.

In this new era, the most satisfactory marriages are based on egalitarian relationships where there is a balance of power between husband and wife. This trend toward equality between the sexes has accelerated from the bedroom to the boardroom. Women are now much more likely to work, even when they have small children. Roughly two-thirds of women with children hold jobs outside the home. With the erosion of wages over the past decade, many families depend on two incomes to maintain a middle-class lifestyle. The increased economic independence of women gives them more power in the family and puts more pressure on the marriage to be mutually satisfying. It also makes breaking up easier if the marriage is not working—since both partners have the potential of being economically self-sufficient.

With these profound social changes, there's no going back to the fifties father-knows-best, go-along-to-get-along marriage. The high divorce rate reflects the tenet of rugged individualism that is a particularily American characteristic. Barring a major shift in values in the United States, family researchers do not expect a significant change in the divorce rate. For all the emotional trauma of divorce and financial hardship that follows a marriage breakup, most men and women come to the decision of divorce with the expectation that it will eventually lead to a more satisfying life. As Madonna sings for her generation: "You deserve the best in life/So if the time isn't right then move on/Second best is never enough/You'll do much better baby on your own/Baby on your own/So don't go for second best baby/Put your love to the test."

But what about the children? If present trends continue, nearly half of American children will spend some time in single-parent households. Research in the last decade has documented the high price of divorce on children who go through their own Crazy Time. A separation may bring much needed relief to one or both partners in a marrriage but can have the opposite effect on children who are often unprepared for the breakup. At the same time, research also shows that preserving a conflict-ridden marriage "for the sake of the children" can cause as much or more damage to the children as well as to the parents. "What really hurts kids is conflict," says Andrew J. Cherlin, professor of sociology at Johns

Hopkins University. "Continuimg conflict really hurts children."

So, how bad do you think your marriage really is? Bad enough? Do you have a choice in whether you break up or stay together? And if you end the marriage, do you think you will end the conflict with your spouse?

Of course, raising children as a single parent—or a stepparent—is nothing new. In fact, the percentage of children in single and "blended" families is about the same as it was in past centuries. In those days, however, the major cause of broken families was not divorce, but death. How well children fare has a lot to do with how well you fare in your post-divorce life.

Divorce, moreover, is not a permanent state. It is a transition to singlehood, recoupling or remarriage. Whether you mate again or stay single, you have to get beyond your divorce in order to build a new life. Most people eventually form new family units. About three out of four Americans who get divorced remarry, usually within three years. Many others form alliances with friends or lovers or colleagues or neighbors. In the process, you create a whole new web of kinship beyond tradition and biology. The American nuclear family, consisting of mother-father-sister-brother, has given way to the extended divorce family of mother-stepfather-former wife, their children, her children, their father-stepmother-former husband, their children, their stepmother, companions, friends, housemates . . . not to mention uncles, aunts, cousins and grandparents from the traditional extended family.

You start to wonder what's "normal" these days. With life expectancy of about seventy-five years for both men and women, "till death do us part" is a commitment more and more people find they cannot and—more interestingly—do not want to keep. "Longevity puts a real burden on couples," says Staples. "Farmers have always known that if you plough the same field year after year, the field loses its power and strength. This is what happens to people in burnout. It's the same in marriages."

Unless you change.

What goes around comes around. You can't escape it. At work you hear a story: A man comes home and his wife says she's leaving,

leaving him and the children and the house and the dog. Bang—it's all over. Then the house down the street goes up for sale. It turns out *he's* living with someone downtown and *she's* taking the children back to her parents in Michigan. Poof—the family is gone.

You pick up the newspaper: Woody Allen and Mia Farrow . . . Congressman "Pete" Stark, Senators Strom Thurmond, Bob Packwood . . . Palm Beach socialite Roxanne Pulitzer . . . boxing champions Sugar Ray Leonard and Evander Holyfield . . . Redskins football star John Riggins . . . songwriting duo Carole Bayer Sager and Burt Bacharach . . . real estate prince Donald Trump . . . "Prairie Home Companion" writer Garrison Keillor . . . sex researchers Masters and Johnson . . . actor Nick Nolte . . . Next it's Santa Claus, you think.

Then it happens to you.

Look around.

Every day, people are lining up at bars, employment bureaus, mental health clinics, gymnasiums, diet centers, travel agencies, budget seminars and marriage counseling institutions to ease their way through the various passages of the marriage crisis.

Breaking up a marriage may be as common as Main Street nowadays, but when *you* finally do it, the psychological experience seems as uncharted as the dark side of the moon.

The terrible morning after my own confrontation scene, my friend Heddy happened to stop by and found me in the shower. I had been in there so long trying to wash away the pain that my flesh was scorched red and my skin was as shriveled as a turkey's neck. Heddy, my college roommate, would be the friend who stood by me through the divorce. You need a friend when marriage ends. You can always find a good lawyer or family counselor, but it is a friend who bears witness to your struggle—and puts the marriage crisis into the larger context of your life.

I was overwhelmed and totally unprepared for what followed. There was no Dr. Spock for getting divorced; no helpful guidelines on adult equivalents of bed-wetting and thumb-sucking; no official protocols for dividing assets or memories; no training manuals on how to decipher the past and build up new emotional skills.

At first I felt like Alice in the wrong Wonderland; I'd eaten this mushroom by mistake. My world was turned upside down. I wanted to protest to the management, I wanted to throw up, get a doctor, drink a magic potion—anything to get back on track, to get back to a universe where things go right, to get back to my dream of falling in love, getting married and living happily ever after. But the mushroom of reality stuck in my throat. Indeed, I began to realize it had been a dream—not reality—I was trying to live.

When I got back from visiting my parents, it was cold in the house and the rooms seemed hollow. My six-year-old daughter refused to say her prayers. The sink in the kitchen stopped up. I knew I had been unhappy in the marriage for a number of years—getting sick those times, repressing relief when my husband had to go away on business, wanting someone else. When we finally confronted each other, the betrayals were too deep on both sides. We had stunned each other by our double lives. The wedding pictures hung in the hall, but we had both "left" each other in a basic way long ago.

And then again, we hadn't. That was the agony of it. Somehow we were still glued to each other. It wasn't just the children whom we both adored and in whom we would be forever linked. We still wanted something from each other. We had started out so much in love. That's what everybody said. Ours was a beautiful wedding on an island in Maine, with bridesmaids in straw hats and the blessing of Great-grandmother's veil. "I have just one piece of advice that my mother-in-law gave me," said my Aunt Melinda on the eve of the wedding: "Never go to sleep on a grudge."

Alone now, I hated the king-size bed and got rid of it. I put away the wedding pictures and took off my ring. The children wanted a puppy. I told them I couldn't handle it right now. The house was always cold. We lived on eggs and granola. At night in bed came the pain in my chest. As I lay there, awake and afraid, my mind racing over the past and back to the future, I tried to bring logic to my despair. In the end, I was haunted by three disturbing thoughts that wouldn't go away: I didn't really know the person I was married to for twelve years; I wasn't too sure what kind of person I was; and I certainly didn't like myself or some of the things I had done.

Most of all, I realized that the official issues that broke us up were not the real ones. Something else was at work, something deeper that neither one of us was able to explain. It was tantalizing, this chimera, this hint that understanding was there somewhere. I felt that if I could just understand what it was—this mysterious something that had come between us—I would not only understand what had gone wrong in the marriage; I could get over the marriage and on to a new life. I also sensed that this mysterious something might be a key to why relationships generally don't work—and why they do.

Ultimately, these questions led to my writing this book. After my own confrontation scene, I entered the limbo of separation and joined the singles' world. Everywhere I turned, I saw relationships ending and new ones beginning. I watched people grope through the lonely nights and bleak days. I listened to their stories and saw how their lives changed—for better and for worse. Patterns began to emerge. The details were always different, but I began to recognize a sameness in the stories.

My search took me across the country. Everywhere I went, I heard: "Let me tell you what happened to me; you'll never believe this. . . . Do you find that this happens to other people too? . . . I don't know why it was so bad. . . . Even now, when we have to talk on the phone, I start screaming. . . . It was the most painful experience of my life—and I was the one who wanted the divorce. . . . You know, we still call each other on our birthdays; my new husband/wife can't understand it. . . ."

Every time the subject of a book on marriage and divorce came up, I found the conversation around me grew louder. It seemed everybody had a story that had to be told. In the end, I interviewed hundreds of men and women. The majority belonged to the middle and upper-middle class. They were doctors and lawyers, ministers, engineers, nurses, diplomats, office workers, teachers, business executives and entrepreneurs. Most of the women held jobs or went to work as a result of the breakup. Just about all the couples had children and had been married at least ten years. They ranged in age from twenty-five to about fifty-five years old. A significant number were remarried with stepfamilies. Sometimes I talked to them right after the separation scene; sometimes many years after they had put the divorce in perspective.

Slowly, from their stories, I began to piece together the give-away danger signs in a relationship and what seem to be the common phases of divorce. The countdown to crisis usually begins earlier than you think—and the buildup to the confrontation scene can take years. Most couples that break up—or at least one half of the couples—undergo intense pain for a year or more beforehand. Then follows the critical stage in the emotional divorce process: Crazy Time. Most people become very disoriented when a marriage ends, and this crazy period lasts about a year, sometimes two years.

The next phase is the recovery period. It's the time when you rebuild your life. You reestablish yourself on the job, you make new friends, you redefine your relationship with your children. This is a gradual process, with stops and starts. For many people, an essential part of the recovery period is falling in love and getting involved in new relationships. This phase usually takes three to five years.

After talking to many people and sharing their experiences, I was reassured that the confusion and craziness I'd gone through myself is "normal." I learned that people who don't get angry are the ones in real trouble; that depression is part of grieving for the past and a dating phase is part of building for the future. I also came to realize that the moment of truth in divorce often comes when you try again in a new relationship.

Some people don't make it. They may get divorced legally—but not psychologically. They are Divorce Flameouts. Like test pilots who get lost in the clouds or fly too close to the horizon, they flame out and crash. Nothing rises up out of the ashes. If you don't navigate successfully through the predictable emotional passages after a marriage ends, you risk flaming out emotionally. You crash into bitterness or get swept up in violence. You see examples all the time in the newspaper:

Atlanta—A millionaire has been charged with arranging to have a rose-bearing gunman kill his estranged wife, authorities said. [The wife] was killed in the foyer of her Atlanta townhouse, hours before a scheduled hearing in the couple's divorce. . . .
(*Washington Post*, January 12, 1992)

Yet despite the pain of divorce, the message of this book is one of hope. Most people can and do adjust to divorce and reestablish themselves in a new life. Most children also adjust to the pain and dislocation of their parents' breakup. In time you look back on your separation and divorce as a devastating but necessary transition in your life. You are forced to learn a few things about emotional warfare and yourself if you are going to survive. Says a woman, forty-two, with three children: "I feel I've been tested in a basic way now. I made it. I don't have to take shit from anyone again." A man, fifty-two, says: "I was furious at the divorce, but now, looking back, I'd say it was a good thing."

I feel the same way. After watching divorce alter the social landscape over the past decade and talking to groups of separated and divorced people, I am convinced that in most cases, divorce has the potential of freeing couples from destructive relationships. It also has a galvanizing effect on individuals to become more self-sufficient and creative—and in the long run, more knowledgeable about themselves, more loving and generous to others.

Perhaps because breaking up a marriage is so traumatic and the suffering lasts for such a long time, you are forced to find strengths and talents that never would have emerged without such a catastrophic crisis. "Almost all growth takes place in the imperative of unhappiness," says clinical psychologist Augustus Y. Napier, director of the Family Workshop in Atlanta. "People have a powerful drive to grow, to break out of the impasse, to live."

It took me a long time to get divorced emotionally—several years of intense desperation in the marriage, a year of total chaos after the separation, and then several years of fundamental rebuilding, with periodic dips back into chaos. I had to start from scratch to establish a new life vis-à-vis children, work, friends, family, sex, love, remating—not to mention coming to terms with my own psyche and learning how to deal with my ex-spouse.

The children and I made it through the bad years. We survived the winter the furnace died and I had to get a home improvement loan at 18 percent interest. We rented out rooms to make ends meet. I threw new-found energy into my job and went regularly to group therapy. The children learned to spell and skate. We painted the living room and listened to the music of Little Feet. In time, there were parties and laughter again. Finally I was strong enough to add a puppy to the household—a honey-colored cocker spaniel. We named him Leggo, after my older daughter's English teacher. The children saw their father regularly and often. He and I didn't yell at each other so much anymore. Leggo learned not to jump up on people. The younger daughter got the lead of Buttercup in her school's production of the musical *H.M.S. Pinafore*. I got a promotion at work. When the bank sent a notice that the home-improvement loan was paid off, seven years had passed since the breakup. It had snuck up on me. My divorce was over.

Nearly fifteen years after the confrontation scene, I stood in front of the fireplace. Next to me was a man with glasses and a special laugh. He had been coming to the house even before we got Leggo. And when the children went away to school, he took over the care of this aging eccentric dog that had become the mascot of our family. It was time. We knew each other well by now. I wanted to get married and so did he. My two daughters, grown women in their twenties, were by my side. The room was crowded: his family, my family—old friends like Heddy who had been bridesmaids at my first wedding; new friends from work and my long period of singlehood; his friends from the journalistic

12

kinship of foreign correspondents; my daughters' friends. My cousin sat down at the piano and the singing started. *We gather together.* . . . The red-headed minister in flowing black robes began the marriage vows.

Another Christmas: Sunlight pours in through the windows. The man beside me laughs and puts on his glasses. We light a fire. We have a new snow village on the mantelpiece. And a new dog. Leggo died of old age, and now the role of family mascot has been filled by a bounding yellow lab named Sulie. The girls are home for the holidays. One daughter is about to graduate from college; the other is working in a far-off city.

What is most different about my first and second marriages is not the husband—though they are very different—it is me.

Robert Kirsch, clinical psychologist in Bethesda, Maryland, puts it this way: "Divorce often forces people to grow up. You get over your divorce by confronting the kind of relationship there was in the marriage. You realize there aren't any victims. You recognize your own complicity in the breakup. Then you learn how to carry on a relationship that works. You can't do this intellectually; you learn through experience."

In time, you begin to discover how many people have gone through a divorce—and not only survived but flourished.

For all those who are now in the midst of a marriage crisis and are thinking about divorce, the following pages describe what getting a good emotional divorce involves. Whether you end up getting divorced or staying together, you have to go through this process of divorcing the old marriage and starting over. There are no shortcuts in this journey.

The job of a journalist is to listen and to make sense of what is heard. The stories speak for themselves. All the names have been changed, as have identifying details, to provide anonymity; the quotes and plot lines remain intact. Some of you will protest: *That's not the way it was for me.* You're right. People don't always fit neatly into categories and stages. In the end, everyone writes his or her own script.

But where do you start? Do you understand what lies ahead?

These stories show how others have made the painful emotional journey of divorce. They have some things to tell you. It's not going to be easy, but you have a chance. The Chinese word for crisis combines the characters for danger and opportunity. In our country, that's the definition of divorce.

PART ONE

CRISIS

Should I, after tea and cakes and ices,
Have the strength to force the moment to its crisis?

T. S. Eliot, "The Love Song of J. Alfred Prufrock"

She picked up her glove and hit his cheek with it,
but so lightly he did not even blink.
"I despise you," she said.
"Quite," said Mr. Mackenzie.

Jean Rhys, *After Leaving Mr. Mackenzie*

1

DEADLOCK

People will ask you: *I didn't know you were having trouble. What went wrong?* You already know the easy answers—they were in the script of the confrontation scene. Then some of your friends say: *I never liked the bitch/bastard you were married to anyway.* You wonder if they know something you never knew. Then you go over the confrontation script again, refining your grievances, sharpening the battles. The main thing is to get this over with and get on with life. You roll the breakup scene around in your mind for a few nights. Your emotional editing process gets to work. You put the story through your memory a couple of times. It's finished, you think. The marriage is dead.

And then the ghosts start dancing on your bed at night. You shut your eyes tight. They stomp louder, laughing. These ghosts, they nag, they question, they taunt, they blast holes in your version. You run from them. You refuse to speak to your ex. You only communicate through lawyers now. The ghosts keep boogying, jeering. You fight over the house, over child support. The ghosts are clapping. You fight about custody, visitation rights. The

17

ghosts are cheering. You get frightened. You thought you had it all figured out. Life is full of beginnings and endings, you tell yourself. After all, more than a million couples get divorced every year. But you had forgotten about the bad ghosts that go dancing in the night.

What was your marriage really like?

You have to stop a minute. *When did it start?* You don't have a lot of time to think just now, with all the new things you have to do—figuring out how to pay the electricity bill, explaining to your mother, hugging your children. But in that spare moment when the house is quiet and your anxiety dulled, you start wondering about what really went on in your marriage. You have to confront those dancing ghosts. Because that's the only way you're going to get through your divorce. Otherwise, you carry the ghosts with you forever.

It begins the day you walk down the aisle, your fears and hopes buried in the rituals of getting married. The wedding march, the ring, the flowers; church and state smiling down on you, the in-laws cautious. Wait. Here comes the bride. A long white satin gown, the distant veil. But something's amiss—an omen. The minister notices first: the bride's wearing red shoes! Her grandmother gasps. The ring bearer giggles. The groom is anxious. *For better or for worse.* You pledge your life to another. Flashbulbs, the rice raining down on you. Someone is crying. Where's the cake? The ushers are laughing. The bridesmaids are dancing. More champagne. *Till death do us part.*

Most people have the dream of falling in love, getting married and living happily ever after. So you barely notice on your wedding day that your future partner wants to live on a houseboat and inclines to believing in the Moral Majority; you don't think about the fact that your mother-in-law is a bitch and wants to move next door. You block out of your mind that maybe you'd like to go to law school in the fall. It's only later that you remember these things—much later, when the dream and the marriage are in shambles.

The time bomb for crisis is set early, often as soon as two people meet. You marry for all the obvious reasons—you look to your partner for stability, warmth, ambition, sensitivity, success, money, mystery. You often marry to complete yourself, ascribing to your partner magical properties that he/she may or may not have. Like a homing pigeon, you marry the very qualities you don't think you have but want to acquire. "Nature leads us to fall in love. It gets us in touch with what we don't have," says Washington, D.C., Jungian analyst Lawrence Staples.

It is here, in the twilight zone of your emotions, that you make the psychological contract of wedlock. You're not aware of it at the time, but in return for those magical properties you need so much, you make the basic marriage bargain with your spouse. The French say there is always one who kisses and one who is kissed. It's a crude generalization, of course, but in general terms it does seem to work out that in the subconscious wedlock contract, one of you takes the dominant position in the marriage and is the "kisser"; the other the submissive role and is the "kissee." One of you assumes responsibility for controlling the course of married life. The other agrees to be pleasing and supportive, the dream partner who fulfills the common wish of the marriage. One of you is the initiator, the pursuer, the seducer. The other is the passive one, swept up by the dominant one. This is the wedlock contract when you start out. The power balance reflects the psychological dynamics between you when the marriage begins.

But as James Taylor reminds you in "It Used to Be Her Town Too": "Nothing lasts forever."

Francesca Livoti is Italian-American, dark and beautiful, from New York City. She once had a small part in a Broadway show. For a while she lived with a British architect. Bill Taylor is an all-American boy from Dayton, Ohio, who has never been out of the country. They meet in his hometown, where she has a job with a radio station. He is going to night school to learn engineering. His people are farmers. His arms seem too long and he's shy. Francesca is six years older. She meets him in a furniture store. A few days later she calls him up. It's not long before she seduces him. To Bill she's the most exciting person he's ever known. He falls deeply in love. They marry. The bargain: She gives him the worldliness and adventure he seeks; he promises her the small-town American security she desires. The wedlock contract: She's dominant—after all, she knows more when they start out; he's submissive—he owes her for opening the door to adventure.

In time, he becomes an aeronautical engineer. They move to California, where he gets a job with an aerospace company. There are overseas assignments: Japan, Germany, Saudi Arabia. He becomes vice-president in charge of government contracts. It's an expense account life: the Asian ruins of Angkor Wat and the Mozart festival in Salzburg. She raises dogs and dreams of a farm in Ohio. He wonders: What happened to that worldly woman with adventurous eyes? She wonders: What happened to that shy farmboy? One day he buys a car without consulting her; then he announces they are moving to New York. She is outraged. How could he do this without asking her first? He smashes a glass in the fireplace and spends the next weekend with another woman. She stays at home and develops a bad back. Who's dominant now? The marriage bargain is betrayed, the wedlock contract broken.

The man is submissive on the way to independence; the woman is dominant on the way to dependence. They each marry the person they want to be. But instead of renegotiating their basic marriage contract as they both changed, they remained trapped in their original dominant-submissive relationship. Instead of a wedlock contract, they have a Deadlock contract in which they are stuck in unequal and opposing roles. As a result, they are not able to negotiate what they need or want in the marriage. She behaves like an aggrieved mother; he like a rebellious child. In this case they break out of Deadlock by breaking up the marriage.

Think back: Who wielded the psychological big stick in your marriage? When you first met, were you the kisser? Or the one who was kissed? As the ghosts dance gleefully around your head, you want to know: *When did it start?* You stare at the ghosts. To more and more family therapists, the genesis of divorce is rooted in the original wedlock contract couples make when they get married.

What attracted you to your spouse? Were you very young? Did you need someone to give you what you didn't get from your parents?

"A lot of people have very low self-esteem when they get married," says Suzanne Keller, professor of sociology at Princeton University. "That means you are going to put a lot on the other person to make the world right for you."

The more you need your spouse to "make the world right for you," as you get deeper into the wedlock contract, the more you will be willing to accept emotional inequality in the relationship.

Most marriages start out on an unequal basis. Perhaps you are five years older than your spouse and you just know more when you get married. So you take the dominant role. Or you are the youngest child and are used to older siblings telling you what to do. You take the submissive role—at first. In time, both partners change and grow; if the marriage is to work, the original wedlock contract must be renegotiated. Sometimes you have to be dominant, other times submissive; your relationship is a seesaw of psychological power. "Equality comes down to a sense of justice, a sense of fairness," says Atlanta psychologist Augustus Napier. "Marriage can only be deeply satisfying if it's a fair, just relationship and each one is treated with respect and has degrees of autonomy."

In marriages that run amok, the seesaw of psychological power often gets stuck, with one end up and one end down. One of you takes the dominant role *all the time* and is on top; the other remains in the submissive role *all the time* and is kept down on the bottom. Now the psychological dynamics of the relationship are frozen. You're in trouble. The seesaw doesn't budge. You are both trapped in unequal—and opposing—roles. At this point, the original wedlock contract becomes the marriage Deadlock contract.

You can muddle through for a while in Deadlock—and many

couples endure for years under such a regime. In these cases, there is enough fulfillment elsewhere that makes up for the Deadlock union between spouses. Then there's a triggering event: you fall in love, a child dies, you get a new assignment at work, you move to a new city, or you simply look at yourself in the mirror. What do you see? You turn to your marriage. What are you getting out of the relationship? More unsettling, what is the marriage taking out of you? You are keenly aware that the social and economic glue that used to keep marriages together is largely gone. Today, you stay in a marriage because of the relationship you have with your spouse. Well, what kind of relationship do you have? Look at the ghosts.

"I'm quite sure that without equality in a relationship, there can be no wanting of each other, no tenderness or respect," says Bethesda psychologist Robert Kirsch. "Sex goes to hell. It's only a matter of time before a couple reaches a crisis in the marriage."

But he adds emphatically: "It is possible to have a truly equal relationship. That's the only way people can get what they want in our culture. Most people can be passive or dominant in a relationship. One person's submissive partner can be another person's dominant partner. Equality in a relationship means switching roles back and forth—being dominant some of the time and submissive at other times.

"When couples come into my office in a state of crisis, I can usually find out how they got to this stage by looking at who is dominant in the relationship and who is passive and submissive. The dominant-submissive imbalance then becomes the focus of therapy. If two people are going to get back together, they have to bring equality into their relationship."

In *The Art of Loving*, Erich Fromm describes the dominant-submissive Deadlock relationship as a *symbiotic union*, the psychic equivalent of a pregnant mother and her fetus. "The *passive* form of the symbiotic union is that of submission," he writes. "The . . . person escapes from the unbearable feeling of isolation and separateness by making himself part and parcel of another person who directs him, guides him, protects him; who is his life and his oxygen. . . . The . . . person does not have to make decisions, does not have to take any risks; he has no integrity; he is not yet fully born. . . .

"The *active* form of symbiotic fusion is domination. . . . The . . . person wants to escape from his aloneness and his sense of imprisonment by making another person part and parcel of himself. He inflates and enhances himself by incorporating another person, who worships him."

In Deadlock marriages, the power balance between husband and wife mimics the psychological dynamics between parent and child, lord and vassal, lady and servant, overdog and underdog, oppressor and oppressed.

There are telltale signs of couples trapped in Deadlock. Look around you. What about your parents' marriage? "You can tell who's dominant by seeing who's afraid of whom," says Kirsch. "'He/she won't let me smoke indoors . . . play the piano . . . work late'—that's the submissive one talking. 'He/she doesn't understand me' is a milder version of the same refrain."

Submissive spouses tend to invest a tremendous amount of power in their mates and sigh a lot. Dominant partners often treat their spouses with contempt and scowl a lot. The power positions may have little to do with objective reality. The husband is a sloppy bore, but his wife is afraid of him and tries to please. Or the husband is vice-president of a corporation but goes outside the house to smoke because his wife doesn't approve. "I see just as many men pushed around by their wives as women afraid of their husbands," adds Kirsch.

With such tension in the marriage, the stage is set for a crisis. Without making major changes, the only way, it seems, for you to accommodate an unequal relationship is through the mutual game of deception and denial. You're not aware of it at the time. You both slip into it so easily. You deceive by living outside the marriage. The real you is on the job, in Harry's Bar or the children's car pool or a motel on the outskirts of town. The level of deception somehow doesn't matter: car pool or motel. It's an escape from Deadlock at home. Meanwhile you deny by not looking at what is going on with your spouse—intuitively you sense that's too threatening. Whatever it is, it must be bad. You don't want to know. You also deny by not letting your spouse see what you're doing, thinking, feeling. It's a psychological standoff.

Through the *pas de deux* of deception and denial, you can keep the original roles of Deadlock intact—until the confrontation scene, when you find out that in the process the marriage has been destroyed. This often comes as a surprise, because the process has usually been subconscious. The Deadlock wars have been waged on a level that neither one of you recognizes. But when you do, you find that all that is left are the ghosts.

Sara Williams comes from Wilmington, Delaware, and has sad, adoring eyes. Her mother died when she was five. As the firstborn child, she took care of her father and siblings; she put herself through school; she lived in Mexico City for a year and speaks Spanish; she took the law school entrance exams. But there's something of the orphan about her. "Oh, for someone to watch over me." Then she meets John Davenport. If he would just marry her, she thinks, everything would be all right.

He is blond and bold, a "comer" from Boulder, Colorado, who loves the sun and mountain vistas. He drives fast, makes jokes about coming from the wrong side of the continental divide and wears tweed jackets with patches on the elbows. He's a cardiologist. People say he's good—good in medicine, good in sports, good with people. Right up the stairway to paradise. He's the dominant man.

They kiss. They marry. A Camelot couple, so bright, so attractive. Sara and John look equal. But in the unspoken, unconscious bargain, she gets a dynamic caretaker to fulfill her dream; he gets a supportive partner to fulfill his dream. Deadlock: She is submissive; he is dominant.

They live with their three children in Palo Alto, California, where John is an associate professor at Stanford University Medical School. He gives Sara an allowance to buy food. As long as she can find a part-time job, she's allowed to have a cleaning woman once a week. So she gets a research job in the department of archaeology. For a while, she's happy. Her boss has warm eyes and specializes in ancient Jewish ruins in Israel. He comes to the house for dinner. John likes him too and they all become friends.

One day at work in the Middle Eastern wing of the museum, as she comes into the conference room, Sara looks at the back of her boss's neck and feels a pulling in her groin. She's shocked; her nipples are getting hard, her cheeks hot. What's going on here? She looks away. He turns around and smiles and talks about Abraham's tomb in Hebron.

Then one day her boss seduces her on the couch in his office.

The affair is brief but it runs deep in her. There is no easy way out of this, she realizes, no lifeboat she can jump to. She's on her own now. She knows in a small corner of her chest that it will never be the same—not herself, not her life, certainly not her marriage. She feels frightened and caged . . . and not so submissive anymore.

Her husband notices that she seems to be off with her own little thoughts all the time—and he hasn't had a good meal to eat in months. Goddammit. He gave her a new cookbook last Christmas. Now she wants a new dress. He writes her a check. Couldn't she buy two dresses this time? she asks. He feels harassed and perplexed. What is happening?

Soon she gets sick and lies in bed. There's a cyst on her ovary. In the hospital after surgery, she's gray-faced and cold. The children get frightened. What's the matter with Mommy? John gets frightened: What the hell is going on here? Where's the stairway to paradise?

Sara says, "We've got to get into therapy." "Why?" John asks, surprised. She doesn't tell him about the affair then; she just says she thinks she's going crazy. John thinks she's probably right. She has been acting strange. He agrees to therapy and they go, but all she does is sit in front of the marriage counselor and cry. When she does talk, she says mundane things like he's always criticizing her, always angry and yelling. Jesus, he thinks, it's like she hates me. All he wants is the living room picked up before he comes home. The counselor nods. "If you don't change, you're headed for divorce," the counselor says. Jesus Christ, thinks Mr. Dominant, now the counselor is crazy. Sara stops crying.

The counselor recognizes what neither of them can see: how deep they both are in Deadlock and deep into deception and denial. The problem is more complex than either of them knows. For one thing, John is having his own affair, which he is keeping a secret from Sara as well as from the therapist, just as Sara is keeping her affair a secret. As John sits in therapy, he thinks to himself that the affair is not that important. He remembers the postcard from Carol this morning. She works in the lab at Baylor College of Medicine in Houston. Maybe he should break it off with her. But next month in Houston is a pacemaker conference and he's so looking forward to a week in the sun with her at Padre Island. . . .

Sara and John muddle along. They try another city—maybe that will help the marriage. John gets a job at Rush Presbyterian Hospital in Chicago. They buy a four-story town house on North Sedgewick Street. Then Sara makes a strike for independence. It's a small thing. In California, they had a joint checking account and John controlled household funds. In Chicago, Sara goes out and gets her own checking account without consulting him. John is outraged. "Why do you need a separate checking account?" he asks. Then she hires a housekeeper and starts teaching full time at the university in the Ph.D. program in archaeology.

A few months later, it all comes out. She tells him about her affair. And he tells her about his affair. They look at each other—perhaps for the first time.

Goodbye, dominant-submissive Deadlock. Sara is the submissive partner on her way to independence; John is the dominant partner on his way to dependence. Because of Deadlock, neither one can accommodate change in the other. He can't stand her rebellious ways and is devastated by the affair—someone he knows, someone he's had to the house. She doesn't see his vulnerability (he doesn't show it). She can't stand his bullying and his rages and is stunned that he had an affair too.

Sara turns out to be a phony submissive just the way John's a phony dominant. But instead of bringing equality to the relationship within the marriage, they go outside. It's not long before they split up for good.

Take a good look at the breakup of your marriage. There's a pattern here. You think your crisis has to do with right and wrong, villains and witches. That's how you feel. You want justice, revenge—and your bones ache with guilt. Look again. It's reassuring to discover there's a pattern in breaking up, a Deadlock imperative to how relationships crumble.

What is striking to many family therapists is that it is the submissive partner who usually becomes the deceiver; the dominant spouse the denier. As the submissive spouse on the way to independence, you go outside the marriage and build up strength—and courage—to equalize the relationship. Like a Samson who has finally grown some hair, you become assertive and rebel. The classic act of revolt is the marriage-breaking affair; initiating the divorce is a final act of defiance. You are the deceiver, the Divorce Seeker.

If you're the dominant partner, you try through denial to hold on to some lost dream kingdom of marriage. That's how you keep control. You don't recognize the symptoms of change in the other spouse—the signals of despair and rebellion. At first you ignore the signs. If that's impossible, you get angry, short-tempered. Maybe this will all go away. The one thing you don't do is try to figure out what's going on. Change means undermining your dominant position and showing your vulnerability. Instead you reassure yourself that you're still on top by getting your own way. What you don't realize in Deadlock wars is that every time you win, you lose. The crisis finally explodes in your face and the marriage is overturned in one final fatal coup. When a couple breaks up, you are usually the one who is left. You seem to be taken by surprise: *I can't believe this. I thought the marriage was basically good. My spouse must be crazy*, you say. You are the denier, the Divorce Opposer.

Sometimes it's the dominant one who changes the most in a

marriage and tries to break out of Deadlock. You are sick of being Mr. Right and Ms. Perfect and playing the role of Super Spouse. It's exhausting to carry the whole burden of making the marriage a happy one. It's like breathing for two when you're not getting enough oxygen for one. Gasping for breath, you run for the door for some fresh air. You cross some emotional red line of self-loathing or contempt for your leechlike spouse and reach the crisis point.

But this scenario seems to occur less frequently, according to Kirsch. Most of the time, the dominant one hangs on to the relationship—not for what it was but for what it was supposed to be.

Deception is a key step in the divorce process. It shows you how easy it is to have a life out of Deadlock. The immediate benefit is that you have the chance to behave differently than you do in the marriage.

How many times have you heard a friend say: *Around your spouse, you seem like a different person.*

In deception, you do new things—on the job, in bed—and get involved in new activities: political rallies, school meetings, football games. You discover things about yourself—what you want, what you need, what you can give, what you expect in return.

The most obvious act of deception is an affair. At first glance, it sounds like a natural solution. Unable to gain equality within the relationship, the underdog goes outside the marriage to redress the balance of power between husband and wife. In spy novels, the balance of power between nations is altered by treachery. It's much the same in wars of Deadlock. It's usually subconscious, but the way it works is that you tip the scales of psychological power by having an affair which will totally devastate the dominant spouse.

But what you don't actually realize at first is that you're playing for high stakes. Once you start the game of deception and denial with your spouse, you're right on the edge. You may not sense it, but the countdown to crackup has begun. How long can you go on like this? As psychoanalyst Herbert S. Strean, professor at the Graduate School of Social Work at Rutgers University, explains in his book *The Extramarital Affair:* "I am firmly of the opinion that an extramarital affair is *never* a healthy or mature act. . . . Although I believe that an occasional one-night stand or short-term extramarital affair can sometimes be viewed as a harmless regression, a prolonged extramarital affair always implies that the adulterer is involved in a conflicted marriage and is therefore a conflicted person."

That doesn't mean that couples can't go on for many years playing the game of deception and denial. There's a certain security in maintaining Deadlock. But the critical process in divorce of separating psychologically from your spouse has begun. You simply start living separate emotional lives. By the time you have the confrontation scene, you have in fact already "left" each other.

It takes two to go the route of divorce. Every deceiver needs a denying spouse. Every denier protects and encourages a deceiving spouse. That way you both subconsciously maintain Deadlock and avoid confrontation. Each of you goes on and does your psychological thing. *You deceive; I'll deny. I deceive; you'll deny.* It doesn't take long to build up a complex web of betrayals and illusions between you.

It's not that simple, of course. Marriage and divorce are never simple. But think back again to how it started. What were your fights like? Or didn't you fight much? Or talk much? And what about sex? The ghosts are dancing again, taunting you, jeering at you.

When the marriage cracks, the past games of deception and denial are exposed.

Mary van Elder, thirty-nine, is a professor of law in New York City. She's a woman with soft brown eyes and a gentle smile. Her face is pretty and smooth. Her voice, like her eyes, is also soft, and sometimes she giggles like a teenager.

But something is very wrong. Mary is roughly thirty pounds overweight. She was once slim and inviting. She had narrow hips and full breasts, and even at age fourteen she knew she was sexy. The color of her hair matched her eyes, and when she smiled, a man would want to dive into her, get lost in her warmth and soft goodness.

Mary comes from Detroit. Her grandparents immigrated from Poland. They ran a chain of fifty dry cleaners which they had built up over thirty years. By the time Mary is born in 1943, her father is president of the company. But her mother does all the books and everybody says—though not out loud—that it's her mother who is responsible for the company's continued success.

Mary is brighter than her older sister and takes the dominant role in the family. At sixteen, she enters the University of Michigan, and four years later, graduates tenth in her class.

Austin van Elder is the first man she sleeps with, a thin man with washed-out blond hair. His family is rich and Episcopalian, from Greenwich, Connecticut. He's also a freshman at the university, the first Wasp Mary has ever known. "I think we were very impressed with the otherness of the other," she says. "I was impressed with this person from a sophisticated background. He was snowed because I was so smart—and showed I was smart."

Austin doesn't know what he wants to do. His father is an overbearing and unsuccessful stockbroker. His mother drinks. Despite the glamour of nannies and summer places, the family has Wasp rot—the slow erosion of trust funds, Scholastic Aptitude Test scores and ambition.

Mary has enough ambition and high test scores for both of them and Austin would fit in perfectly with her future. She wants to be a judge. Her favorite book is *Clarence Darrow for the Defense* by Irving Stone. She has a scholarship to Columbia University Law School. She knows she will do well. She always has. She also knows that she and Austin will marry. They have to, now that they are sleeping together. She feels happy and secure with her destiny.

Everything goes according to plan. Only once during the college years is her ordered world shaken, a harbinger of things to come. It happens in her senior year. With her good marks, she has the chance to spend a semester at the University of California at

Los Angeles. By this time, Mary and Austin are very much a couple, spending happy student hours in bed together. Everyone likes Austin—except her roommate. Mary ignores her.

While Mary is at UCLA, she and Austin write long letters back and forth and telephone regularly. But she senses something is wrong. For the first time, she feels real panic. It turns out that her instincts are right. Austin has taken up with her roommate. "He kept saying that the relationship with her didn't count," she recalls. "I was very cool about it most of the time, but at one point I just went off the wall—I lost my temper and began screaming. I remember feeling: I can't trust him. He's not reliable."

But Mary quickly buries the crisis. After all, he says the relationship with her roommate doesn't count. It's better to believe him than to have her whole world crash. The way to take care of this, Mary thinks, is to get married, to get a legal commitment to each other that can't be broken. She starts planning the wedding with even more determination.

"Just before the wedding date, Austin said to me, 'I'm not sure we should go through with this,'" she recalls. "Well, I threw another temper tantrum. I felt very strongly. I made up my mind I was going to marry him, and by God, I was. That's the way it was going to be.

"So we got married. I think I expected: O.K., now you live happily ever after."

On the outside, everything goes along according to plan. Mary finishes law school and has a baby. Austin is sweet and has charm. But inside the marriage, something is wrong. Here she has everything she wants: a law degree, Austin and a baby. But Mary feels the panic welling up in her. She goes to a psychiatrist. She explains to herself it's just the pressures of bar exams, plus diapers, plus making Austin happy while the baby has colic. Meanwhile Austin is wondering what to do in life. Maybe he should try being a painter. He likes art. Why not take a year off somewhere? It sounds like the perfect solution. Mary is glad to put off bar exams for a year. She can relax and Austin can paint. They decide to rent a house in the South of France.

It's a dream setting. Looking at Austin, Mary thinks of Rubens, Braque, Rothko. But it takes him six months to get the right paints. Mary begins to wonder whether he could paint the dining room, much less a canvas. Meanwhile she is pregnant again. Another baby so soon? They hire a babysitter from the village. Mary feels sick and gets tired easily. Austin grows impatient. The baby seems to cry all the time and he can't stand the mess in the bathroom. All Mary thinks about is the baby, he mutters to himself; and her breasts always smell of sour milk.

But the French sky is spectacular. And they now share a dream: a house overlooking the Mediterranean, a man in a dark-blue beret standing by his easel, a pregnant woman, a baby, a maid.

Yet, the Deadlock gloom sinks over them. It's still not working. Mary is very unhappy. She doesn't know why. She feels heavy and starts putting on a lot of weight. She feels depressed and tired and goes to bed early.

Austin likes to stay up late. It doesn't matter that Mary retires early. The maid stays up and keeps him company. Danielle is plain-looking, with wide eyes and a hooked nose. Austin teaches her English and tells her stories about America. He is used to servants. They always made a fuss over him when he'd come home from school, Aggie waiting for him with a batch of chocolate chip cookies, giving him pantry love during those dismal adolescent years when his father stayed in town on business and his mother stayed in bed drunk.

"There were times I'd dream about Austin and Danielle having an affair," Mary says. "I would be in bed trying to go to sleep. They'd be in the kitchen, talking. Time would go by. I'd hear strange noises. Then I felt guilty about having such thoughts."

Mary denies the gradual breakdown in the marriage. She decides not to face Austin's attraction to Danielle. In fact, she suggests that they bring the maid back with them to the U.S. to take care of the new baby—even though she already finds Danielle a difficult and lazy worker. Austin agrees it's a good idea.

Austin gives up painting and buys a bookstore in Princeton,

New Jersey. Mary lines up a part-time job at Columbia University Law School. The baby is born. The bathroom is still a mess. Danielle is still difficult and lazy. Mary has to keep after her to do the laundry and clean the guest room. Mary's also studying for her bar exams. She's got to pass them this year. Over the next few months, Mary tries to fire Danielle three times. Always Austin intervenes. "He'd say to me, 'How can you do this to her? She loves you so much.'" That stops her.

Soon the battle for control turns into guerrilla warfare. With a weak man's instinct for the jugular, Austin knows how to get to his wife. Every time Mary says she wants to fire Danielle, Austin points out that Danielle doesn't have her green card. If she loses her job, the poor girl will have to leave the country. And think of the children. By now they are used to Danielle's homemade bread and French nursery rhymes. Surely Mary wouldn't subject poor Danielle and the children to the trauma of firing her?

Mary gets frightened. The tables are turning. She feels very vulnerable. She's also quite fat now. Two babies in two years. Austin nicks at her on every level. She remembers the incident with the toothpaste. Seemingly an insignificant thing, it was a symbol, an omen. "Early in the marriage, we decided Colgate was our brand of toothpaste," she begins. "Then one day, Austin went out and bought a giant tube of Crest toothpaste. I felt betrayed. Somehow that we should have this difference was very threatening."

Despite these signs, Mary never faces the reality of her marriage. In fifteen years of marriage, she recalls, they never got angry. They never really talked. Mary completely buries Austin's relationship with Danielle. Yet she knows something is terribly wrong. She feels depressed all the time. There is no more sex between them. In fact, the last time they had intercourse was the night before they left France. And yet they are still bound to each other.

"It was a situation where we both wanted the marriage to work," says Mary. "We were both in love with the fantasy of the other person. Neither of us could confront that it was a fantasy.

We had so many expectations, but no understanding of reality."

Then a radical change takes place in the marriage *à trois*. Danielle gets her green card. That means Mary can fire her—which she does. After all, Danielle is lazy and difficult. Austin's response is to retreat into the bookstore. Then Danielle announces that she's getting married and wouldn't they both please come to the wedding? Mary gets a wedding present for the bride and groom. Austin cries throughout the ceremony. A few months after the wedding, Danielle leaves her husband and has a nervous breakdown. This time, Austin doesn't withdraw. He goes to the hospital to take charge of Danielle's care and rescue her from her aborted marriage. Mr. Submissive Deceiver becomes Mr. Dominant Life-Saver.

"Even at that point, I denied that I knew there was any real relationship between them," says Mary. "I told myself: This is what employers do for their servants."

Mary takes the children to visit her parents in Florida over spring vacation. When she returns, she finds out that Austin is living with Danielle.

Reality finally crashes in on her. Deadlock is broken. And the breakdown of the marriage is complete.

Most people take a long time to make the final step of breaking up a marriage. Despite the rhetoric about people rushing into divorce, research shows that people who initiate the breakup have usually contemplated the possibility of divorce for a long time—more than a year—before they take a firm stand.

In one of the most thorough studies of divorce, the California Children of Divorce Project, Judith S. Wallerstein and Joan Berlin Kelly found that most people in their study of sixty families had endured years of emotional starvation and abuse before deciding to separate. As they described in *Surviving the Breakup: How Children and Parents Cope with Divorce*, they talked to individuals about the problems that led to divorce and concluded: "The question that inevitably formed in our minds about their plight was *What took you so long?*"

Well, how do you answer? *What took you so long?*

The hooker in divorce is that in order to get over a marriage, you have to go back to it. To go forward to a new life, you have to go backward to the past. That's the agony of breaking up a marriage. It's not over yet. Take a deep breath. Whether you stay in the marriage or get a divorce, you have to deal with your Deadlock ghosts.

It begins with the confrontation scene. There you are—husband and wife—like two strangers on different trains: twelve years of marriage on the average and 2.2 children between you. The two trains come into the station and stop. After the long ride in separate compartments, you both get off, and on the platform between trains, you face each other—perhaps for the first time. This is the watershed of a marriage—the moment of crisis when you confront your spouse and acknowledge the breakdown of the relationship.

2

CONFRONTATION

Some couples talk for months about splitting up. Others seem to break up on impulse, not daring to let a second thought intrude. Sometimes people are resigned to the doom of divorce; sometimes they seem to be taken by surprise. Shocked and bewildered, they say: *How can this be? Maybe it will all blow over.* Most people are desperate; many are ambivalent: *I think we should separate for a while and think things over.* All are confused and hurt.

When the crisis hits, the basic structure of the marriage relationship is altered. With the confrontation scene, you are forced to renegotiate your psychological contract with your spouse. Some people are able to break out of Deadlock and stay married to each other. In a sense, they divorce their old marriage and try to form a new one. But for many couples, by the time they get to the confrontation scene, they are too estranged and too battered by the relationship to remain in the marriage.

There are several common plots in this process of uncoupling. For most people, the path from the confrontation scene to separation to divorce is rarely straight. Sometimes you can't make the decision to separate in a vacuum. You need to have another relationship to turn to. Many couples discover that one or both has had an affair at some point during the marriage. "Husbands and wives who had had extramarital sex were more likely to break up, whether it happened at the beginning of the marriage or after many years," conclude sociologists Philip Blumstein and Pepper Schwartz in their 1983 study *American Couples: Money, Work, Sex.*

The marriage-breaking affair is a cliché for good reason. But these affairs are transitional. Often they collapse once the miserable process of getting out of the marriage is accomplished. But whether they are short-lived or lead to a second marriage, they play a key role in the divorce process. These relationships help destroy the Deadlock balance of power between spouses and often become the triggering event that forces a confrontation.

Terry Sanford, forty-four, looks as though he stepped out of a Marlboro ad. He sails, plays tennis and works as a trust officer in a New York City bank. He went to Yale and belonged to Skull & Bones. He married Eloise, the girl next door. She plays tennis, too, and is rich—in fact, she's a lot richer than he is. Her parents died in a car accident when she was thirteen and left her with an inheritance. The Sanfords have four children.

On the outside, Terry has all the trappings of success—prestigious education, prestigious job, prestigious wife. Why is he so miserable? It's as though he's always in the position of trying to please his wife—he's always been a good boy and done well—but he never seems to get an A from her. The sense of failure builds up in him. She doesn't even seem to notice how he's struggling. She says, "If you want to be in international finance, be in international finance." Or: "If you want to run the Chicago office, I'll buy a house in Lake Forest." In the Deadlock contract, Terry is submissive; his wife is dominant.

Finally, after seven years of marriage, Terry has a fling. "I was seduced by a gorgeous Swede," he says. "Sure I wanted to be seduced, but she did the seducing." How else is a submissive guy like Terry to make the initial break? For the next five years, Terry and his wife play cat and mouse: he deceives her with other women; she denies what's going on. "I went through a series of one-night stands," he says. "My wife almost tacitly agreed to that. I felt like I had permission. Now that I think about it, what she was really telling me was: I don't care enough to give a damn." The Deadlock ghosts start dancing.

The flings don't help. He feels life closing in on him. He doesn't like his job, his marriage, himself. His friends tell him he's having a midlife crisis.

After a period of assessing his options, Terry decides to make some real midlife changes. He's happiest on his father's Friendship sloop—the exhilaration he feels on the weekends when he gets the sails up and heads out of the harbor; the lapping of the water as the bow cuts through the waves; the pull of his pale-blue jib against the white sails going before the wind. He used to win all the races when he was growing up. His favorite book is *Moby Dick*. Part of his problem, he muses, is that he should have lived a century ago.

He devises a plan. What about leaving the bank and moving to the Virgin Islands? He could set up a charter boat service. To hell with the bank, the Shetland sweaters from Bloomingdale's, the private schools. Lady Dominant thinks it's a terrific idea. It's a new life for them. It's trendy. She buys an old plantation house on Saint John that looks out on the sea. It's a perfect setting. She buys new furniture and puts in air conditioning. The children are thrilled about living on an island and they love to sail. The blue-green sea, the sun, a life of sandals and bathing suits. No more Manhattan hassle, no more commuting, no more martini lunches.

Once they are settled, Terry buys a boat that sleeps ten and bases himself in Saint Thomas. He asks his wife if she'd like to come along and be his crew—be chief cook and bottle washer on the charter cruises. He laughs nervously. She looks at him as though he's crazy. He sure didn't get A+ with that suggestion; and so he starts the season alone on his boat with the tourists.

Very quickly a double life takes shape for the couple. Eloise stays on Saint John in the dream house with the children. Terry goes to Saint Thomas to take the pale faces from Chicago and Boston out for three- or four-day cruises. Then he goes home to his family in Saint John. His visits home become more infrequent. As the season progresses, she makes cracks about the boat being a tourist tub—too big to be classy, too small to be impressive. Terry resents her remarks. Love me, love my boat, he thinks.

Meanwhile the weather is beautiful and there are lots of visitors and parties. From December to June, Terry and his wife host a continuous house party. Everybody drinks rum and dances and relaxes. On the outside, it looks like a perfect life.

But Terry is not happy and neither is his wife. There is an emptiness that gnaws at both of them. Eloise wants to do something significant and starts teaching reading in the local school. She worries about the children growing up with the island mentality. Whatever happened to the work ethic? She looks at her husband. He's very tan and boyish. Sitting on a boat is work? Yet he's always complaining and seems tired. Tourists are obnoxious, he says, rude, difficult, condescending. "Well, this is what you wanted to do," his wife reminds him. "You just don't understand. You've never had to work for anything," he snaps back.

Eloise suggests they get into therapy. They obviously have marriage malaise. Everybody has it. Now they talk a lot about their problems in relating to each other, their problems in communicating, about their friends' problems. A heaviness sinks over both of them, over the dream house and the weekend parties. Terry gets into a routine of more one-night stands on Saint Thomas and heavy therapy-related weekends at home.

Then, it happens! Terry falls in love at first sight—a real *coup de foudre*, or bolt of lightning romance—with Marianne, a civil rights attorney who takes cases from all the U.S. islands. Marianne, with full lips and a schoolgirl body, is twenty-seven and just out of law school. Terry imagines her in a green tunic playing field hockey. She looks vaguely like his wife and makes all the arrangements concerning their social life on Saint Thomas— where to eat, whom to see, when to leave the restaurant.

While Terry is terrified that his wife will find out, he is much happier with Marianne in his life. How can he get an A from Eloise, though, if he's fucking around? He is ambivalent: he wants out of marriage—and he doesn't. Fear creeps up in him. He's not ready to break out yet. What about his children? He doesn't want to lose them. He misses them intensely when he's away from home. Maybe he should give the marriage another chance.

In a burst of conscience, he breaks off with Marianne and decides to go home to make a new commitment to the marriage. A storm is coming up and planes aren't flying between the islands. He gets a charter ferryboat to make the trip and hires a taxi to go across the island. It's close to midnight when he staggers through the front door.

A party is still going on: half-filled ashtrays, spaghetti-encrusted plates on the floor. His wife is sitting on the sofa in a low-cut black chemise and laughing with an old friend of his from Yale. He senses they've both had too much to drink and he's tired and wants to go to bed. But she's having too much fun to stop now.

"I had beat my brains out all week long, had turned down Marianne, had battled my way to get home—taking taxis, chartering a boat—finally making it out to the house, and then to have her sitting up all night getting drunk with somebody else? It just said to me: Is there any use? I really felt I'd been had."

Crisis takes shape in his mind: "One of my problems is that I never stood up to my wife. I never told her she was full of shit. I always took her seriously," he says. That night he leaves her partying in the living room and goes up to bed without saying a word. He's not ready to stand up to her, not yet. His anger may still be buried in silence, but his conscious commitment to the marriage has been snapped.

Later, on the boat in Saint Thomas, he calls up Marianne. She is eager for him. She believes in him—believes that he's talented and good and right. She gives him A+. His self-esteem improves, and for a while he thrives on his double life. It goes on like this through the summer, until Columbus Day weekend in October.

That Sunday, Terry and Eloise walk on the beach and look out at the stark blue sea and the whitecaps in the wind. They look out on their dream—beautiful, cold and choppy. "I said to her: 'I want to separate.'

"I don't know what prompted the split just then," he continues. "I came home that weekend and I found I just wasn't there anymore. It was over. And the attraction of Marianne was so great. To have someone sympathetic to you, caring for you; to have someone really love you.

"I wouldn't have done it if there hadn't been someone else to jump to," he says.

Still he's cautious. "At that time, I didn't want a divorce," he continues. "I really felt that separation was the only way to shake things up, to fill my needs, to keep me from going insane. I'm really quite proud of myself. I finally behaved intelligently."

His wife is not surprised. She's not too happy in the marriage, either, and she's sick of analyzing what's wrong with their relationship. In a way, she admires him for making the decision. A separation will get them off dead center.

Then she throws him a curve ball. As they stand on the beach, she says to him, "I hate to think I'll never be on the boat again." He is shocked. "I couldn't believe what she said," he says. "I thought she always hated the boat."

He looks at her closely—perhaps for the first time. Who is she? Maybe he doesn't know her as well as he thinks he does. Fear creeps up in him.

Six months later, his wife finds out about the affair with Marianne. By that time, Terry has broken off with Marianne and is involved with someone else. The marriage-breaking affair is over, having served its purpose in giving him the courage to precipitate the crisis.

But the marriage isn't finished yet, though they are now living separately. They still go to a marriage counselor. They want to get to the bottom of things. What about the affair? Can they get beyond it? Terry finally tells Eloise about how upset he was that weekend he came home and found her messing around with his old friend from college, how that catapulted him out of the marriage. "What?" His wife is shocked. "Nothing happened at all," she says. He doesn't believe her. She's covering up, he thinks. After all, her messing around catapulted him out of the marriage, right? She wonders out loud: "Why didn't you say something at the time?"

Then the rage wells up in her: "What right do you have to be so self-righteous, coming home all hot from little Miss Legal Affairs of the U.S. Virgin Islands?" She lashes into him. Terry feels guilty. She's got a good case against him. But wait a minute—if you are happy in a marriage, you don't stray, right? "You made me do it," says Terry. Now she really gets angry and starts screaming at him. He screams back: "What right do you have to yell at me like this?" Both are yelling. The dream is crumbling. The psychic demons of Deadlock are screaming *Mayday! Mayday!* It's not long before Terry and his wife switch from the marriage counselor to two separate divorce lawyers.

When the crisis hits and you have your confrontation scene, you probably aren't aware of your Deadlock ghosts. You think you are trapped in a very unique situation. You don't see how predictable your crisis is. Years go by before you can unravel how you got to the meltdown point in your marriage.

For many people, getting out of a marriage is an act of desperation. Like a political refugee, you leave everything behind and jump over the wall. *I would have died if I had stayed in that marriage,* you say. Your eyes are haunted. *It was a question of survival,* you say. People look at you strangely. They don't quite understand: a question of life or death? *I would have died if I had stayed in that marriage,* you say? Only those who have been there know what it's like. You have no choice. Not now anyway. Maybe later, much later, you'll see it differently. But right now you have to get out to survive. You can't explain why you feel so driven.

Your life takes on a certain drama. It's as though you have a part in a soap opera; it's not really you, it's bigger than you. You can't believe what's happening to you.

Janet Kelly, forty-three, is the kind of woman who always believed that if she lived in medieval times and the feudal lord came riding through the village, she would never have been picked out among the maidens. Her hair is dark and her skin is very pale. She grew up quiet and shy and has lived all her childhood and married life in Worcester, Massachusetts. Though she doesn't know it, she's a good-looking woman with haunting green eyes.

She marries her high school sweetheart, Jack, when they are both twenty, both in college; both are Catholic. "In the community, his family is not as—quote—refined as mine although his father made as much money," she says. He plays football and is outgoing. She doesn't have a lot of dates and she looks to him as her salvation during those painful "What! You're not going steady?" years of adolescence. He asks her to marry him. She says O.K. "Jack was the only person I went out with. I married him because he asked me. I was not particularly attractive. I know I didn't love him. I didn't know what love was," she says.

In the marriage, he decides what they are going to do. She agrees. In the Deadlock contract, he is dominant, she is submissive. Janet doesn't expect much in life. It doesn't occur to her to wonder whether she's happy. The babies start coming. Her husband has a good job at Sears and teaches Sunday school at church.

After twelve years, they have three children and a house that looks like a Sears display catalog, with a Sears washer and dryer, Sears bedding, Sears lawn furniture. In the afternoons, after the housework is done, she daydreams about famous people—Jane Fonda, Jennie Churchill, Cleopatra, Madame Curie.... She imagines a big house with antique furniture and a light-blue velvet loveseat. A restlessness begins to build up in her, the sense that life is passing her by. She remembers how she used to get good marks in school—better marks than her husband.

When the last child enters first grade, she takes a part-time volunteer job at the hospital. She brings messages to patients and reads the Bible to them. She finds she's good with patients—especially the dying. The hospice movement is just getting started and the hospital encourages her to take a course to get a certificate in social work.

At first her husband is proud of her. She's not so awkward anymore. At parties, she tells stories and people gather around her. She looks better too. She's cut her hair. He watches her go up to strangers and start a conversation. What happened to his shy little girl who couldn't look anyone in the eye?

The power balance in the relationship starts to shift. Enough of this, he thinks. She's different now. He starts sniping at her. Dinner is late. The children haven't done their homework. Janet reads newspaper stories about the women's movement out loud at breakfast. Jack pounds the table. "Ball-breakers!" he yells, spilling his coffee. Janet just sits there like Mona Lisa. She's spending a lot of time at the hospital now and has a glow in her eyes. Jack gets scared. Something very threatening is happening to his world. He's got to stop this. "He really fought me," she says. "He didn't want me to work at the hospital. It wasn't in his plan. I was out in the world and it was threatening. It wasn't the world he understood," she says.

In April, the hospital asks Janet to go to a conference on hospice care in Providence, Rhode Island. It's the first time she's traveled outside the state on her own. She buys a new suit. Her husband drives her to the bus station.

The conference brings together physicians, nurses, ministers, priests, rabbis, social workers and psychologists. Janet is enthralled. Then it happens. She meets a Lutheran minister from Pennsylvania, who has soft brown eyes and is running a geriatric counseling program based in his church. He invites her to dinner. She thinks back to the feudal lord riding through the village and smiles; they drink wine and talk and talk. He takes her to his room. She can't believe this is happening to her. Here she is, in mid-life, the mother of four children, and a good woman too, in bed with a man—a minister yet!—who is not her husband. And she's never been so happy. The sex is good and they spend every night of the conference together. "I thought I was frigid before," she says.

The conference comes to an end. So does the affair. She

knows the man is married and she tells herself she doesn't want to get into that. She also knows she's in enough trouble just by herself. A grimness comes over her as the bus travels back to Worcester. Between her work at the hospital and her adventure in Rhode Island, Janet begins to feel trapped in her web of deception.

Back home, she staggers along for two more years in the marriage. She and Jack start having long, nasty fights. "He always criticized me," she says. "He'd say, 'Look at the children; if it weren't for me, they'd never have a shower.'" They stop sleeping together and she moves down into the basement. She keeps on working at the hospital and starts seeing a therapist without telling her husband. There are no more affairs, but the idea builds up in her. She wonders what it would be like to do the unthinkable and get divorced. Jack glowers at her, makes cracks about her preferring the dying to the living. She realizes she hates him now, but she's still afraid of him and his rages.

One night, in those dark months before she gets up her courage to leave him, one of those heavy August nights, they are sitting out on the front steps, talking. "I realize now he had an unhappy childhood," she recalls. "His parents' marriage was troubled. My husband grew up determined he was going to have the perfect family. I see now that's what I represented to him. I think his rage is in proportion to how strongly he held on to those ideals and how devastated he was to have them taken away." They sit there listening to the cicadas. The clouds come up in the sky.

"I said to him, 'Why have you always been so critical of me?' He said, 'I guess I just wanted you to be perfect.' I was shocked. I said, 'By whose lights? What does that mean?' He said, 'I guess I loved you so much, I just wanted you to be perfect.'"

Who's the strong one in the marriage now?

As long as her husband maintains control of the marriage through criticism and rage, he can keep his wife "perfect" and perpetuate his dream of having a perfect family and living happily ever after.

Finally, on Thanksgiving, Janet dares to broach the subject of separating.

Mr. Dominant Denier slams the door to her prison shut. "He wouldn't hear of it," she says. "He said absolutely no. He said he would never leave the house."

Janet continues in therapy and sleeping in the basement. The children start to plan for Christmas. Janet hears Christmas songs on the radio and gets more desperate. She and her husband rarely speak to each other anymore.

By mid-December Janet knows she has to make the break. "It was a question of survival," she says. "I had to leave or I wasn't going to survive."

She decides to tell him she wants a divorce. But still afraid of Jack, she wants to tell him on neutral territory—away from the house with all the Sears bric-a-brac, away from the photographs of all the children as they entered first grade, away from the preparations for Christmas. Janet suggests they go out for a drink to a new bar in the neighborhood; she needs people around; she needs the padding of strangers. What if he tries to hit her?

They sit at the bar and face the layers of bottles. A plastic face of Santa Claus is lit up over the window.

"I said to him, 'I'm going to leave in a week.'" She goes on to tell him that it's all arranged. She will go to her friend Tricia's for the weekend and then just not come back.

Her husband is silent. They finish their drinks and get up to leave. He says nothing. His lips are tight shut, mere thin slits. They get in the car and start to drive up the street to their house. Jack never looks at her. Suddenly he screeches on the brakes, turns the car around and drives in the opposite direction. When they get to the Greyhound bus terminal, he stops the car.

"He turned off the engine and said to me, 'If you want to leave, you leave right now.'" He is hissing at her through his teeth. Both hands are clutching the wheel. What better way to keep control of the situation than by turning the tables and telling her *when* to leave?

The battle is on. She strikes back. She doesn't have any money for a ticket. She isn't packed; she doesn't even have a toothbrush. She looks up at him submissively. How can a decent person put a poor little thing like her out in the cold?

That does it. Jack bangs the wheel with his fists, starts up the car and heads for home.

The next day, her husband is taking the children to the church fair. She decides there's no question he's a better parent with the children. He remembers their lunch money; he likes to go to parents' night at school. "Bye, Mom," the kids yell as they go out the door.

She sits alone in the house. "I telephoned Tricia. It was now or never. I couldn't wait until next weekend. Then I wrote a note: 'At Tricia's. Need time to think things over.'"

She can't believe she's doing this. She walks out the door with a suitcase full of clothes. She feels as if she's in an underwater movie, watching herself take long, slow leaps over giant boulders that rock back and forth in a green sea. Maybe she isn't really leaving. It's all in a dream. Is she really out of the house? Out of the marriage?

Tricia arrives and they drive away. Is it as easy as this? Seventeen years and this is all it takes? "Suddenly I realized that I'd forgotten my electric hair rollers." She starts to grin at the memory. "I can't live without my rollers." She tells Tricia they have to risk going back to get the rollers. Her husband probably isn't home yet. "I just had to have my rollers," she says. The rollers are now a symbol. She must go back into the house to prove to herself that she is really leaving.

"It was like a thriller movie," she says. Tricia turns the car around and speeds back to the house. "Will Jack and the children be home yet? Will they catch me in the act? Will they try to stop me? It was exciting." Janet sneaks in the back door while Tricia turns the car around for the getaway. Janet runs upstairs to the bedroom, grabs her rollers from the dressing table, races downstairs and slams the door.

They speed off, two middle-aged women shrieking and giggling like teenagers. It's true, it's true. Escape at last.

Janet gets a job as head of social services in a hospital outside Hartford, Connecticut. Before she leaves Worcester for good, she has a farewell session with her therapist. "At the end I said to my therapist: 'You know, it's hard to be a grownup!' My therapist said, 'The only thing worse is being a kid.'

"I'm not a kid anymore," she says.

Janet builds a new life for herself in Hartford. The children stay in Worcester with their father and she doesn't see them for three years. Janet looks away. She worries about the children. The battle for control with Jack has shifted to the children, and the rage and bitterness continue. Will it ever be over? Janet shudders. Right now she has to concentrate on herself and her job and making her own way.

Many people, like Janet, are forced to grow up through upcoupling and greatly improve their lives, but the turmoil is great. For Janet, it takes years simply to find ways to communicate with her ex-spouse so that she can reestablish herself as a parent with her children. In time, she accomplishes this and at no point does she think her marriage could have turned out any other way.

Confronting a spouse with the end of a marriage may break Deadlock, but it does not resolve the problems in the relationship. In many marriages, the confrontation scene is like a declaration of war, especially for the spouse who at this point does not want to let go of the old relationship. It can also create new problems for children who are not shielded from escalating conflict in the separation period. "We have to come to grips with the fact that what is good for the individual is not necessarily good for the children," says Jeffrey Evans at the Center for Population Research at the National Institute of Child Health and Human Development.

A number of people who get divorced are like passengers on an airline who follow the safety guidelines on oxygen masks: When traveling with small children, be sure to put your mask on first and then adjust the mask for your child. If you lose consciousness—or Flameout in your divorce—you're no help to anybody. But after the crisis is past, you may find there's a lot of catching up to do with your children.

For people like Janet, the desperation and pain of Deadlock are so overwhelming that staying married becomes life-threatening. Janet looks back on her marriage and speaks for many marital refugees when she says: "I think I would have died if I had stayed in that relationship—maybe not literally, but certainly metaphorically. I was becoming nonexistent somehow."

Those are the give-away words of a dead marriage. *I was becoming nonexistent, somehow. . . . I would have died if I had stayed in that relationship.*

To many therapists, the panic of *becoming nonexistent* is a common characteristic of what happens to at least one spouse in a Deadlock marriage. The crisis may seem to hit all of a sudden but it has been building for years. As Staples explains: "If in your marriage you live within the boundaries of what's allowed, no matter how nice it is to be loved, it isn't worth the sacrifice of hiding an important side of yourself. If you have a partner who can't tolerate the way you are, it's going to be really hard [to stay in a marriage]. It means your partner has determined for you not to become yourself. If the self is going to emerge, you have to take risks." With the confrontation scene, you take enormous risks in exposing yourself to your spouse in ways you never did before.

3

SEPARATION

It is the seminal moment in a marriage when one of you packs a suitcase and leaves the house. Sometimes months or even years go by between the confrontation scene and the decision to separate. More often, at least one of you has already packed a suitcase psychologically and is ready to separate by the time the confrontation scene takes place.

Perhaps the breakup does not seem very dramatic. You decide to leave a marriage because it seems the best thing, the only sensible thing to do—for you, your spouse, the children. It's the mature thing to do for all concerned, you think.

There is no "other" person. You look at yourself, what you've become in the marriage. You think about what lies ahead—within the marriage and outside it; you assess your accomplishments and the lack of them, you think about your age and examine your changing body. Your decision becomes less a rejection of your spouse than a rejection of the self you don't want to be anymore.

Often the decision to separate gets played out as a duet. Each of you has a part to sing as you break down the past in Deadlock harmony. The irony is that when two people finally confront each other, they can end up getting closer together.

You are forced to look again at your spouse. The person you thought was drab and dependent is suddenly a fiery rebel. Perhaps you find out that your spouse has been having an affair for five years and *you never suspected a thing*. You are forced to do some reevaluations of the marriage . . . and your partner and yourself.

There is an Alphonse-Gaston quality to this unstructured decision-making process, with each partner nudging the other to make a stand. The classic scenario has one spouse reveal an affair that forces the other one to say: *I have no choice but to ask for a divorce.* That way the responsibility—and guilt—for initiating the breakup is shared jointly.

In many cases, the confrontation evolves over a period of time as the couples go around and around the decision tree.

The Alphonse spouse says: *I think we should separate. You don't love me. (I don't love you.) There's nothing here anymore.* The Gaston spouse replies: *Oh, no; I really love you.* The Alphonse spouse says: *What? You do? Really? Well, I love you too. Let's not separate.* The Gaston spouse replies: *Well, I've thought it over. It's not going to work. I want to separate.* And so the circle is closed. Who is breaking up with whom?

Joan Ellsworth, forty-one, has been a military appendage all her life. Her father retires from the navy just short of making admiral. She is first daughter. She wants to marry someone who will be an admiral. She finds Sam Ellsworth III. He will do, even though he's in the army instead of the navy.

Joan is very tall and blond, with hazel eyes and good-tanning skin. Her husband is a redhead with freckles. In the Deadlock contract, she is dominant; he is passive. They have four children and live all over the globe: Germany, Japan, Australia, Italy. Now they are stationed back in San Diego, where Joan begins to think she's living out a script from "General Hospital." She's getting terrible migraine headaches and Sam is staying out later and later. They are both seeing a marriage counselor and going to group therapy. "My group says I should stand up to you more," he says. "My group says you're treating me like shit," she says. They seem to be stuck on an escalator headed for disaster. She says if things don't get better, she wants a separation. *He* quickly starts up an affair with a woman in his group. *She* ends up in a motel one afternoon with a new man in her group. "It was awful. It was really awful," she says.

The don't tell each other about their double lives. Instead, they fight now all the time; they fight about the children, about fixing the room in the basement, about being shitty to each other; about her headaches and his drinking. They fight about everything except the one thing that's driving them crazy: their relationship.

The break comes when he goes away to Puerto Rico on assignment for three weeks. Joan is alone with the children. She looks in the mirror and examines her life. "I felt that something came over me during that time. I became hardened and at the time I felt like a zombie. It set in motion the decision to separate—the hardest thing I ever had to do in my life. Those three weeks while he was gone, I went crazy with activity. I always found something to do—the movies, lectures, dinner out. When he came home, I knew what I was going to say."

It's about ten o'clock at night when her husband gets home. They have a drink in the living room. "I said to him, 'I want a separation.'"

Her husband looks at her. And then he throws her a curve ball. "He cried and said he loved me. He said that I was the most important person in his life. He said things he'd never said before," she recalls.

"We made love," she continues. "He was more gentle and giving. He was able to sit down and talk to me." Sam stays on in the house and in the following weeks he seems like a different man. He plays with the children and makes love to his wife. "Those few weeks were better than the last several years," she says. "I was still in love with him on some level. Things seemed to be better. So I asked him to stay."

Now they are halfway round the circle.

Her husband smiles and stays another week.

Then he throws her another curve ball. He tells her that he's thought it over and he's decided not to stay. He thinks he needs time to be by himself, to work things out, to learn how to be on his own. She looks at him in disbelief. He moves out and gets an apartment. Three weeks later, Joan hears that a woman has moved in with him. "So much for learning how to be on his own," says his ex-wife.

The circle is closed. Who is breaking up with whom? Joan and Sam get divorced, and Sam quickly remarries.

Now Joan has had time to look back at her marriage and listen to her Deadlock ghosts. A different scenario of the breakup emerges: "So much of my life was wandering around full of jitters and self-hate—of somehow not being whole or real," she recounts. "I remember lying down on the edge of the bed with tears rolling down my cheeks and never saying anything. There was something I wasn't getting that I wanted but I had no idea what that was." She pauses.

"I was the classic case of a woman who thinks it was all his fault," she says. "I was pushing him to do things I was afraid to do myself. I was pushing on him because he wasn't stronger, because he wasn't an admiral, because his eye twitched and that looked like weakness to me. I was becoming a bitch and a nagger, but my God, he looked like such an asshole to me." The ghosts grow quiet.

What Joan observes about herself is revealing. *He looked like such an asshole to me.* Joan's contempt for her husband is borne of disappointment. It is a classic scenario in Deadlock marriages: one spouse pushing the other to be a kind of supermate and then blaming the pushed spouse for not measuring up. "When you fall in love, you have unrealistic expectations," explains Washington psychologist Martha Gross. "People often have the illusion in marriage that the other spouse is going to take away the pain. When the person falls short of expectations, you feel alone. How people handle disappointments is the best barometer of how good the marriage is going to be."

Spouses in Deadlock may subconsciously test each other with impossible tasks. *I was pushing him to do things I was afraid to do myself.* With Joan, it is only a matter of time before her disappointment turns to loathing not just of her husband but of herself.

Gross continues: "Do you have empathy for the other's weaknesses? Do you say 'I can see you can't make $500,000 a year . . . I can see you can't deal with my mother. I can see you are not going to take away the pain and hurt.' Can you say 'My spouse can't do it; I understand why. I guess I'm on my own here' rather than 'you are responsible for this, you asshole.'"

In time, Joan becomes the kind of woman you read about in magazines, the woman who "finds herself" and makes a new life after divorce. She takes a course in business and forms her own public relations firm, specializing in computer technology. Instead of pushing on a husband "because he wasn't stronger, because he wasn't an admiral," she pushes on herself to be successful—and reaches her goals in her own right.

Sometimes when you break up, you have only half a confrontation. You tell your spouse you want to separate, but you don't tell the whole story. Usually the whole story involves a commitment already made to someone else. But you don't want to appear to be such a rat. And you don't want to give your spouse ammunition to stop you.

In this scenario, you have usually psychologically left the marriage a long time ago. You have made some fundamental changes in yourself and started a new life outside the marriage. You have moved into another relationship that is satisfying. You don't really want to look at your spouse in any depth. And you don't. You just leave. The old marriage is dead; long live the new one.

Bill Daniels, fifty-eight, approaches his wife with caution. They've been married twenty-five years. The children are grown and married. He works at a large paper company in Michigan. He met his wife, Joyce, when he was in the army. "I was attracted to her and I wasn't," he explains. "Apparently she was very attracted to me—something I was not accustomed to." Joyce is the kisser; Bill is the one who is kissed. Joyce makes plans for the wedding. Bill has doubts about the relationship, but doesn't want to hurt her. "I didn't want to marry her and yet I didn't want to leave her standing at the altar, either. That would have been a crowning disappointment." For the next quarter of a century, he tries not to disappoint her. "She had the attitude of 'I married you, I'm going to reform you; I'm going to whip you into the kind of shape I want you to be in,'" he says.

After seven years of marriage—there must be something to the cliché—Bill is seduced by another strong, domineering woman. "In retrospect, I see she used me terribly to hold herself together," he says. "Her husband was a little bit like my wife. He'd say, 'You better wash yourself before we have sex, I want you to be clean, I don't want the smells.' Now, she wasn't like that at all. Before me, she had been involved with a well-known neurologist in town. His idea of fooling around was to take off her high-heel shoes and beat her."

What a roller-coaster ride for a shy man. "It was very exciting with her, very secret, very risky, very dangerous," he says. "That was the thrill of it. She was so alive. I wasn't getting anything at home. It had been a year since my wife and I had touched each other."

The affair takes on a life of its own, and Bill is swept up by the James Bond adventure of it. To this day, he remembers the night he had to jump from the second-story window. "The husband was always taking business trips in his own plane; the airport was just ten minutes from the house. We knew he never flew at night, so that's when I went over there. We were just miserable devils, the way we went at it," he says with a leer. "One night we were lying in bed and we heard the whir and roar of the airplane overhead. She turned white. My heart stopped. We put our escape plan into operation. I whipped on my pants, jumped out the window, got in the car—I always parked down the street—and drove away. I think it took about three minutes," he says with a certain amount of pride.

The affair lasts twelve years. Then the woman moves with her husband to Kansas. By this time, Bill is totally removed from his wife. For the next ten years, he continues to be seduced by other women. "I didn't go out looking for it," he says. "These things just happened." It's still his style to defer to women. Joyce, the denier, pretends that everything is fine in the marriage, and he still defers to her.

He gets passed over for promotion in production and moves to a new section at the company, retail sales. In late September, he goes to a convention in Los Angeles, where he meets a woman with sharp gray eyes and close-cropped blond hair. She's twenty years younger and works for the tourist agency handling convention arrangements. He's staying at a hotel across town in Beverly Hills and she offers to drive him around the freeways. "I liked talking to her," he says. He invites her in for a drink; they have dinner and talk endlessly. He is sad to see her leave. They saw each other every day of the convention and spent every night together.

"Something sparked between us," he says. "As a result, I conducted an aggressive campaign—scarves, perfume, books—but mostly I wrote her very long letters."

The tables are turned in this relationship and Bill is the aggressor, the pursuer, the seducer. he goes west again and asks her to meet him in Santa Fe. She says yes and for ten days Bill is tour director. He knows the art galleries. He knows the pack trips in the mountains. "I showed her things she'd never seen before," says Bill, the teacher with her, the leader. No longer is Bill in the position of deferring to a woman. He learns how to take charge. He likes this new feeling.

Several months later, his wife conveniently goes to visit her brother in Atlanta. He continues his campaign: "This time I asked her—my paramour, my friend, my wife-to-be—to come here and see what it would be like to live with someone very much her senior—never mind the glamorous restaurants and secret rendezvous." Bill is the initiator, the mature one. They have a glorious two weeks together. She looks at him and says yes. She'd like to live with him forever; yes, she'd like to marry him.

Now it's up to Bill to take the lead and confront his wife.

"I knew the next move would have to be made by me—and I did it with incredible courage," he says. "Jesus Christ. I congratulate myself. It took nerve, it took the fact that I felt strongly about my new life.

"The same way that I didn't want to leave my wife stranded after twenty-five years of marriage, I didn't want to leave my wife-to-be stranded before we even got to the altar."

It's Sunday morning and his wife is still in bed. "I walked into the bedroom and she said to me, 'Is something wrong? Why don't you stretch out and I'll rub your back?' She must have realized something was happening," he says.

He sits down on the edge of the bed and looks at the floor. It's a painful moment. "I said to her, 'I can't take it. I can't take it anymore.'" He starts to cry. She has a good idea of what "it" is.

"Let's talk at breakfast," she says, still the controlling one.

Soon they are sitting in the breakfast nook. "I told her I wanted a divorce," he says. "She started screaming: 'You're sending me out to pasture!'

"I said nothing about the new arrival," he says. "I was afraid. My wife is very hysterical; I thought she'd go crazy if she knew. It was cowardly, but not completely. I knew she would exact a terrible price if she knew. She'd delay the divorce and try to destroy the relationship with the other person.

"So I thought I'd just tell her half the truth—that I felt closed in in the marriage, folded up; I was unable to move. This was the God's truth.

"She said, 'Maybe we should see a marriage counselor. Maybe you need some more therapy.' I thought: Always me, always *I* have a problem, *I* need a doctor; it's never her problem." The anger rises in him.

She asks, "Is there someone else?"

He looks at her straight and says, "No."

Then she starts to sob. "What am I going to do? I haven't worked in years." He's never thought of her as helpless, this dominating dragon lady. Guilt gives way to anger and he says, "I never said you couldn't work. I thought I was doing you a favor. You could stay home and read and take care of the cats."

The scene escalates into a screaming match. "Where am I supposed to go?" she says. "What am I supposed to do? Am I to get lost? If I can't trust you, who can I trust on this earth? I'm finished with everyone." She looks at him pleadingly now and says:

"You know I love you, I trust you, and look what's happened!"

Bill feels he's being torn apart. He thinks his wife looks quite pitiful now, blubbering away, blowing her nose and crying. He feels awful, guilty and insensitive. But he doesn't repent. He wants out. He's already gone.

Who's calling the shots now? Deadlock is broken.

Bill has what is known as a messy divorce.

The decision to separate is like Martin Luther nailing his theses to the door. You stand up with your list of past grievances and new expectations. You break with your past. You start on your own emotional reformation.

So does your spouse. No matter who makes the decision to split, both of you face enormous personal—and practical—changes. You enter the emotional never-never land of separation. The marriage is finished—but not over. At this point, you probably don't know whether you're going to get divorced or stay in the marriage.

The thing is, you don't have to get divorced to break out of a destructive relationship. Some couples go through the uncoupling process and stay together. They are able to face their Deadlock ghosts and renegotiate their marriage contract. It is a long and painful process. But even at this blackest moment of confrontation, when the bubble of betrayal and illusion has burst and you know the worst, it's important to know that you don't *have* to break up the marriage to change it. As Ann F. Leahy, director of the Marriage and Family Institute in Washington, D.C., puts it: "If the two people are decent but the [marriage] contract isn't working, is it possible to grow and change within the system?"

You may end up getting divorced, you may want to get

divorced or you may have no choice if your spouse wants out. But when crisis erupts in a marriage and a couple separates, divorce is not automatically the inevitable outcome.

"I can rarely predict who will go on and get a divorce and which couples will stay together," says Kirsch. "Often the worse the relationship and more open the battle, the better the chances are of keeping the marriage together. The purpose of therapy is to get people to focus on how they contributed to the breakup."

That's the hope in listening to the dancing ghosts. You can unravel the Deadlock contract you made with your spouse. You can understand how and why your marriage broke down.

Kirsch tells the story of an angry, violent man who gets so mad he starts fights in traffic. He is enraged at his wife because she's changed from a decent, pleasing woman to a rebellious women's-libber who won't even let him hold the door for her. He calls her a "bitch" in front of the children. From the sound of it, you'd say he was the villain in the piece; he's behaving like a wife beater and a bore. The couple gets into therapy. What helps most is to have her recognize that she is afraid of him, that she has put on him all the expectations one would have of a father. He feels hurt and rejected because she can only respond to him as a lecherous old goat, whom she finds repulsive. In the course of therapy, she becomes more confident and assertive. She is able to break the psychological power he holds over her and become less afraid. Meanwhile, he becomes more vulnerable. He doesn't have to be her father anymore. He comes to see that when he gets his way, he is really losing in the relationship. He learns to depend on her.

It takes eight years of therapy to renegotiate their original Deadlock contract. They get a good emotional divorce from the way they were—and stay married to each other.

There's no such thing as a quickie emotional divorce. It takes years to straighten out your Deadlock habits. Not everybody can do it and stay married to the same person. How can you tell which way you are going to go? You can't. You just have to live it through.

For many couples, by the time they reach the confrontation

scene, it is simply too late to reestablish a love relationship. "Usually what happens is that people enter a period of conflict. There is so much anger and hurt when they arrive at the therapist's door, it's far too late to change the patterns," says developmental psychologist Lindsay Chase-Lansdale of the University of Chicago. The years of separate emotional lives have worn you down too far; the list of hurts is too long. There's no tenderness, no respect left between you. You've tasted the promise of a new life; you just can't go back and try again with the person you started out with—not at this point, anyway.

In many ways, the politics of uncoupling mirror the politics of nations. As Russian poetess Zinaida Gippius-Merezhkovaskaya wrote in her diary in early 1917, some eight months before the Bolshevik takeover in October: "It is too early for revolution but too late for reform."

For many couples who separate after the confrontation scene, it is too late to reform the marriage—but too early to overthrow it by divorce.

PART TWO

CRAZY TIME

A time to kill, and a time to heal; a time to break down, and a time to build up.

Ecclesiastes 3:3

4

ON THE EDGE

Divorce puts you right on the edge of sanity. Some people go over the edge and destroy themselves and their families. They are like kamikaze pilots in a marital war where the death of their shared past can be the only victory. Although most people manage to get through this period of stress, a significant number of divorce casualties are the victims of murder, suicide, and madness. Other times, it's a slow inner death. The weapons are softer, less crude, more socially acceptable, but just as deadly to your psyche. There is a little bit of kamikaze craziness in all divorces.

You don't have to commit suicide or murder your spouse to know how crazy you feel. Just about everybody goes through a black period, a lonely *Walpurgisnacht*, when psychic demons gnaw at your brain and you think about murder and suicide. Perhaps it's not a very serious consideration, you say. It's just a game you're playing with yourself. Basically you're a normal person—but certain thoughts go in and out of your head. You wonder if things wouldn't be easier if your spouse had a car accident . . . or choked to death eating a piece of steak.

You can't help thinking about it. Actually you haven't been able to afford to eat steak in quite a while. One of the biggest shocks of breaking up marriage is financial: You're a lot poorer than you were before. It doesn't seem fair; to suffer so emotionally and then to suffer financially just when it would be nice to have some extra money to help ease your way through the trauma. If you're a man and worked for twenty years to have the good life, perhaps you're now renting a furnished efficiency apartment; back where you were when you started, and what with child support you think you'll be lucky if you ever have a decent place to live. If you're a woman who's been primarily a homemaker for the last fifteen years, you find you can't even get credit, let alone a job. How are you supposed to go to work when there's nothing you know how to do, and besides, who's going to take care of the children when they come home from school? Life takes on a very grim edge. Winter comes and the pipes burst. The car breaks down, the refrigerator conks out. You shake with hate, and after a trip to the bank and more debt, you sink down inside yourself. Maybe you're not going to make it. Maybe you're not ever going to have a decent life. In desperation, you think to yourself that if things get too impossible, you can just end it. Then you try to imagine what it would be like to be nothing, a vague blackness. The funeral: What would people say? Would anybody come?

The world is turned upside down; you've lost your center of gravity. You can't get your feet back on the ground. Instead you flip-flop in slow motion like astronauts in space. You don't seem to go in any particular direction; not forward, not backward. You just float and sink, float and sink again. Sometimes you're the Cheshire cat looking down on yourself. Other times you're trapped in a deep hole looking up. You go to a therapist who tells you what you already know: Divorce is a disorienting experience. You wish you could just press a button and stop the emotional roller coaster you're on.

He sits alone in his basement apartment. A .38 caliber revolver is on the table. He keeps the bullets back at the house. On the week-

end when he picks up the kids, he takes the revolver home and brings the bullets to the apartment. He's very careful not to have the revolver and the bullets in the same place. He likes to play a game with himself. He puts the gun to his head and pulls the trigger. "The old self is dead, long live the new!" he cries.

This is Crazy Time. It starts when you separate and usually lasts about two years. It's a time when your emotions take on a life of their own and you swing back and forth between wild euphoria and violent anger, ambivalence and deep depression, extreme timidity and rash actions. You are not yourself. Who are you? At times you don't want to know. You think about going on a sex binge and fucking anything that moves. Or you lie very still in bed, your muscles tense, your breathing shallow, your imaginings as dark and lonely as the night.

Then at the height of Crazy Time, you may get a reprieve. You fall in love—a *coup de foudre*—and the block of lead in your chest miraculously melts; you can't believe it, you laugh, you dance. You know it's too soon, too much like jumping into a lifeboat that you know leaks and has no oars. But you smile, feeling so good after feeling so bad for so long. Therapists call this the search for the romantic solution. But it's usually not a solution. You crash. Puff, the magic dragon of love is gone. Now you're really scared.

There seems to be no end to this wild swinging back and forth. You can't believe how bad your life is, how terrible you feel, how overwhelming daily tasks become, how frightened you are: about money, your health, your sanity. You can't believe that life is worse now than when you broke up. You thought you were at the end of your rope then.

In all the feel-good rhetoric about divorce being a growth opportunity for the new super you, nobody tells you about Crazy Time. Yet this is usually the very painful transition period you have to go through before you can establish a new life for yourself. It's equivalent to the mourning period after death and catastrophe.

Divorce *is* death and divorce *is* war. It's no wonder you go a little crazy. I had an uncle who used to say about World War II that some people came back from the war and were on one foot ever since. It was as though they had seen things and done things that were too much to bear. It's the same with divorce. You see things and do things that are too much to bear.

The loss through divorce is massive. It is the death of a relationship, a war with your past and the confrontation with your dreams of how you wanted your life to turn out. You learn things about your childhood, about your family and your friends. These are the dark secrets of divorce. Sometimes it's too much and most people go a little crazy for a while.

"Things are likely to get worse before they get better," says E. Mavis Hetherington, head of the department of psychology at the University of Virginia and a leading researcher on the impact of divorce.

"At the end of the first year, our divorced mothers and children were functioning less well than they were two months after divorce. And they say, 'My God, what's happening to me? I thought I would gradually get better, but here I feel worse.'

"Eventually things do get better; most of our people were functioning quite well after two years," she says.

Results of the California Children of Divorce Project confirm these findings. After separation, most of the one hundred and twenty men and women in the study went through a very turbulent period that lasted two years or more. In addition to widespread anger and depression, researchers found a startling incidence of profoundly disturbed behavior. While Deceivers who initiated the breakup were often paralyzed with guilt and low self-esteem, the Deniers who opposed the divorce were usually the ones who turned to violence.

"These men and women seemed catapulted into a period of chaos in which primitive, regressed, and uncontrolled behavior erupted unpredictably," says Joan Kelly, co-director of the project.

One fourth of the men in the study experienced this type of severe disorganization, the report continues. These men engaged in "acts of spying, breaking down the doors at night, obscene and frightening phone calls, physical beatings, vandalism and attempted childnapping," says Kelly. "A similar number of women became severely disorganized."

North Beach, Md.—A town councilman killed his wife, his 9-year-old daughter and then himself with a shotgun today in their home in this quiet southern Maryland community, apparently because of deepening domestic problems, according to State Police. . . . The daughter had recently told a little neighbor boy with whom she played that "she was moving uptown with her Mommy and new Daddy."

(*Washington Post*, August 25, 1981)

As much as you want relief from the misery of your marriage, as much as you thought about it and planned it, you usually aren't prepared to break up when you separate. Lack of preparation is linked to major emotional problems in the separation period. Studies show that most husbands and wives, including those who initiate the separation, are not really psychologically ready for divorce at the time. In one study, only 37 percent of the husbands and 30 percent of the wives reported having been prepared for the divorce—in spite of the fact that 53 percent of the men and 47 percent of the women had undergone at least one trial separation before the final breakup. Directors of the California Children of Divorce Project conclude that who initiates the breakup is often an important predictor of psychological trouble in the immediate period after the breakup. The one who is left—the Divorce Opposer—is usually the least prepared and the most vulnerable to violence and severely disturbed behavior.

Farwell, Mich.—Seven members of the Post family were murdered Tuesday night. . . . Both George W. Post, head of the family, and his wife were killed. With them in the family kitchen was Garnetta Haggart, 23 years old, Mrs. Post's daughter by an earlier marriage. She was also killed by a shotgun blast. In front of the Post farmhouse, police found the bodies of Helen Gaffney, Mr. Post's 29-year-old daughter from his first marriage, and her children, Angela, 10 years old, Tim, 8, and Amy, who was 4, also killed by blasts from a shotgun. . . . Sheriff Ghazy H. Aleck of Clare County today issued a call for the arrest of Robert Lee Haggart, 31, the estranged husband of Mrs. Haggart. . . . Mrs. Haggart arrived from Brandon, Fla., over the weekend. She was to attend the County Court Wednesday for a final decree in the divorce.

(*New York Times*, Feb. 18, 1982)

Crazy Time is when you get very close to Flameout. If you're lucky, you survive the trauma and learn from it. Often you discover your strength during this period, an emotional staying power that lays the foundation for your future. But it's close. Looking back, you realize you could have gone either way. It's important to remember that you're not alone. Most people who get divorced go over the edge for a while.

Margaret Simmons, forty-eight, remembers what it was like. She's very thin and has a passion for bright silk designer blouses. She's made it now: She's a reporter for a New York daily; she has an apartment overlooking Central Park, a lover, and a country house they own together.

Twenty years ago, she was in the hospital emergency room in Detroit, Michigan, her stomach being pumped out. Her chart read: "Attempted suicide." Margaret grew up in an academic community. Her father was a professor of American history in Michigan; her mother worked for Planned Parenthood and wrote book reviews for the local paper. Margaret was raised in the intellectual bohemianism of the fifties—the protective cage of a warm academic family.

Her freshman year at the university, she falls in love with Joseph, a man four years her senior, with sad brown eyes and prematurely graying hair. He's very bright, a kind of legend on campus, but there's a shadow over him, she knows. His mother committed suicide when he was twelve. Nobody talks about it. She's fascinated by his darkness. It's as if he's lived before and knows more than she. He also tells her that he's going to be the most successful real estate tycoon in Michigan.

They marry just before her twentieth birthday. In the unconscious Deadlock bargain, she gets the Great Man; he gets the perfect Helpmate. He is dominant; she is passive.

"The excitement of building *his* career was the glue," she says. "We loved each other very much for a long time. I worked while he went to school. We had a small apartment; spaghetti and Beethoven—it was very romantic. He graduated first in his class and I felt I was getting the diploma."

True to his word, Joe gets rich very fast. He develops shopping centers, apartment houses, indoor air-conditioned malls. They buy a big house with a swimming pool in Grosse Pointe. Seven years after the wedding, Joe is written up in the newspapers as the hottest real estate developer in Detroit. Margaret has three children, two dogs, two maids and a bad case of depression.

"He was flying and I was nothing," she says. What happened to that bright bohemian child who used to write plays and listen to her parents discuss the poems of Wallace Stevens at dinner? "Being a mother was fine, but it wasn't intellectually stimulating," she continues. "I was restless. I had never seen the world. I went to see the movie *The Graduate* and I said to myself: 'My God, all my life I've been too young. Now suddenly I'm too old. What happened to *my* time?'"

There's another thing she wonders about. She has never had an orgasm with Joe and he's the only man she's ever slept with. "I thought there was something wrong with me," she says. "I was undersexed or something." Joe starts staying out late at night and gambles. It's what the Very Rich do, he tells her. It's good for business.

For the next two years, the marriage slides downward. "We separated twice. We reconciled. We went to a marriage counselor.

Then finally one night I said, 'I don't want this marriage any-more.'"

She is twenty-nine years old, with children aged eight, five and three and nothing else. He is thirty-three and sitting on top of the real estate heap in Detroit, his dream having come true: money, fame and status, backed up by the lovely home with a lovely wife and three lovely children. She was a good Helpmate. He kept up his end of the Deadlock marriage contract and became the Great Man.

Now Margaret has betrayed him. By breaking up the mar-riage, Margaret destroys the foundations of his dream—or that's the way it looks to him. How could she do this to him? The dark shadow over him grows longer. He feels haunted by his mother's suicide, which no one talks about, his earlier link to madness. Now this. He could kill Margaret for exposing him.

"He was enraged," she says. "He made me suffer. He put a tap on my phone. He had me followed. He came after me with a gun once."

Her husband fits the pattern: the dominant one who denies problems in the marriage, he opposes the breakup and reacts to the separation with violent rage. She also fits the pattern: the submissive one who is aware of problems in the marriage, the one who initiates the separation. But she is so unused to independence she becomes paralyzed by her new responsibilities—and her husband's craziness.

He moves out of the big house in Grosse Pointe but refuses to send alimony or child support. Because he is so well known, she becomes convinced she can't get a lawyer to represent her. One afternoon she watches from her bedroom window as he smashes the dashboard of her car. She calls the police, but they won't come. "The sense of isolation was excruciating," she says. Fear turns into paranoia. She feels she has no control over what's happening. Everyone is against her, she thinks, no one under-stands how she could want to divorce such a successful man. "Just because you're restless?" her friends ask. She doesn't know how to answer. Even her parents back off. "What's happened?" they ask. She doesn't call them anymore. Guilt overwhelms her.

"For six months all I did was cry," she says. "The children's friends would come over, I'd open the door and tears would be streaming down my face." Then the bank notifies her that the house is in foreclosure. She takes a job as a hatcheck waitress in the daytime, trying to juggle children and baby-sitters.

"It was over for me. I had given up any chance of having a life. I was twenty-nine and my life had ended. I couldn't see my way out. My self-esteem was at an all-time low. I had terrible responsibilities. It was bleak. With nothing to look forward to, I thought of killing myself."

It is around nine-thirty in the morning. The children are in school. She stares at the bottle of aspirin. It won't take long, she thinks, lots of people do it this way. She takes five tablets and then another five. It's not long before she swallows all 150 tablets. "I tried killing myself and nearly succeeded," she says. "A girl friend happened to stop by," she continues. "She knocked on the door. I said, 'Go away!' But she came in. She took one look, grabbed the phone and got an ambulance."

Margaret stays in the hospital for several weeks. A complete nervous breakdown, say the doctors. Everything stops.

In retrospect, cracking up saved her life, she says. "Sitting there in the hospital was my turning point. I had been trying to do too many things without adequate resources—material or emotional resources. Fortunately, I found a genius of a psychiatrist."

She goes into therapy for several years. In time, she gets a lawyer to represent her side. The divorce comes through a year later. Meanwhile she takes the children to Saint Petersburg, Florida, and gets a job writing headlines for the *Saint Petersburg Times*.

"The violent phase ended after about two years," she says. "My ex-husband remarried soon after the divorce. He and his new wife were living in the big house in Grosse Pointe. They had everything. The children and I had nothing. We had literally three pots in the kitchen and five holes in the ceiling. But that was a most recuperative time in my life. We had nothing but it was *my* nothing. I was on my own.

"I learned that the only way you can make it is to take responsibility for your own actions. Not to be dependent emotionally or financially," she says.

Even after almost twenty years, her ex-husband is angry and still hangs up the phone on her when they talk about the children. His second wife looks haggard. Margaret rolls her eyes with a hint of malicious satisfaction. Then she smiles. Margaret is glad to be out of it.

Not everybody is as fortunate as Margaret—or as young and talented when they start a new life after divorce. But she doesn't come out of Crazy Time completely free of wounds. She's still cautious in relationships. What if it happened again? It was so crazy. To this day she doesn't understand what so enraged her husband. She remembers thinking: This can't be happening to two "normal people"!

A big part of Crazy Time is the ambiguity you feel. You aren't sure you really understand what's going on. This causes enormous anxiety. You don't even know how you really feel or what you want now. You feel so many conflicting emotions. Your own ambivalence is mirrored by your ex-spouse. He/she is acting as crazy as you. You look for clues. Separation scenes flash by. Where are you? You listen to the words of separating—that's you talking now—and you hear the sounds of rage and despair. But there is hope and humor in this too. After all, you've spent most of your life together. There were good times too, you remember. You look harder; if only you could be sure. . . . You are out of the marriage—yet you aren't.

It is a psychological earthquake, this feeling of being in two places at once, with no firm footing. "You feel split, especially if there are children," says Robert Kirsch. "You feel insane, crazy, strange—never where you're supposed to be."

In many ways, the disorientation of the post-separation period is similar to the pain and confusion of adolescence. People between the ages of sixteen and twenty get out from their parents geographically, but it's often not until they're in their thirties that they leave psychologically, therapists point out. Separating from a spouse is analogous to leaving home. It's the beginning of a weaning process. You may have slammed the door shut, but you haven't made the psychological break yet.

Separation may also trigger unresolved issues buried from childhood. If you haven't psychologically left the home of your parents yet, you have unfinished business to do. You may find you have merged the emotional landscape of your childhood with that of your marriage. When the marriage breaks up, you have to leave both your parents and your spouse—a doubly painful weaning process.

It's like being rolled over by a wave on the beach. You are turned upside down and ground up by a jumble of conflicting feelings: Love-hate. Tenderness-rage. Innocence-guilt. Regret-hope. You are caught in the psychological stalemate of Double-feel, and there seems no end to it. She wears the scarf you gave her last Christmas. He picks up the children and offers to mow the lawn. Now where are you? You dream more than you sleep. You can't stop the wild emotions flowing through you. The Dead-lock ghosts fight fiercely through the night.

John Ritchie, fifty-one, of Cleveland, is sitting in church. It's just before Christmas and he and his wife, Carol, are separating after eighteen years of marriage. "I closed my eyes during a prayer period and had this vision," he says. "I was riding a rocket up into the sky toward a great big hole. Carol was in front of the hole. I ran right through her with the rocket. As I was traveling through the other side of her, she looked at me kind of surprised. She was doubled over and held her stomach where I had gone through her. Then she climbed up on the rocket and went with me through the hole."

He smiles.

"After that vision, I came home and without even thinking I suggested we try again. I felt it could work."

The twisted logic of it: *I have to destroy my spouse to save the marriage.* But that's the logic of Crazy Time. John feels put down in his marriage. He wants Carol to see that he's really strong and decisive. He wants to hear that she needs him and wants to stay with him; she wants to climb on the back of his rocket for a change. He's also so angry at her for all those years she pushed him around, he could kill her. He has to run right through her with a rocket to bring her to her senses. Then they could go off in the clouds together.

The leap from hate to love is par for the course in Crazy Time. Therapists know that by exploring conflicting feelings, instead of blocking them out as irrational, you can come to terms with a situation and make decisions. It seems ironic, but when you acknowledge your Doublefeel in divorce, you can break the power these wild and contradictory emotions hold over you. If you're persistent and lucky, you ultimately can gain some control over your emotional life.

The problem with John Ritchie is that he only acknowledges Doublefeel in his vision. He doesn't explore these feelings in the real situation. That way he remains in control of the script.

Carol doesn't get the Doublefeel logic of his vision. She's in her own Crazy Time. So when John tells her of ramming her through with a rocket and then asks for a reconciliation, she looks at him in horror and says: "Are you crazy? Are you trying to kill me?"

Orlando (AP)—Suspended Orange County Commision Chairman Ed Mason testified Monday that he was irrational at the time he shot and killed his estranged wife. Mason, 36, is charged with first-degree murder* in the slaying of Diane Mason, 34, who was shot five times on the balcony of a southeast Orlando condominium May 17. . . . Mason told police he shot his wife after she laughed at his offer of reconciliation and that he later tried to kill himself in a traffic accident. . . . He blamed affairs he had had with other women [for the breakup]. The couple separated twice, the last time in February. He insisted he loved his wife.

(October 13, 1981)

This is the dilemma. To get through Crazy Time, you have to let yourself be out of control for a while—in order to gain control

---

*He was subsequently found guilty of second-degree murder.

of your life. You have to explore these conflicting feelings you have, even though they are the cause of so much pain and anxiety. That's the only way you're going to get over the past and let go of the marriage. If you try to stay in control of your emotions, you might be able to block out the craziness of Doublefeel for a while. That might make you feel better temporarily, but in the long run it prevents you from working through your emotional divorce. You remain trapped in this stage of the divorce process. Then you start acting really crazy.

People who don't make it through Crazy Time usually are the ones who won't let go and accept the divorce. They refuse to confront the emotional disorientation of the marriage breakup. They try to stay in control of the situation—until they burst out in uncontrollable behavior. Murder and suicide are futile, fatal attempts at control; in the last analysis, violence is the loser's way out.

Violence can also be a form of denial. If you oppose the divorce, for example, you deny that it's happening by destroying your spouse, whom you see as the agent of all your troubles. In effect, you shoot the messenger of emotional bad news. Or you shoot yourself: *See what you've done to me* are your last words.

It sounds as though Ron and Ingrid are simply in the middle of divorce, another sad, messy divorce. She is the thirty-three-year-old daughter of a black American GI and a white Austrian schoolteacher; he is a thirty-four-year-old printer's son from rural Virginia. They live in an orange brick house in the Maryland suburb of Camp Springs, their dream house they worked so hard for in their fifteen years of marriage.

They have married young. She is seventeen, he a year older. They dream of ballet lessons and bicycles for the kids, a station wagon in the garage, a swimming pool in the backyard. He works as a printer; she has three babies and joins the police force. "He said his wife was going to leave him . . . he didn't want the family to break up. He looked kind of sad . . . but I don't think he ever gave up," says his friend in the neighborhood. She moves out and stays with a friend. They put the dream house up for sale. "Yes, it's a dream house," he tells the real estate agent.

The police find her lying dead at the bottom of the stairs, shot in the head, neck and chest with a handgun. Five other bodies were found in the house, including two daughters. There were so many wounds that the medical examiner who did the autopsy said it was almost impossible to count them.

(Based on reports in the May 10, 1981, *Washington Post.)*

There are subtler ways to destroy your spouse and yourself: You go to court and testify that the spouse is an unfit parent. You make threats over the phone and in letters. You drain the joint savings account. You tell mutual friends about the drinking, the fooling around, the embezzlement that was covered up . . . in short, what a bastard/bitch the ex-spouse is. Or you kill yourself slowly: you take drugs, ricocheting from doctor to doctor; you start drinking, ricocheting from one bar to the next. That way you turn your ex-spouse into a distant murderer.

After a while, you forget that you are involved in a power struggle with your ex-spouse—and yourself—to accept the death of the marriage. You are still playing Deadlock wars. You live in the past. It's not long before you become a Divorce Flameout. By having the last word through violence—whether it's murder, suicide or the more subtle forms of destruction—you lose.

Everybody gets very close to the edge in Crazy Time. For most people, violent behavior is usually expressed only in fantasy. It's still an attempt to control the divorce battle. Even in fantasy, the taste of violence gives you a sense of mastery over what seems like an intolerable situation. You're taking care of this your own way. Your own crazy way.

Carl Hillings, forty-one, a pin-stripe lawyer from Seattle, has developed an overwhelming hatred of his wife and spends a whole summer plotting her murder. He sits in a bar with his colleague

Ron Kraus and fantasizes. Their wives and children are spending August together on one of the San Juan islands in Puget Sound. The two men stay in the city and meet every night at a bar. Halfway into their martinis, they plan the murder of Cal's wife. It starts out as a joke, but day by day the fantasy grows. Ron, who's been there, knows what Carl is going through. Ron's marriage broke up five years ago and now he's remarried with two kids under three.

Throughout August, these two gentlemen lawyers stop at the bar after work to talk of murder. Poison, fire, guns. They devise a number of plans. "At first it shocked me," says Carl. "Then I began thinking about it. I came up with the perfect murder. I would get her to go out kayaking in the moonlight. She can handle a boat but she's not very strong. We'd get a little chop in the open sea. Then I'd tip her over. A perfect murder. How could she survive, several miles offshore—at night?" He smiles, reliving the thrill of the fantasy.

Carl gets through the summer—and through Crazy Time—without acting out his fantasy. In the marriage, he is the passive one. He feels his wife always calls the shots. During Crazy Time, he says those mental murders were a secret psychic weapon that gave him strength when he had to deal with her. By recognizing how close he is to the edge, he remains just this side of sanity.

As you plunge deeper into Crazy Time, you start to feel better. Your life takes on a certain drama. Only the good love affairs die young, you say. The rest is sham. You go to the movie *Casablanca* and relive the doomed love between Humphrey Bogart and Ingrid Bergman. You listen to Italian opera. In some ways the trauma of separation is a welcome contrast to the boredom that underlies many marriages. You talk to fellow travelers on the divorce trail. You find your personal problems seem not unique. You are part of a new Lost Generation—not in war or art but in divorce. You remember the verse from Oscar Wilde's "The Ballad of Redding Gaol": "Yet each man kills the thing he loves. . . . The coward does it with a kiss, the brave man with a sword!"

* * *

Getting an emotional divorce after the death of your dreams takes time. But it finally happens. After a while, Crazy Time comes to an end. The marriage is over. While you're going through this period, you can't believe it's happening to you. Looking back, you can't see how you and your ex-spouse could ever have a working relationship again after so much kamikaze violence has passed between you. But even after the worst of Crazy Times, you can put this bitter period behind you and rebuild a working relationship with your ex-spouse.

Sandra Holton, forty-eight, remembers what it was like. When her marriage breaks up, she is thirty-five, alone in a new house in Indianapolis with three children under four, an escapee from a twelve-year marriage to Roger, a self-made man in public relations. Premarriage, Sandra is a rebellious flower child before the sixties made the combination trendy. Sandra comes to New York after junior college. She goes out with truck drivers. She pickets the Greyhound Bus Terminal. Then she marries Roger, who comes from Arkansas and belongs to the Young Republican Club.

"I felt I was marrying an old friend rather than a great passion," she says. "I felt comfortable. I felt safe. He was a very strong figure. I had an insecure childhood. I knew he would balance the checkbook and take care of all the stuff I wasn't good at." In the unconscious marriage bargain, he gets class and she gets a caretaker. Roger is dominant; she is submissive.

They move to Indianapolis and join the up-and-coming young-married set. Roger doesn't let her picket bus terminals anymore. He wishes she'd stop wearing dirty blue jeans and grow up. It's not long before Sandra has the Deadlock-breaking affair. "I just fell into an affair," she says, still trapped in the submissive role. "I didn't go out looking for someone. I happened to meet him at a party. He was a very strong, outgoing person. He made me feel terrific." Meanwhile the marriage disintegrates. "I was leading a double life and it was very serious," she says. Roger and Sandra don't sleep together anymore; the last time they had intercourse was when the younger child was conceived three years before the breakup. "We'd just pass in the halls, turn our eyes away and say, 'Oh, excuse me.' It was unbearable."

She goes to a psychiatrist. Desperate in the marriage but too insecure to leave it, she lets the psychiatrist talk to her husband about breaking up. Roger refuses to consider it. "Forget it. There's never been a divorce in my family before," he tells Sandra. "You're not going to destroy this family." Ultimately, with the help of her psychiatrist, Sandra leaves. She picks up the children, asks her parents for money and moves into a house nearby. But as is the case with many submissive people who initiate the breakup, that first strike for independence has demanded so much of her strength, Sandra feels exhausted and overwhelmed by the new set of problems that face her.

And now Roger goes after her.

"The worst moments were when Roger would call up drunk and say he was going to kill himself. He went through a serious drinking problem when he was at his lowest. He'd call up at eleven at night and say, 'God damn you, you bitch,' the words slurring, desperate. 'I have nothing to live for. I'm going to kill myself. I'll make it look like an accident—and you better not interfere with this.'

"I thought, Oh my God. What have I done?"

She tries to find out—indirectly—how serious he is. "I'd call a friend of his. He said Roger never missed a day of work or anything."

Sandra waits it out. Roger doesn't kill himself, but he still carries on the battle for control. He tells the children that the breakup is all Mommy's idea; it's her fault; she's responsible for all this trouble. He tells his mother, her mother, their friends, the bartender at Harry's, the tax accountant, the lawyer, the judge. When he comes to pick up the children he says, "The children look dirty—per usual." Or: "So-and-so saw you down at Murphy's Bar—are you sleeping with everybody down at Murphy's? You're fucking all over the place, aren't you, slut?"

It goes on like this for about two years. "Gradually things got better," she says. "He moved to Chicago and we began to communicate in a more normal way."

Sandra and Roger have been divorced for more than ten

years. The children are teenagers. They spend every summer with their father and he comes to see them once a month in Indianapolis. Roger and Sandra discuss math tests and plans for college. When she decides to open a shop, he helps her find a good place. "Nothing lasts forever," not even the bitterness of Crazy Time. "Now it's almost like we're old friends," says Sandra. "Last Christmas, Roger was here with his girl friend and we all sat around and had a drink. Sometimes I can't believe it myself."

It's important to know that Crazy Time is normal. You are not alone. It's a time when helpful friends say, "Come over for dinner"; when helpful parents say, "We'll take the children next weekend"; when you repeat to yourself, "Take one day at a time."

This is the time to be good to yourself, to spoil yourself, even if that only means taking a long bath as you sip a glass of wine and listen to the sound track of *Chariots of Fire*. You're not going to conquer Crazy Time in a day. You might as well take things slowly if you can. When you feel yourself going over the edge, stop a minute. *This too shall pass.*

It's also, for many people, a good time to get into therapy if you haven't already sought help. People are more likely these days to get counseling when problems arise in a marriage. There is also a wide range of counseling services, from traditional psychotherapy to support groups affiliated with community centers and churches. You need guidance and support when a marriage ends. You need to have someone you can turn to, someone who knows about Doublefeel, who knows when you're getting too close to the danger zone of violence and despair.

Give yourself about two years. This is the tough part of your divorce journey. This is also the period when you grow the most and you lay the foundation for a new life. So try to take each phase as it comes. Let your family and friends know you need their support. Unless they've been through it themselves, they probably can't comprehend what your life is like now. You need to help them along.

5

RELIEF/DISBELIEF

In the dark, you wonder: Is it true? Is this really happening? Suddenly your life no longer seems to belong to you. You're in a television soap opera. Someone else is writing the script. What kind of part do you have: Good guy? Bad guy? Martyr? Do you know your lines? Does the audience like the show? What's going to happen next? Will you triumph over evil and agony as your world turns? Or is the scriptwriter going to drop you one day and you'll just fade away?

Maybe in the morning, you think, all this will go away.

You are in shock. This is the first phase of Crazy Time, an interlude of numbness that usually occurs right after the breakup. Perhaps it's the psyche's way of giving you a rest after the traumatic decision to separate. For most people, the numbing phase is a combination of relief and disbelief, a phony calm before the real *Sturm und Drang* of Crazy Time takes over your life. An initial period of shock lets you build up strength to face the pain and turmoil that lie ahead. There's no such thing as a painless divorce—unless it wasn't much of a marriage to begin with. For two people who invested their basic dream in marriage together, who had children together, who lived for a decade or more together, breaking up is nothing less than a death.

At first you feel a mixture of relief and disbelief—more or less proportional to your role in initiating the separation and the degree to which you were "left." For Divorce Opposers, the immediate reaction is usually disbelief. *This can't be happening to me!* Disbelief is often an extension of denial. You refuse to accept the decision to separate. *This can't be real!* Disbelief dulls the pain and humiliation from being "left" and found inadequate—for a while.

For Divorce Seekers—and those who subconsciously welcome the decision to separate—the initial reaction may be one of relief. The bubble of marital misery and dishonesty has finally burst. You are still raw from the months spent agonizing over whether or not to terminate the relationship. You don't yet know what the new set of problems will demand of you, but still you are relieved. You just stop and take a deep breath. The sense of relief replenishes precious psychic energy that has been drained away in the months preceding the confrontation scene.

In many ways, relief and disbelief are emotional twins. They are stalling actions. Feelings of *I don't believe this* and *Thank God, it's out in the open now* are psychological soft strokes to get you started on the right foot in the separation process.

There are enormous practical problems: Who moves out? Who pays for math tutoring? What do you tell the children? Your friends? Your parents?

There are also enormous psychological problems: Who are you? What went wrong? Who is to blame? Those Deadlock ghosts are going to wake up soon and start dancing. Over the next five years or so, you will probably not only re-examine yourself, your marriage and your past but revise your basic dream for the future as well.

It's too much to cope with all at once. Besides, at this point you may not know if you are going to end up getting a divorce or not. An instinct tells you not to make any major decisions just now.

This initial phase of Crazy Time can last anywhere from a couple of days to several months. For some people, this period when you accept the decision to separate is the most important—and most difficult—phase of the uncoupling process.

For both Divorce Seekers and Divorce Opposers, there may be a manic quality in this period, even a sense of euphoria and a tremendous release of energy. You throw yourself into activity—movies, bars, picnics; you take on a new assignment at work, you paint the spare bedroom, you civilize the children with trips to the museum, the theater, the zoo, you buy a new wardrobe.

You wallow in your soap opera. It becomes a time of high drama—the forbidden thrill of telling the news. "You know, John and I are splitting up—this is the worst thing that's ever happened to me," says Mary. Yet friends notice she's never looked better; she has color in her cheeks, a light in her eye. She repeats the phrase as though she were trying to convince herself that it's really true. "John and I are splitting up!" Her eyes look around the table—is there a "no" from anyone in the group? Only nodding heads, she sees. She forgets that she's telling the news, not listening to it. "John and I are splitting up," she says again. Everybody nods. They say they're sorry. The split must be real.

Other times, you look haunted, your face the color of a dead fish, dark circles around the eyes, hollow cheeks—your hands shake, you can't look anybody in the eye, your lips don't seem to connect with words. You are locked in your agony and you know that probably everybody knows but you can't talk about it yet.

Meanwhile, you cling to familar rituals. In the evening, you watch the nightly news on television—just as you always do. You put the trash out on Tuesdays and Thursdays; you go to staff meeting on Mondays; you drive the car pool on Fridays. Just as you always do.

There's a curious sameness to your life—despite the fact that it is turned inside out with the separation. Perhaps it dawns on you that you always watched the nightly news on television alone. You realize there will always be a staff meeting on Monday. The President announces more budget cuts, the launch of the space shuttle is delayed, the Rolling Stones come to Philadelphia. It all goes on, whether you get divorced or not. People who are strongly opposed to the breakup of a marriage usually have a very difficult time in the beginning of the separation period—especially if you haven't recognized the signs of crisis in your marriage. Mr. Dominant. Lady Denier. You are used to being czar. Now your whole universe is turned upside down. Who can you trust? Is there anything you can count on anymore? You have a lot of psychological catching up to do in Crazy Time. You don't know where to begin. So you buy time for yourself. Disbelief is not only a socially acceptable response, it's a protective emotion—as long as it doesn't last too long.

For Bailey Wadsworth, his wife's decision to divorce him is the most unbelievable thing that has ever happened to him.

Bailey, fifty-five, thinks of himself as one of a dying breed of self-sufficient gentlemen. Born in Boston, he wears the somewhat shabby mantle of old Wasphood. Cold showers. Dirty sneakers. Sweaters with patches at the elbow. His face is square; he has a Talleyrand nose, black hair and blue eyes. The emphasis in his growing-up years was on character. People from Texas may be richer, but he knows that Bostonians have cornered the market on good character. Having started out realizing he has an edge on life, he relishes it.

He meets Catherine at a house party in Saunderstown, Rhode Island, given by his favorite aunt, Helen. Bailey is in his first year at Harvard Law School. Catherine is the daughter of one of Aunt Helen's old boarding school friends from Virginia. "I didn't think she looked terribly pretty," says Bailey of his first meeting with Catherine. "A nice-looking woman, but essentially I felt she was rather plain."

It turns out she is studying music at the New England Conservatory. That fall, he is an usher in two weddings—for his brother, who is two years younger, and for his Groton roommate. It seems natural that he, too, will soon get married.

"I wanted to get married," he says. "Basically what I had in mind about Catherine was that this was a marriageable woman. For one reason or another—social pressure or loneliness—I just wanted to get married." It all sounds very legitimate: marriage, family, community, character.

"The marriage started out on rather pragmatic principles as far as I was concerned, and therefore it seemed to me it could work that way indefinitely," he continues. "I guess I wasn't very concerned about her feelings—once one is married, I thought, one is married. The idea of divorce never really occurred to me."

In the unconscious marriage bargain, he gets the good wife he thinks he is supposed to marry and she gets the respectable husband she is hoping to marry. In the Deadlock, he is dominant, she is passive. "I definitely thought I was dominant," he says. "I never really thought about it—it was just the way things were."

They get married and live in a walk-up apartment. Bailey finishes law school, spends two years with the Justice Department in Washington and then they disappear to Minneapolis for three years. By the time he returns to Boston and joins an old-line law firm, he and Catherine are firmly welded, with four children. Back on home turf, they quickly slip into rituals of Sunday lunch, Labor Day weekend with Aunt Helen, season tickets to the symphony.

His home life is solid and not very interesting. But Bailey never expected it to be interesting. His excitement lies in his job. He moves up in the firm and takes over some new projects. He travels often and there are month-long separations in the marriage. He loves to be on the road and enjoys the time away by himself. He has the perfect job, he thinks, the perfect life. He's finally getting his finances under control after so many years in law school. The struggle is behind him. He has a couple of insignificant affairs. The oldest boy is ready to go away to school next fall. Bailey and Catherine celebrate their eighteenth wedding anniversary with good French champagne.

Then, driving to the headquarters of a new client outside Mexico City, Bailey sees a flash of silver in the road ahead and swerves the rented Peugeot to one side. He avoids hitting a tree and curses. When he looks back up to the road, all he sees is the silver radiator grating of a truck coming in through the windshield. He doesn't remember the crash, the Mexican voices, the ride to the hospital. "Spinal cord injury," it says on his chart.

He is flown back to Boston on a stretcher. The doctors tell him he will never walk normally again. His hospital room is filled with flowers. The office keeps his job open. He comes home and Catherine nurses him for the next year. He enters the world of braces, crutches, canes and wheelchairs. The doctors smile at him. They say he's making much more progress than they ever expected. But Bailey doesn't smile. His dreams are broken.

"This damn accident," he says, poking a crutch at his shriveled legs. "I was completely out of control. What I had planned to do was to begin to have some fun in life, to take vacations, to go traveling. That's what I was building up to, what I was working so hard for. I had to get things under control first. Then the accident. I couldn't do anything. I was totally paralyzed and Catherine had to take care of me. It was a shock. Six months of intensive care. I was near death."

Bailey starts to get better. He learns to drive a specially equipped car. He goes back to work. The excitement builds up in him again, the excitement of new clients, new colleagues, new trips. He gets so he can move around pretty well with a cane. He goes to parties and tells funny stories. There are times he forgets he's been in an accident.

Then Catherine says she wants a divorce.

Here is a woman with four children and a paralyzed husband, a woman burdened by duty and hardened by the lack of warmth in her emotional life. To be sure, Catherine is a woman of character, a good wife. But it's too much for her. In the midst of this, her mother develops cancer. The sting of dying is regret. Catherine drives her mother to the hospital, she drives Bailey to physiotherapy, she drives the children to soccer games and skating parties, she makes calls for the coalition against nuclear war, she works one day a week at Planned Parenthood, she sends out Christmas cards, she takes the cars in for tune-ups, she writes letters to her congressman. Her mother dies. Bailey gets better. The children get older. Catherine is forty-one years old and doesn't want to be married any longer.

At first Bailey plays it cool.

"I had more or less recovered," he says. "My mental faculties were never impaired and I had recovered physical control and could get around with a cane. Then the discussion came up. We had a few fights and started to talk seriously about getting divorced. At this point I had a lot of general anger. All my plans had been interrupted by this horrible accident. I was furious at the world.

"So when Catherine suggested we get divorced, I thought: Oh, well, what the hell. My reaction was: Oh, sure—let's do it. We don't really love each other anyway.

"It never occurred to me that she would go through with it," he continues. "My feeling at the time was I could more or less stay married indefinitely. My perception of Catherine was that she probably couldn't really handle a divorce and so she would come back and say let's start again.

"I felt I was in a one-up psychological position. I could hardly walk. I had just been through this horrible experience. I could not imagine that anyone would pursue a divorce in that situation. The fact that she did was a complete violation of my code."

Bailey's disbelief gives way to fury as it becomes clear that Catherine has every intention of getting the divorce. They sell the house in Dover. He moves downtown. Catherine and the children move out to Hamilton on the North Shore.

"Because of the original basis for the marriage and because I thought the household was my creation, to have the whole thing destroyed seemed absolutely outrageous to me," he says.

Boom—his world is gone. The anger wells up in him. He can't help it. He finds he is furious over money. All the rage he has—at the accident, at the breakup of the marriage, at Catherine as the agent of destruction—comes out in dollars. Four children. Four college tuitions. Four pairs of dirty sneakers. Four sweaters with patches on the elbows. So much for good character, he thinks.

The days turn into months. He can't believe it. The divorce is final. He is stunned . . . outraged . . . and panic-stricken. For the first time in his life, he goes to a psychiatrist.

"I thought something was wrong," he says. "Something had to be basically wrong with me, because all my fundamental Anglo-Saxon Wasp principles had been blown up in one bang."

It's the beginning of a painful journey. He goes into analysis. His legs continue to get better and he fantasizes about a new life. He gets a second wind at work and goes to Argentina on a special legal project. He takes up painting and photography. But the overwhelming rage stays with him for several years. He bellows in the dark at his fate. How to accept the unacceptable? His paintings start to attract some attention: wild abstract pieces in bright colors. He sells a few paintings to friends. Then he falls in love, perhaps for the first—but not for the last—time in his life. Even his attitude toward Catherine changes:

"I had to do some reassessment of this person who did not seem so terribly impressive during the eighteen years or so we were married. Yes, she changed. More important, my attitude toward her changed. I like Catherine a lot now. I can't stand her intellectual positions—she's simplistically antiestablishment, a limousine communist who believes in God and lives next door to my mother in polo country. The inconsistencies in her position are not obvious to her!" He stops and laughs. "I guess I enjoy the fights we get into over this—and I admire what she has done."

He still walks with a cane. He still wonders what happened to the Wasp values he grew up with. There's something about the old world neatness of arranged marriages that he likes. Do Prince Charles and Lady Diana really love each other? Then he smiles. He knows there are possibilities for enjoyment and happiness that didn't exist in his marriage or in his imagination before the breakup. It's been ten years since the accident, nine years since the divorce. "On balance, I'm glad we were divorced," he says.

For Divorce Seekers who have wrestled with the notion of divorce for a long time before they do anything about it, the greatest period of stress may have already occurred. In a University of Colorado study of one hundred and fifty-three recently separated adults who asked for a divorce, the highest incidence of stress symptoms—weight change, upset stomach, headaches, nervousness and general weakness—occurred six months before the separation.

Getting separated often brings much-needed relief from the extreme stress that led to the breakup. In the California Divorce Project, more than 50 percent of the adults reported significant relief at the time of the separation—including some of the spouses nominally opposed to the breakup.

Sometimes a marriage crumbles for a very specific reason. Louette Sullivan, for example, spends seven years married to a man who is homosexual. In that period, they never have sexual intercourse. Had she been Catholic, she says, she would have gotten an annulment. She was raised a strict Presbyterian and divorce was unheard of in her family. But separating from her husband brings to an end several years of acute distress in her marriage.

She was a virgin on her wedding day. How could she have known? Although she knows the marriage is over as soon as it begins, she feels she has no choice but to stick it out. She's from Naperville, Illinois, an outsider in her husband's hometown of Charleston, South Carolina, living next to mama and paying court to Beauregard Culture, that nostalgic view of Southern gentlemen on horseback with medals and mammies. It was supposed to be a good match. He had charm, he ran the family business. Louette was just out of college, a bright and serious young woman who never lost her strong faith.

The wedding night passes. They go to Australia for a honeymoon. He never touches her. When they return to South Carolina, her husband tells her that he always spends at least four nights in town each week. It's not long before she hears the whispers. She doesn't say anything to anyone. She doesn't even tell her parents. She tries to make the best of being Mrs. Beauregard. She considers the idea of divorce unthinkable.

They drift along, paralyzed in mutual loneliness. It takes her several years to get to the point of considering divorce as an option—even with supportive counseling from a minister. It takes another year to make the decision—and another year to put it into action and leave her husband.

It's a scandal in the community. Her husband is outraged. Damn Yankee, he says. But Louette feels as though her life is just beginning. Separated now for several months, she says, "The main thing I feel is relief—just relief to be out of it. I don't know what I'm going to do or where I'm going to go. But I'm just so happy."

Sometimes the marriage is so destructive that breaking up is a cause for celebration. Usually one partner has a problem that makes family life untenable. Your spouse may be addicted to alcohol or drugs and refuses to stop the abuse. You may find yourself sucked into a netherworld of violence and crime. Has there been physical or sexual injury to you or your children? If so, you don't have the luxury of choice or time to consider your next move. You need emergency help to protect you and your family from further harm.

Such cases of domestic abuse are the extreme. For most people, the reasons for breaking up a marriage are much less obvious. The injuries in Deadlock marriages are subtle and psychological. Spouses are more evenly matched and the bond between them is more complex. Breaking out of Deadlock is a welcome change. But the feeling of relief is temporary, like spending the night in a luxury hotel after a long unpleasant flight, before you change planes for the rest of the journey. It's a passing phase in the divorce process, when you take time out.

Jane Riccardo, of Denver, Colorado, looks back on her relief period as a psychological vacation. She is a born worrier. She worries about her figure, she worries about her job at the state education department, she worries about toxic wastes and the environment. Her children are grown and she's about to remarry. It's been five years since she and her husband broke up; they were together twenty-two years.

"For the first three months after he left, I just had a euphoric period," she says.

Jane has green eyes and always wears her reddish-brown hair in a pixie cut. Her marriage takes a lot out of her. Her husband, Michael, has an artist's look, black hair and a thin nose, is very bright and unsure of himself. They marry while he's still in graduate school studying economics. Her father is a well-known professor of economics. Her husband is going to be one too. She's going to make it all turn out right. In their unconscious bargain, she gets someone to be as successful as her father; he gets a strong agent to make things go right. She is dominant; he is passive.

She reads his papers and drills him before exams, has his colleagues over for dinner and makes sure he does well. His colleagues say he's on the fast track. But behind closed doors, Mike comes to depend on her excessively. If she doesn't take care of him, it seems, he won't make it.

The babies start coming. Mike gets a job at the University of Colorado. To the world, he is a brilliant professor of economics. At home, she says, "the marriage became a power play for control."

They fight about little things. Housecleaning. Who gets the car. The kids' schooling. She's very strong. He starts drinking. The competition grows. Isn't he lucky, friends say, to have such a strong, supportive wife to see him through? She criticizes his papers, reminding him how important it is to publish. He stops writing and spends the afternoon watching football games. They go to a cocktail party hosted by the chairman of the department and he gets drunk. She covers for him, making conversation on economic theory with the department chairman. He trips over a rug in a hall. She runs to his side: "Did you hurt yourself, honey?" He glares at her. She's winning. Everybody can see that. She's the gallant wife of a professor who drinks too much. He doesn't even grade papers now. It comes as no surprise when he doesn't get tenure.

Jane can't stand it anymore. In this case, it is Jane, the dominant one, who decides she can no longer carry her dependent spouse on her back. For the next few months she and Michael talk about separating. Finally she sets the date—Thanksgiving.

They all have Thanksgiving dinner together. Afterward Michael leaves and spends the night with faculty friends. The next day, Jane changes the locks on the doors. Separation begins and her first response is relief.

"I felt terrific at first," she says. "I took stock of myself. I read four or five books a week. I played the piano—I hadn't done that in years. I let the housecleaning go—Mike always insisted on neatness.

"There were ridiculous little things—like having the whole bed to yourself. To be able to read as late as you wanted to. He always hated that and insisted the lights go out when he went to sleep. I bought a skirt for myself and didn't have to sneak it into the house. I was free to make decisions," she says. "It was a tremendous relief."

Jane revels in his absence. This period lasts for three months.

"Then I crashed," she says.

The divorce honeymoon is over. Jane plunges into Crazy Time. "I was alone, I didn't have a job, the roof leaked," she says. "I started going out with a few guys. It was awful—dating like a teenager. Life seemed to be easier for my husband. I felt like killing him. Then I got scared, really scared. Maybe I wasn't going to make it."

Jane's initial response of relief passes in the face of the new realities of being separated. Although Jane doesn't regret her decision to divorce, she goes through a stressful two years before accepting the end of the marriage. She is still plagued with free-floating guilt, especially when it comes to the children. And she still worries about her ex-spouse. Mike never gets back on his feet after the divorce. It's as though Jane is still his lifeline. His disintegration after the divorce is twisted proof that she pulled the plug on him.

In those five years after the divorce her life improves. She gets a job, she has her share of romances and one-night stands, she goes into therapy. After a while, she meets a man and thinks about remarriage.

There is some hesitation in her eyes, a wariness that divorced people carry with them. Will it work the next time around? Then she smiles. "It's different this time," she says. "I don't worry about him all the time—how he's feeling, what he's doing, why things at work aren't going better."

It takes Jane a new relationship to break out of Deadlock. The future is hopeful. But she doesn't forget the pain of Crazy Time. "If it hadn't been for those first few months when I felt so good, I think I would have lost heart. Those months were precious to me. I learned to like myself."

For most Divorce Seekers, the period of relief ends all too quickly. There's no escaping the stress of Crazy Time. But sometimes for Divorce Opposers, the period of disbelief goes on too long. The art of denial perfected during the marriage works too well. You get stuck in this first phase of Crazy Time—and if you're not careful, you risk flaming out. The people who resort to violence are obvious casualties. But there are subtler ways of becoming a hostage to your past. The result is you never accept the end of the marriage.

It takes Howard Richards eight years to get divorced after he and his wife, Janice, separate. During that time he lives in a fantasy world of the marriage he thinks he still has. He's the dominant one—so dominant that he thinks he creates reality for two. He thinks he has a good marriage. He doesn't notice that his wife disagrees. He doesn't even register that the marriage is in trouble when she picks up and moves to a different city. He always thinks: Maybe she'll come back. They still spend every Christmas together; they celebrate the children's birthdays together. They share many things—but not their marriage. It is finished, but he can't accept that fact.

Howie's a big man, six feet three, with black curly hair, brown eyes and full lips. He admits he loves sex: the Vietnamese babysitter, the women's lib pilot, the buckaroo club blonde at the Roy Rogers where he takes the kids on Thursdays. Thank God, that's one thing that's always been easy for him. He's never had any trouble with women—except for Janice.

He lives in Austin, Texas, and works for a small oil-rig equipment company. The way it's worked out, he has the house and the three children. Janice lives in Dallas.

He grew up in Hightstown, New Jersey, where people headed for Princeton get off the New Jersey Turnpike. He didn't know anyone in Princeton. His father, a dull bureaucrat, worked his way up in the state registry of motor vehicles in Trenton. His mother, a large complaining woman, used food as the only emotional currency in a listless marriage. Howie doesn't care much for his family. He is seventeen when he heads out on his own for California, never to return.

Howie obtains a student loan and goes to the University of California at Los Angeles. Working toward two degrees—one in business administration, the other in eighteenth-century English literature—he doesn't get out of school until he's twenty-five. Then he takes a job with the oil-rig company in Texas. It's a good salary and lots of travel. He loves his life. He also loves his wife, Janice.

She is seventeen and he is twenty when they meet. "She was absolutely beautiful and we immediately fell in love," he says. "That's why I'm so nostalgic for beautiful young girls. They remind me of Janice.

"It wasn't like other divorced couples who really don't like each other," he says. "We adored each other. It was a beautiful relationship."

He is the good-looking guru who is going to change the world. She is the beautiful child who looks up to him. At first she supports his dream.

He spends more and more time away from home. There are always women around, wanting him. "When I was on the road, I had other women but it was no big deal," he says. "Out of sight, out of mind. I never said anything about it. It was as though it didn't exist for me and Janice."

It goes on like this for ten years, the game of deception and denial. What Howie doesn't realize is that it's a game Janice is playing too.

She doesn't tell him that she knows about the other women. She doesn't reveal how much it hurt her at first. She doesn't speak about the rage she feels. Then something changes in her. One fall weekend, she says she wants to go to Dallas and work at a radio station.

"I didn't realize we were splitting up," he says.

"I said to her, O.K., you want to do your thing. We're a modern couple. Let's give it two years."

She leaves him with the children. He drives her to the airport and they all wave Mommy goodbye. Friends tell him Janice has split for good. Wives of his colleagues tell him she's split. His secretary tells him she's split.

"I just didn't believe it," he says.

For the next two years, Howie and Janice live in limbo, seeing each other on weekends only. She has an apartment in downtown Dallas. She gets on the air and finally becomes a regular host on a daytime talk program. She never asks for any money from him. She wants to do it all on her own.

Everything is going great, he thinks, a great two years. Until the last weekend in November. That's when they really have their confrontation scene—except that she's not there and no words are spoken.

He is visiting her in her apartment for the weekend. She has gone out shopping and on the table is a notebook, a desk calendar from several years ago. "It was right out for me to see," he says, "so I opened it. It was as though she had put it there on purpose. There were names written down. Men. People I knew—people I worked with. She must have been sleeping with guys—friends of mine. It was when we were still living together.

"Suddenly the illusion crashed. I realized that when I was away those times, she wasn't waiting patiently at home. We lied to each other all those years—not by what we said but by what we didn't tell each other. She knew about the other women and never said anything. But the names on the calendar were my friends. That was the worst moment. It killed me," he says.

Howie is shattered by reality, but his habitual reaction of denial is so strong that he puts mutual betrayal in a back corner of his mind and clings to the marriage even more.

Like a man facing a terminal illness, he goes from disbelief to the bargaining phase. He's going to turn this situation around. Janice is doing just great in Dallas, he tells his friends when he gets back from the weekend. All he has to do is change and everything will be all right. He admits it—he was an insensitive male chauvinist pig; he had driven Janice to do this. If he could just be a little nicer, more sensitive, more supportive, the marriage could work and they would live happily ever after.

He goes into therapy. "I became much nicer—I was gentle and sensitive and supportive and willing—I was Jesus Christ," he says. Hell, he recalls, he would have done anything to put off the idea that he and Janice had separated for good. For years he holds on to the dream of being married to the beautiful young woman who is only seventeen when they meet.

All the while, he takes care of the children. Janice continues to visit on weekends. They draw up the settlement agreement themselves. Eight years after Janice packs her bags, the divorce is final.

But he still thinks of them as a family. It's just a legal split. They still spend Christmas together and go to Mexico for a family vacation. The typical American scene: mother, father, three children. They play ball together on the beach. They have a real Christmas dinner and make toasts to each other. The day after Christmas, Howie says he's going jogging. Instead he goes out and buys more presents for everybody. He buys a doll for the younger daughter, a calculator for the son, a silver pin for the older daughter—and a sunflower necklace in silver and turquoise for his wife. He comes back in time for supper, and as they sit down at the table, he pulls out his bag of surprises.

"The presents were a big hit; the kids loved them. There was great excitement," says Howard, who is doing anything he can to keep the marriage together—to deny that he and his wife are separated and divorced.

Then, as they are finishing up the meal, Janice says, "I am seriously considering getting married."

A cold splash of reality is thrown over the family scene.

Howie is stunned. "I couldn't believe what she was saying. I still don't," he says. There they are all together, supposedly in the Christmas spirit, and he's just finished being a super Santa Claus; that's when she comes out with a statement like that. Does she just want to hurt him? Is she still mad at him for the other women? Can she really want to marry someone else?

For Howie, facing the breakup of his marriage is like seeing a UFO land in his backyard. It's just too unbelievable. Besides, as the dominant one, he feels he has control over the situation. He thinks that if you mow your lawn and have porch furniture, there's no room for a UFO. It's the same with marriage. If he goes into therapy and buys presents there is no way the relationship can break up. He doesn't see that the UFO has already landed.

Instead of providing a brief period of psychological rest, his reaction of disbelief deepens his anxiety and frustration. It goes on too long, locking him into an emotional purgatory between marriage and divorce. He is neither in the relationship nor out of it.

It takes him a long time to break the habit of denial and get on in the divorce process.

Some people never do get out of this initial stage. You find them in bars and bridge clubs. *I never thought this would happen to me. . . . You'll be shocked when I tell you this. . . . I just can't get over the fact that . . .*

A woman in her seventies still talks with surprise about how her husband up and left her in 1945. She remembers exactly what he said, what she was wearing, how they had tickets for the theater the next day. She describes the scene as though it were yesterday.

These people are Divorce Flameouts—the ones who get stuck in one stage of the divorce process and stay stuck. They never move on to the next phase, Crazy Time, and work through the different stages of divorce to arrive at a new life. For them, the marriage is never over—despite the legal badge of divorce.

How many months has it been since you separated? In time, most people get through this initial stage of relief and disbelief. You accept the decision to separate and are ready to move on in the divorce process.

6

DEEP SHOCK

Some people are paralyzed by the breakup of a marriage. Instead of relief/disbelief, you go into deep shock. You simply don't respond. You can't function. You drop out of life for a while. Like biblical prophets, you take time out in the wilderness to think things over. Your friends and family don't understand. They think you're behaving very strangely. You say you can't talk about it now. You have to put your life on hold for a while and go off by yourself. When you come back from your personal wilderness, you are ready to confront your marriage and your past. But you need that period of psychological hibernation to prepare yourself.

For Chicago internist Garry Lehman, dropping out of life for three months is the critical healing passage in his divorce journey. Friends say that's when he went a little crazy. Garry smiles. He is forty-five, with stark blue eyes. His hair is almost frizzy; he wears granny glasses and has no children. After his marriage of twelve years goes up in smoke, he moves into a run-down studio apartment in a marginal neighborhood. The apartment consists of one big room. The floor is covered with art deco linoleum. In the center of the room is a potted lemon tree. Otherwise the room is bare but for a mattress with a single sheet and a patchwork quilt. There is no hot water. He makes do with a hot plate, a sink, two can openers and a large supply of tuna fish.

Despite this austerity, Garry is not hurting for money. He has a reputation for being the sharpest diagnostician in Chicago. The hard cases come to him. He's a clue man; he sees all the clues in a case, clues that nobody else sees. For a single symptom, there are a thousand explanations. He sees them all and like a good bookie he picks the diagnosis that fits the patient. His patients love him. They think he's a miracle worker. He shrugs. It's a genetic habit, he says. Instead of looking at reality in three dimensions, he sees three hundred dimensions. Nothing escapes him. That's why he always figures out what's going on. . . .

Except with his wife and his marriage.

It comes as a terrible shock that what he thought he knew best, he knows least of all. How could he, the good doctor, miss the signs of the end in his wife, in their relationship, in himself? The crisis in his marriage forces him to question everything in his life.

He starts with his past.

His parents were Jewish immigrants from Germany and he grew up in a kosher household in the Flatbush section of Brooklyn, New York. It's no mystery where he gets his habit of looking for clues. When he is eight years old, he asks his mother why the Rosenbergs are being executed. It's in the papers. Julius and Ethel Rosenberg . . . selling secrets to the Russians . . . charged with espionage. The family is sitting in the kitchen and his mother says: "It's because of anti-Semitism and it's the start of another pogrom."

His older brother, president of his high school class and more American than George Washington, says, "No, it's just the McCarthy era—and besides, maybe the Rosenbergs are guilty."

His father says, "Lower the window; someone might hear us talking."

Garry learns early that there are many interpretations to every event and he grows up suspicious about everything. This quality may make him a good doctor, but it leads to his downfall with women. In the end, his suspicious nature keeps relationships at bay. Instead of unraveling the clues he sees in a woman to find out who she really is—the first step toward getting close to someone— he backs off. So wrapped up is he with his suspicions, he can't see the woods for the trees. That way he can keep his distance from women. He goes to Harvard and on to Harvard Medical School, and despite his success he comes across as a shy, cautious man.

Interestingly enough, he doesn't fall in love until he's twenty-four and a lieutenant in Vietnam. Then it happens—wham! The woman is Eurasian—a mysterious neurotic lover who sweeps away his caution. He can't believe it and for several months they live together. Later he finds out that she was working for the CIA the whole time. He is quite stunned. "I realize I never really did know her," he says.

Although the affair ends after a relatively short time, Garry carries his physical longing for a mystery woman with him for many years—even after he marries Alice Terry, a slightly disorganized granola princess with dirty-blond hair and riding boots; a woman who loves his intricate mind and his gentleness; a graduate of Vassar College who writes mystery stories; someone, like him, in quiet rebellion against her origins.

"We were best friends. It was not a passion. We were like brother and sister," he says. "What I loved about her was that she was so up-front. I was so suspicious of people, so distrustful. I loved her for being so straight."

The unconscious bargain of the marriage: he gets someone he can trust, someone who relieves him of being so wary and insecure about life; she gets his mind and his sweetness—and they both get exit visas from their pasts. In Deadlock, she takes the dominant role, he the submissive one. As he says: "I was the specialist in internal medicine. She was the specialist in social relations. Since internal medicine doesn't come up too often in relationships, I left most of our life up to her."

Garry looks up to his wife, her confident style, her lack of inhibitions. Yet they are both cautious. What else is a mystery writer but a professional collector of clues and suspicions? It takes them a long time to make a commitment. They live together for four years before they get married. They both have careers and decide not to have children until later. She is writing a screenplay from her last mystery novel. He joins Chicago's leading private clinic in internal medicine. They have busy, separate, exciting lives. Looking back, Garry thinks those years were almost perfect. The two of them were such close friends; they talked about everything together; they respected each other's work. Who would have thought he could have such a good life?

But things are changing for Garry. After a while, he starts getting bored at the clinic. He's making a lot of money but he's seeing patients less. He finds that running the office is like running a grocery store. Are the secretarial salaries competitive with those of other clinics? Will the nurses stay? Who can fill in for the receptionist during vacation? What about getting a new computer billing system?

Garry starts drawing political cartoons. Alice knows the editor of the main newspaper in town. They all have dinner and soon Garry is doing a cartoon every week. Alice and Garry celebrate with champagne. The idea comes to him that maybe he should change careers. It's a first step toward breaking out.

In the midst of this he is suddenly asked to come to Washington, to a glamorous job in the Department of Health and Human Services. He finds himself in the nation's capital, advising the President on Medicare, kidney dialysis, a national policy for the aging. He works long hours. It's a bad time for Alice. She has a deadline on the screenplay. She stays in Chicago.

Then it happens again. He gets seduced—another mysterious, neurotic woman.

"I just fell in love," he says. He thinks about the mysterious women he lusts for. He thinks about Alice, his wife. He realizes he's been the passive one with women; he sees how he waits for them to seduce him, to marry him. That way he doesn't have to make the commitment. The women make it for him.

Slowly he rebels. Although he doesn't realize it yet, he's in the process of changing careers. He's also not aware of how much he's changing in the emotional arena, and with this affair, he uses passion to strike down the dominant-submissive Deadlock of his marriage. "What could be a greater act of passive aggression than to go out and have an affair?" he says.

The affair peters out. There's a change of administrations in Washington. He goes back to Chicago and to Alice and internal medicine. He still thinks of his wife as his closest friend. They always talk about everything together. It seems natural to tell her about the affair.

At this point the script of his fantasy marriage stops and reality cracks the relationship open. Alice is no longer the understanding companion he has put on a pedestal. She is devastated, outraged. The betrayal is basic. There is no understanding. A few weeks later, she goes out and has an affair—and then tells him about it. Deadlock is broken on both sides.

"I guess we should separate," he says, still thinking this is the way the script goes. He must feign significant distress to match her devastation. Now the score is even. They can get back together again, he thinks.

"You'd better move out," says Alice, not following the script.

Garry is stunned. "Are you serious?"

He can't quite believe it. Alice files for divorce. She remarries immediately and has a baby. It's as though their marriage never existed.

Garry goes into deep shock. He moves into the studio apartment. The office calls: "When can we expect you in, Dr. Lehman?" "Later," he says. A magazine from the West Coast calls about his cartoons. "Later," he says.

His routine is simple. He takes a hammer and a chisel and starts pulling up the floor. One inch at a time. Then he walks around the potted plant in the center of the room. The office keeps calling: "The blood tests are back and Mrs. Gwaltney is coming in for a CAT scan next week, Dr. Lehman." "Later," he says, and he goes back to the floor. There is good hard wood underneath. Sometimes the mystery woman from Washington comes to Chicago and he sleeps with her. After a while, he grows not to like her very much. Besides, she thinks he's gotten a little odd.

Every day he pulls up a little more of the floor. It's as if he's pulling up his psychological roots, pulling up the layer of clues that somehow kept him from knowing the truth. After he gets up half the floor, he realizes the ghost of the mysterious passion is finally dead. Then he starts thinking about Alice. Who was she?

One day slides into the next. The office doesn't call anymore. He doesn't shave. Probably he smells. He chisels up the floor for a while and then walks around the potted plant. He goes out only for groceries. He can't believe this is happening to him. Alice gone? His marriage over?

After three months, the floor is bare. Autumn has turned into winter. He goes for a walk. People stare at him on the street. The glare from the snow hurts his eyes.

"I thought I knew Alice better than anyone else in the world," he says. "She loved to read. I thought if she couldn't read, she would die, the cells in her body would disintegrate. I once took her to a bar mitzvah and she was reading a book while we waited for our coats.

"Now she's married with a baby. All she can do is write her mystery stories and take care of her family. She has no time to read. Yet she seems pretty happy.

"This is devastating to me. I lived with her for twelve years and I had the arrogance to think that I knew her better than anyone else in the world. Now it turns out I didn't really know her at all.

"What that means is that maybe if I had known her as she really was, we could have made it."

The ghosts of the past prick up their ears. *If I had known her as she really was, we could have made it.* It's a haunting admission. It's also the key to getting a good psychological divorce. Garry sees his own responsibility for the breakup. It's not a question of right or wrong, good or bad, fair or unfair. Morality is not at stake. It's more a question of knowledge—knowledge of each other and knowledge of self.

After he emerges from the wilderness of his one-room apartment, he goes back further in his past, goes back to his roots. He returns to Brooklyn, where his brother now runs a chain of record stores. His father has been dead for ten years. His mother is dying of cancer in a nursing home. He visits her; she is weak and the chemotherapy makes her brain foggy. Her eyes wander and talk is painful.

"I think I'll have chocolate ice cream for dessert," he says. Suddenly her eyes snap, cold and sharp as marbles, and she raises herself up on one elbow.

"But you always liked strawberry ice cream," she says.

He smiles. He doesn't tell her that he now sees where his panic comes from when clues in life are inconsistent; he doesn't tell her about pulling up his habit of looking for clues along with the floor in the Chicago wilderness. It's too late for his mother. He says goodbye and hugs her and tells her he loves her and will see her again. Her eyes wander.

Garry had to lock himself away for three months to begin his painful journey through Crazy Time. Now there is sadness in him—and great warmth, especially when his eyes sparkle and he laughs. He still sees Alice. They talk on the phone at least once a week and he comments on her stories, just like before. She's pleased with his cartoons; he's given up medicine almost entirely. He has a girl friend, but he feels no real commitment. It's hard, he says, to break the habit of looking for clues in the trivial inconsistencies that keep intimate relationships at bay. But he's working on it. He thinks he knows this woman pretty well. Something holds him back. Maybe he just doesn't like her that much. Then he breaks into a grin. Eight years later he gets married and has a baby.

Going into deep shock is a protective strategy. Sometimes, it's the wisest thing to do. Fate is giving you a beating just now. It's not only your marriage that's breaking up. You have other traumas to face. Sometimes these crises are overwhelming. Perhaps in the midst of this, a parent dies, your brother or sister is disabled in a car crash, your child develops leukemia. It's too much all at once. An instinct tells you that you won't make it through the coming winter of your life with your nerve endings so raw and bruised. If you started to cry, you think, you would never stop. It's all you can do to notice day turning into night. You put your emotions on ice until you're stronger. You learn to say "no" to the competing demands on your time and emotional energy. You withdraw into the psychological cocoon of deep shock and block out part of your life.

Sally Barnett doesn't go to her sister's funeral because it would mean emotional overload. If she opened up to the outer tragedy of her sister, she'd have to face the full magnitude of crisis in her own marriage. She can't fight the demons on both fronts, not with two children and the panic she feels right now. She doesn't think about it. An instinct guides her. She simply blocks out her sister's death.

Sally, thirty-five, is supposedly living the golden life of the Southwest in Flagstaff, Arizona—that's what she's been writing her family in Thomaston, Maine, for years. Her parents would be disappointed if they knew what was really going on, she thinks. She is a proud woman, the oldest daughter, who looks as if she just stepped off Plymouth Rock, with her square jaw and straight, sandy-colored hair. Her husband, Clint, is a slight man, tall enough, at about five feet eleven, but thin, with red hair and a quick grin. He's with the U.S. Geological Survey.

Sally and Clint elope their last year at Middlebury College in Vermont. "We fell in love," she says. "It was a college romance. I was sure I was going to be married for the rest of my life. I was sure this person had all the things that I didn't have in terms of marvelous qualities. I was totally unrealistic. We were two kids, two babes in the wood doing our thing. We didn't have children for seven years. We went out to California for a while, we went to

Mexico, we built a beach house in Florida, we went to Europe. We were spoiled brats in a way—no responsibility. It was very romantic."

Then Sally decides to have a baby. "Once I had the responsibility for one child, I went and had another one," she says. As the oldest child who used to take care of her brothers and sisters, she carries over her dominant role into the marriage. She runs the family, including Clint. Inside their Deadlock relationship, she is the mother; he is the child. From the outside, he looks like a rising young star with a strong wife.

"Once we had children, I couldn't cater to my husband—and he began to show the signs of not being catered to. My loyalties were divided," she says. It is the middle of the sixties, a glamour time, with everybody smoking grass and hashish. There is a young single crowd at the Survey. People begin to invade the household. There are lots of parties. But Sally doesn't have any fun at them. "I put up with it like an all-loving mother for a while and then I totally withdrew. I didn't want to have any part of it."

Now Sally and Clint scrape at each other in little ways. He is the popular geological guru with a gaggle of admirers. She is more and more alone. As they lie there together in the cold bed, she feels a steel band is wrapped around her head, growing tighter and tighter, squeezing her brain. Suddenly the band snaps behind her eyeballs, exploding, and she wakes up screaming: the repeated nightmare of her marble eyes turning into a million red fish eggs that splatter against the bedroom mirror. Clint is sound asleep. He doesn't hear her screaming. He even smiles in his sleep, the leaden look of a well-fed baby. She takes the pillow and beats him around the head. He wakes up. Jesus, it's four in the morning. What's going on here?

They agree to get into therapy. "Because I was so lonely and so desperate, I went into analysis. She was an excellent therapist and psychologically I began to transfer my dependence from my marriage to the analyst," says Sally. The young crowd keeps coming to the house, young women steeped in the poetry of William Carlos Williams, young women who bicycle to the door at night, young women who don't have children and don't go grocery shopping. "Clint went into analysis at my request," she continues. What she doesn't know for sure, but suspects, is that Clint is in love with one of his young assistants.

Then, on a Friday morning, Sally gets the phone call from her parents. Her sister Rachel has been killed in a car accident. A head-on collision on Route 1. A boy from Brunswick was driving. It was foggy. Sally knows the place well, just north of Thomaston on the way to Rockland. The funeral is on Wednesday.

Rachel. Clint. It's too much, she thinks. She feels that cotton balls are stuck in the back of her throat. She can't swallow. Clint is bending over a duffel bag; he's taking a group on a field trip. She thinks of the square-angled clapboard houses in Thomaston, all white with shutters, and the widows' walks facing out to sea. Here in her yard, it is red and dusty and she stares at the stucco bungalow next door. She knows the elm trees on Main Street in Thomaston are dying; they were green giants when she was growing up, Yankee symbols of power and plenty, and people living happily forever. Rachel was the youngest in the family, baby Rachel, twelve years younger than Sally. The children only met Rachel once, when they all went back east for Christmas five years ago. Sally always thought she'd get to know Rachel later. They were too far apart in age to know each other when they were growing up. She remembers the heavy sadness of August in Maine when summer ends and the elm trees used to get so dark and heavy.

Clint is staring at her. Sally tells her parents on the telephone she can't come back for the funeral. "I couldn't face Rachel's death. My mother was furious. She's never forgiven me for not coming back to the funeral. I was just incapable of doing that. I was traumatized," she says.

It's all too much right now: the death of her marriage, the death of her sister. How can she comfort her parents over Rachel and at the same time tell them about the problems with Clint? What could she say? How can she face the loss of her sister when she can't yet face the loss of her marriage?

Over the next few weeks, Clint tries to cheer her up. What's needed is to invite some people she likes. And so Clint brings home a string of appropriate men to pay attention to Sally so he can be with his group. It's only a matter of time till the charade explodes. "A couple of weeks after Rachel died, I found out that Clint was indeed having a relationship with this trainee, Debbie. It had been going on for about a month and a half. What I had feared most was true—that was the worst moment," she says.

For a while, Sally and Clint bargain with each other. "Clint was saying he would rather give up the affair than break up the marriage, but that didn't work. This person was there where he worked. He saw her every day. She'd never been married and you know how young people feel about their bosses. I couldn't bear to break up the marriage after so many years and two children. But then he wouldn't come home until very late at night. All the little subterfuges. You know perfectly well what is going on, but you don't want to face it."

Then fate strikes at her again. Sally and Clint are still having sex together, despite the affair. Sally discovers she's pregnant. "I thought I couldn't possibly have a baby in the midst of all this, and so I decided to have an abortion."

First Rachel dying, then learning about the woman, now the abortion—all in the space of a couple of months. Sally finally confronts her marriage. "After a while, I knew it was just a veil of illusions," she says. "You can't put it back together, no matter how nostalgic you feel."

Clint says he'll move out. Everything's shifting inside; maybe she'll just explode like a volcano. "Too many things had happened all at once. There was too much on my crisis chart," she says.

In the end, Clint and Sally get divorced within a year of Rachel's death. He remarries very quickly. Debbie is now his wife. He drops out of the Survey and they move to the beach house in Florida. How she must have pushed him, Sally thinks. It takes her several years to build up her strength and start a new life. Slowly she puts the pieces together.

Six years after the divorce, she remarries. She gets pregnant and has a baby girl. She calls her Rachel. "I still haven't come to terms with my sister's death," she says. "Naming the baby Rachel helped me to start dealing with that. I realize that Rachel's death was a symbol for me. I couldn't cope with her death at the time, but it catapulted me out of the past. I had to face the marriage first. I couldn't do both."

The next summer, she takes baby Rachel to Maine. She drives by the Knox mansion, where her mother always took summer visitors. She sees that a few of the elm trees in the square have been saved. "If I had come home to the funeral, I know I would have cracked up," she says.

Sally's period of deep shock allows her to take one trauma at a time. In this instance, her denial at the time of her sister's death is a coping strategy. Sometimes it's the only way to get through catastrophe.

In studies of Nazi death camp survivors, for example, Harvard Medical School psychiatrist Dr. Joel Dimsdale points out that a period of denial and psychological numbing is an effective coping response to massive trauma—as long as it doesn't go on too long.

"Paradoxically," he says, "denial can be both a mark of useful coping and poor adaptation to stress. The distinction has to do with how long the denial persists. In the short run, it may be helpful for a person to numb himself emotionally while experiencing massive stress."

Eventually Sally gets over the breakup of her marriage and confronts the death of her sister as well.

Most people don't go through such a pronounced phase of shock. You are not able simply to drop out of life for a while or withdraw into an emotional cocoon. Sometimes you have to fight the devil on two, three fronts. You have no choice. You have to respond to the demands of your new situation. But a little bit of shock when you separate is good. You may not notice how numb you are as you put the house on the market or go out for a job interview.

The message of deep shock is important: You must look after

yourself in Crazy Time. Shifting from being a couple to being a single person is a horrendous transition. You must let yourself go limp in little ways as you gather strength—like spending a day in bed listening to old Beatles records; going to a French movie and not looking at the subtitles; taking a warm Sunday afternoon and walking around the neighborhood.

Take your time getting used to the idea of separating. You'll get blasted out of this initial numbing period soon enough.

7

ANGER

It's not long before the shock wears off and you plunge into the depths of Crazy Time. Intense anger is a key phase in this period. You feel it as you drive down the highway; you feel it in the morning while it's still dark; you feel it standing in line at the bank; you feel it when the phone rings with a plea for the needy, when your lawyer sends a bill, when your child nearly gets run over while crossing the street without looking.

The feeling starts in your gut and rises up through your chest to your neck. A rage so dark and ferocious it scares you. Why should you feel so angry—especially if you know you weren't happy in the marriage and you aren't particularly opposed to getting a divorce?

Be reassured. It's a predictable—and probably necessary—stage in the psychological process of divorce. Without anger, you can't mourn the loss of your marriage and let go of the past. You find that screaming with rage is a good way to quiet down those Deadlock ghosts. Go up to the top of a hill and shout.

This wellspring of basic anger comes from the feeling of

being betrayed—by fate, by your spouse, and indeed, by yourself. For a while you are overwhelmed with hatred and rage.

"Intense anger associated with the failed marriage and separation is one of the hallmarks of the divorce experience," explains Joan B. Kelly. "For the majority of spouses, bitterness and conflict *escalated* rather than diminished following separation, and for many, the unexpected intensity of anger added significantly to their initial level of stress."

In the California Children of Divorce Project study, 20 percent of the men and 44 percent of the women were described as "extremely and intensely angry or bitter." An additional 60 percent of the men and 46 percent of the women were found to have "moderate but not extreme anger." This means that four fifths of all the men and women showed visible anger at separation. In general, women were found to be more hostile than men.

Divorce is the death knell for your basic dream: a cozy home with a fireplace; bicycles for the children; a second honeymoon when they are grown. You thought you were doing your best. Divorce shatters all dreams, all illusions.

Says a forty-year-old architect in Atlanta who has been separated from his wife for five years: "I think I was ready for a good marriage—to give a lot and to appreciate and receive a lot. The idea of being happily married, of cooking together, making a house together, going to concerts—I wanted that. Now I don't live in as nice a house. I'm not with my children. Money is a constant problem. As for women, my trust is so low, they all look like crocodiles to me." His lips are thin, pressed tightly together. The muscle in his cheek bulges in and out, the flashing light of his barely controlled anger. Breaking up the marriage took away his dream and he hasn't replaced it yet with a new one.

As you delve into your broken marriage, you question your whole value system. What about your standards of right and wrong? Honesty and deception? Dignity and corruption? Compromise and revenge? Are the wicked punished and the good rewarded? Is divorce ever fair? Does evil win out? What happened to "gentlemanly" and "ladylike" and playing by the rules?

How do you shift from the playing fields of marriage to the street wars of divorce? It was much easier to follow your old value system of good fairies and wicked witches—never mind that it was a child's simple view of the world. Divorce forces you to look at reality; you didn't need a president to tell you life is unfair. The reality is smacking you in the face.

You get furious and blow up. The target is easy to mark. There sits the ex. The deep anger you feel over the loss of your life's basic dream and the shattering of your value system is directed at your former spouse. After all, you think, you wouldn't be in this situation if it weren't for that rotter/dragon lady, that bastard/bitch. . . .

Like burn victims, separating spouses usually cannot even breathe on each other without precipitating a crisis. If you think the relationship was bad during the marriage, you may find it's often worse after separation. For a while, the raw rage of Crazy Time infects what relationship is left. Very few couples can make a clean break. Hell hath no fury like two people who have separated.

Beth and George Gellard are separated. They live in Saint Louis and have a middle-class house, middle-class children and middle-class dreams. Beth calls up George:

"Hello, uh, George."

"Yes, Beth."

"George, we just got back from the dentist. Sarah's tooth— she fell off a ladder and chipped her tooth. She couldn't help it. She was bleeding and crying and we went to the dentist. (Pause) Well, it's bad. She has to have a root canal done, but first the root has to be treated because she's so young. The dentist says—"

"Beth, do you know how much this is going to cost?"

"Look, what do you want me to do? Take up dentistry?"

"Now calm yourself, Beth. I'm not getting mad—I'm just saying it's not what we need right now. Goddammit, I'm not blaming anybody. You're so defensive."

"Well, if I'm defensive, you know why. You make me feel defensive. I shouldn't have to. It's not my fault Sarah fell off the ladder."

"Well, your feelings are *your* problem—"

"No, it's your problem, because the dentist also thinks we should take Sarah to the orthodontist. She needs braces."

"Oh, for Christ's sake, Beth."

"And I have four impacted wisdom teeth, you son of a bitch, and I want my front tooth recapped—"

"O.K., Beth, that's enough. Jesus Christ it's worse being separated from you than it was being married to you. I don't know how much longer I can go on with this."

Every little thing blows up in your face. You can't escape the rage, the urge to kill. It's not just the present. Separation and divorce release a stockpile of anger between the spouses that has been repressed over the years during the marriage. Your fury erupts suddenly, like a geyser of oil. You scream at each other now, you scratch and kick, you smash glasses on the floor. Your arguments are venomous: *Remember the time when . . . you bastard . . . you bitch*. You say the terrible words you thought you'd never say in your life. Perhaps you never fought much in the marriage. Always circumspect. Well, things are different now. Welcome to the boxing ring of divorce; the bell goes off and you come out fighting in ways you thought you never knew. There are no Marquess of Queensberry rules left.

When you open up the past, you are in for surprises. You realize how little you knew your spouse, how far apart you were all those years that you sat side by side thinking you were a picture of Christmas card togetherness.

Mary and Cliff Thompson have been married for ten years when they break up. They married when Mary was not yet twenty, Cliff twenty-five. He's a sales representative for the Ford Motor Company in Minneapolis. Mary takes the little-girl role. "I realize I was being treated like a child," she says. "No one was allowed to tell a dirty joke in my presence. Cliff would say, 'Don't tell that dirty story now; Mary's here.' And everybody would laugh and think it was cute." She is the first one to get married in her crowd.

One day she remarks to a friend that she has to go grocery shopping. "No you can't," replies the friend. "Cliff's not here to tell you what to get."

One of the hallmarks of Deadlock is what family counselors call "older generation" language—speaking like a parent, teacher, judge—using phrases that have an I-know-better quality. "Control is maintained through language," says Atlanta psychologist Napier. "Instead of commands—*you should* and *go get me*—say *it would be important to me if. . . .*"

But Cliff and Mary don't tell each other what's important. Deadlock gets to work on them and the marriage starts to crumble. They go through the motions: three children in five years; good years selling automobiles; bad years selling automobiles; continuous parties with the old crowd.

Mary pretty much does what Cliff says she should do, but she has one quirk, it seems, and everybody talks about it. "I'm against Santa Claus," she says. "Christmas is really Christ's birthday. Santa Claus is just a symbol. We give presents in Santa's name, but tell the children the presents are from Mommy and Daddy and the people who love them." The children never have a chance to believe in Santa Claus. When Cliff and Mary go out to parties, Cliff says, "Mary, tell them about Santa Claus." When she presents her theory, he amends it: "We do it for love."

Ten years after the divorce, Cliff and Mary are arguing over college tuition for the children. Both are remarried. Mary says Cliff should pay the tuition fees. Cliff says he didn't agree to that in their settlement. "But they're your children," says Mary. "Why don't they go to a state university?" he says. "Don't you want the best for your children?" says Mary. Cliff could kill her. He's done more than most fathers would do, he says, and it hasn't been easy, with her as the mother. "Bullshit," says Mary. "You drop out of their lives for ten years and now you claim you're the big sugar daddy." The Deadlock ghosts are dancing, clapping, singing. They reach an agreement to share the costs of college. As they end the discussion, Cliff stands up and yells at her: "And another thing I hate you for—that Santa Claus business really got to me.

Joey was only three. You took Santa Claus away from the children. You and your damn liberalism. You made me hate Christmas."

Mary is stunned. "When we were married, he always said it was so cute," she says.

For all the fury and devastation, the release of repressed anger represents an important psychological shift in Crazy Time. You are used to thinking of yourself as a twosome. You make decisions based on what you think is best for the two of you. You fall into the trap of Siamese-twin psychology. When the marriage ends, you discover your twosome self is a myth. During the separation period, you start learning how to think as one—perhaps for the first time in your life. The emotional ground rules immediately shift to self-interest. Anger is a way to identify yourself as a single person.

If you were the dominant one and usually got your way, you are now enraged to have to give ground to your spouse. You thought you were acting in the best interests of the marriage. You feel betrayed; you don't understand this. You are the White Russians of bedroom politics who suddenly have to deal with the demands of the Red Guard. If you were the passive one who always gave in for the good of the marriage, you are now furious over all those years of being ripped off emotionally. You want to strike back. Divorce is nothing less than a psychological revolution, and as with most political revolutions, the upheaval is fueled by anger. It's almost necessary to have a major angry blowup with the ex-spouse if you're going to get through the separation period. Like the confrontation scene, it's a milestone in the divorce journey. You let all the rage and hate come out of you. You kick and scream and spit and shriek. It's a way to break with the past and establish a new basis for the post-marriage relationship you must develop with your ex-spouse.

The task during Crazy Time is to learn how to use anger constructively. It's a potent energy source. You don't want to go overboard and end up as a newspaper headline. But you want the world to know how angry you are. For some people, especially those who never used to show rage in the marriage, learning how to get angry is one of the most essential lessons of Crazy Time.

Rachel Simms of New Orleans never got angry during her ten-year marriage. Now, after two years of separation, she is officially divorced. Still she feels guilty and depressed. Her shoulders are hunched over. After all, she was the one who initiated the divorce. Her husband is angry at her; he was the dominant one. He wants her to suffer, and suffer she does. With three little girls, no job, no money, she never raises her voice. He owns a successful chain of appliance stores but he refuses to send her any money. She creeps around. Her face is pale, she doesn't look people in the eye; she buries herself under a blanket of guilt.

Her first experience with Crazy Time anger takes place when her ex-husband starts coming late to pick up the children. He's just remarried and has moved, he tells her, to a small house across town. First he's an hour late; then two hours. One day, he's five hours late. She calls his house to find out what's going on. A maid answers the phone. She gets the address from the maid and drives the children up to the house in her battered Mustang. "It turns out that this small house sat on a small lane in Metairie, just outside the city of New Orleans. It was surrounded by a brick wall. There was even a phone outside at the gate. It was a goddam estate. Here my children and I were hungry; I had no money. This man would not send alimony or child support and he was living like a king!

"I let the children out. They were dressed beautifully. Let him take them in for a while. I got back in the car. Then I screamed nonstop until I got to Annunciation Street—a twenty-minute ride. I just screamed and screamed and screamed. It was the best twenty minutes I'd ever had."

From that moment, she makes some essential changes. She doesn't feel so crushed by guilt. There's nothing like a good dose of rage to get rid of a paralyzing guilty conscience. She takes legal steps to get child support and finds a job instead of making a career out of being downtrodden and depressed. She spends several years in therapy. "The biggest thing with the psychiatrist was how to deal with anger," she says. "I love anger now. I use it as an energy source. Learning how to get angry was a key lesson in my divorce experience."

Sometimes the burst of anger has to be witnessed. Martin Lowenstein is a good Jewish boy who does things right, who makes law partner before he is thirty-five, who plays racquetball and keeps trim, who loves his three children, but who hates his wife, Naomi. She is the dominant one. They never have fights. It's not good to fight, right? Not in front of the children, right? If you can't say anything nice, don't say anything at all, right?

A few weeks after Martin leaves his wife and the children, he finally has an occasion to let loose at her for the first time in his life. It's his younger son's birthday. They are in the backyard in the tense togetherness that family occasions demand of separating parents. There's no reason they can't fulfill their obligations as parents just because they are separating, right? His wife brings out the hot dogs and rolls. The children wear paper birthday hats. Martin gives his son his present, a big kite—a red dragon on white silk, the package says. The boy, age four, unwraps the thin sticks, the string; he likes the dragon, the yellow flame of fire from the dragon's mouth, the black paws. He starts to put the sticks crossways. Naomi has her hands on her hips. It's quickly apparent that the boy can't put the kite together and he begins to cry. Naomi hisses: "Schmuck! It's just like you to bring home a gift that can't be used without calling in an aeronautical engineer."

That does it. Martin blows up. "For the first time in my life, I threw a fit," he says. "I slashed the kite. I was so incensed with this bitch I was ready to mop up the floor with her. I yelled and yelled." The children hide under the patio table. His wife looks at him with horror. The guy's gone berserk. He keeps yelling. Bits of red dragon are littered over the yard. He breaks the sticks. He throws the ball of string at the tree. It goes on like this for about ten minutes. "I never felt better," he says. "One of my problems was that I never got angry with Naomi. I never told her she was a pain in the ass. I never told her that sometimes she was just plain wrong."

The birthday party's over. Martin stops yelling. A few days later he calls up and suggests they all go out for a real birthday dinner. He promises he'll get his son another kite. Maybe this weekend. He'll put it together for him and they can go and fly it together.

"Once I was able to get angry with my wife, I was able to deal with her better," he says.

The danger in Crazy Time is that there's a very fine line between constructive and destructive anger. As you know, some people are so fired up by rage that they turn to physical violence, the obvious Divorce Flameouts who end up in prison or in the morgue.

The less visible Flameouts turn to various forms of psychological warfare to wreak revenge. In Little Rock, Arkansas, an enraged husband sends a perfumed letter to his estranged wife on the day they go to court to fight over their divorce. It's a sympathy note for the baby girl they had twenty-five years before. The infant was born with a congenital heart defect and lived only ten days. *Gotcha now*, the note is saying. How many ways can you put the dagger in the heart and twist it hard?

Most people don't resort to such twisted forms of destructive behavior. But they get very close to the edge. The temptation in Crazy Time is to become very bitter and vindictive. You live off your rage the way a diabetic depends on insulin. You want to be vindicated. You long for revenge. Sometimes your rage persists for years; you use it to ward off despair and depression. If you don't feel angry, you think, you won't feel anything. You'll be deadened. At least being angry is being *something*. You're no wimp. You have been violated, betrayed. It's only right that you should rage like a wounded bull. Where is justice?

The key is how long you spend in Crazy Time rage.

* * *

Tricia Reynolds is the golden good girl. She grows up in Mount Kisco, New York, playing field hockey and shopping at Lord & Taylor. She gets good marks and is president of the senior class. She goes to Smith College for women. Her best friend is Muffy. They wear plaid skirts and go to football games. Her senior year, Tricia is president of the student council. That year (it is 1959), three undergraduates are caught drinking on campus and having boys overnight in their rooms. As head of student council, Tricia recommends the girls be expelled. She comes away more convinced than ever that right is right and rules are rules.

Twenty years later, Tricia is in her mid-forties, her light brown hair is going gray. She sits in her narrow-gauge town house in Chicago and chain-smokes. She is divorced. Her ex-husband, Cal, is married to her ex-best friend, Muffy.

Her story has a familiar ring. The four of them used to do everything together, she says, Tricia and Cal, Muffy and David. After college, Tricia and Muffy go to Chicago and share an apartment. Within two years they are both married—both to lawyers. They both have children on schedule: two children, two years apart. They go on skiing trips together; they spend Christmas Eve together; they share a summer place on nearby Lake Geneva, Wisconsin.

Inside the marriage, Tricia carries on her role as class president. Right is right and rules are rules. They pass through the seven-year-itch and approach the terrible twelves, the twelfth year of marriage. Tricia and Cal are sniping at each other. She thinks the problem is that he's drinking too much—not to the point of being an alcoholic, but it doesn't look good to get bombed at parties. Cal never complains. She's the dominant one. A viciousness creeps into their fights. The children are teenagers now. They don't do enough homework. Cal's law practice isn't doing so well. Tricia decides to go back to school. One night, she blows up and confronts Cal about his drinking. "It was just kind of an explosion," she says. "One of us said something about divorce. There was great anger and bitterness. One thing led to another. We decided to separate."

She goes to a lawyer to draw up a separation agreement. She plays by the rules: generous visitation arrangements, joint property split down the middle—a civilized divorce between two civilized people. About three weeks after signing the legal settlement, she goes to a Smith alumnae dinner. Between sherry and casseroles, she catches up with old friends and agrees to provide housing for three Smith girls working in Chicago over the summer. Then she sees a former classmate who just moved in from California. "I'm really sorry," the woman begins. Tricia is about to say something about alcoholism when she hears: "Frankly, I can't believe Muffy would do such a thing." Tricia brushes the remark aside. Muffy is not at the dinner. As a matter of fact, she hasn't talked to Muffy in ages; she's been too wrapped up with Cal. That night when she gets home, she calls Muffy. Cal answers the phone.

"At first I was shocked. I didn't believe it," she says. Her husband and her best friend living together?

"Then I just went crazy. I was hysterical with rage. I wanted to strike back. I said he could not have the kids over there. I would not allow that. He could visit the children at home or take them out, but not bring them back to Muffy's.

"It was a control battle. My sense of control was completely violated. My best friend? My rage was more directed at her than at Cal. I really felt betrayed by both of them. I also felt very threatened by her—not only because of Cal but because of the children. She was godmother to the oldest." Tricia is devastated—and panicked that she is being replaced not only as a wife but as a mother. Talk about breaking the rules. . . .

"According to my rigid sense of right and wrong, Cal had done something very very bad and he should be punished. Something terrible should happen to him because of this. If my system works, he should be struck down. So I waited for lightning to strike." She lights another cigarette.

"Of course it never did. But somehow I wanted to be vindicated, to be proved right. I waited a long time."

For the next three years, Tricia wages total divorce war. "We fought over everything. We went to court over visitation rights, over child support. It came to the point where I consciously knew I was using him as a battering ram. If I was in a bad mood about something, I would call him up and pick a fight. I knew what I was doing. He would retaliate two days later. It went on like this for three years—a constant screaming match. It took me quite a while to understand what the price was," she says.

The danger is that you may stay locked in an endless screaming match. The more you feel you have the "good case," the more you feel entitled to your anger. You never stop to question your rages. Like Tricia, you wait for lightning to strike, for God to avenge you, for your friends to rise up and stone your villainous spouse. You find out you might have to wait for the rest of your life.

It's important to recognize the paradox of rage in Crazy Time. You don't see it at first, but your anger is not entirely personal. You direct your fury at your ex-spouse, but the source of your rage is in you. By always putting the blame on your former mate, you never come to terms with your anger.

Tricia fortunately gets out of this phase. After several years she is able to confront the marriage for what it was—how imbalanced she and Cal were in the relationship, with her running the show, the dominant mother type, the president of the student government, the last word in right and wrong, a schoolmarm expecting great things from her husband without giving him much of her time or interest. And besides, whom do you fall in love with but the person who is around all the time? She understands that now. It's always the best friend, the colleague at work. She smiles. Like murder, love rarely takes place between strangers. It's been six years since she discovered Cal with Muffy. She doesn't feel so angry anymore.

"I began to focus on myself and stop hearing about Cal and his new life and who was right and who was wrong. I then got into feeling more of the loss, the real loss of the marriage. It's interesting, I defend terrifically well. At first I denied that being divorced made any difference in my life and assured myself I would manage perfectly well. It's only been recently that I can admit that I have confronted real loneliness."

The ashtray is full of cigarette butts. She still buys her clothes at Lord & Taylor. She still keeps up athletics, with her regular tennis games and aerobic dancing sessions. She still believes in right and wrong, but she knows you can't just expel wrong from your life and expect to live happily ever after. And her standards of right and wrong are very different now.

As you go through this phase of anger, you should ask yourself certain questions: How long have you felt *consumed* by anger? Three years? Five years? Are you still waiting for some psychological day of atonement when you will be proved right? Do you feel pure hatred and nothing else—no feelings of ambivalence, guilt, depression, sadness? Does your conversation always zero in on the terrible injustices that have befallen you—even though the breakup occurred ten years ago? If all your answers are yes, you may be stuck in the rut of anger. In time, anger turns to bitterness and spite. Friends and family take a deep breath when you walk through the door. They wish you'd meet someone nice at church, on an airplane, at the bus stop, in a bar, anywhere, so you wouldn't talk about your divorce all the time. Perhaps you need some counseling, they say. As the years go by, they don't call you so much. You're alone, flamed out in your own anger.

What complicates the phase of anger is the legal process of divorce. You find that aggressive behavior is encouraged by the country's legal system. Despite advances in mediation techniques and divorce counseling, the adversarial system in divorce law usually pits one spouse against the other, *Kramer vs. Kramer* style.

Although the emotional divorce is distinct from the legal divorce, many people try to use the legal system as an instrument in getting their emotional divorce. You look to the law to fill twisted needs for revenge and restore your material and emotional well-being. Very often the legal settlement reflects the power balance of the deceased marriage: The spouse who was done in during the marriage usually gets done in when it comes to negotiating a settlement.

Most people get legally divorced within two years of separation—just when they're going through Crazy Time. A great deal of anger and guilt is played out in the details of the property settlement and custody agreements. The rejected Divorce Opposer is not only devastated and angry at being left, but regards the legal ability of the departing spouse to take half of the couple's joint worldly goods as the final insult. The Divorce Initiator, on the other hand, may get locked into a settlement out of guilt or fear that favors the other spouse so much that it can't be realistically maintained in the post-divorce period.

A minority of divorcing couples go to court to wage war. Litigation sometimes substitutes as a civilized form of murder for Divorce Flameouts bent on vengeance. You don't need a lawyer to tell you that litigation is time-consuming, expensive and emotionally stressful. Worst of all, it rarely proves who's right and who's wrong. As Washington, D.C., divorce lawyer Peter Sherman says: "The function of litigation is not to do justice. Sorry. It is to resolve the dispute." Endless court battles usually end up intensifying your rage. "If I thought I hated my wife before the divorce, I sure hated her afterward," says one divorce court casualty. It's no surprise that the main beneficiaries of litigation are the divorce lawyers.

At the same time, you don't want to be too civilized when you draw up a divorce settlement. You just postpone your rage until later. Some people say they never really felt angry over their divorce. Watch out. This can also be an emotional hazard. Just as destructive angry behavior can cause Divorce Flameouts, *not getting angry* can also lock you into the mental prison of an unresolved divorce.

"I never felt anger," the woman says. "Getting angry takes too much out of you. I really think someday he's going to get his. I don't have to do anything."

Gwen Miller takes a long sip of Scotch at the out-of-town

bar. Her divorce was the worst divorce in Louisville, she says, the worst. She is very attractive, soignée, she doesn't look her years, all her friends tell her. She's forty-five, her hair is blond, she's had an eye tuck, her figure is good and she knows how to dress. He husband, Frederick—what she had to go through. She covered up for him once when he was accused of embezzlement. She knows now that he lied and cheated. Now he's even turned the children against her. He's very manipulative, very charming, from a very good family. But people are on to him now, she says. He has no friends left in Louisville. He can't even get a job there. They went to court over the settlement. They owned an antique business together. Even his lawyer said he was being unfair. In the divorce decree, she got to keep the membership to the swimming club. Nobody at the club wanted him. A friend once asked her: Do you think he was into kinky sex? She brushes the notion aside. She just thinks he is crazy. All their friends are on her side. He doesn't see any of them anymore. He doesn't even see his family; she's much closer to his mother than he is. As horrible as the divorce was, there never was a time she lost her temper or felt she wasn't going to make it. "I continued to work in my antique business and function the whole time," she says. She looks around the bar. Sometimes her voice gets shaky. It's only been six months since the divorce was final.

Stuffed in her pocketbook is a newspaper clipping from the local paper: "Frederick Miller, a prominent business leader, was shot and wounded today by his estranged wife, Gwen, police reported today. . . . Miller was resting comfortably when the police arrived at the scene. Mrs. Miller was pressing towels to the wound. She had reported the incident to the police herself and accompanied Mr. Miller to the hospital. . . ."

Gwen doesn't show anyone the clipping. She never talks about the shooting. She didn't go to jail; all she got was a reprimand by the judge. She doesn't think anyone outside Louisville knows about the shooting.

I never felt any anger. . . . Getting angry takes too much out of you. I really think someday he's going to get his. I don't have to do anything.

Gwen asks for another drink. The bar is silent. When you don't see the connection between shooting your estranged spouse and feeling angry, you're very close to Flameout. Gwen Miller is lucky she only wounded her husband. She still has time to confront the reality of herself and her marriage. But she has a long way to go. Her eyes look frightened. She doesn't know why she shot him; she cared for him, took him to the hospital. She can't figure it out. But one thing she's sure of—she's never been angry.

If you find yourself sitting at the bar saying you can't be bothered to feel angry; it's too gauche, it's a waste of time and energy; you have other things to do with your life, no matter how hard you try, you just can't get angry—then it's time to call a family counselor and put away all sharp objects in the house.

You're right on the edge. Not feeling any anger at all raises a red flag in Crazy Time. Sooner or later the anger is going to come out.

8

AMBIVALENCE

The problem is you're not sure. You're just not sure that you should be getting a divorce. Is it necessary? Is it the right thing to do under the circumstances? Obviously you think it's the only way to go, or you wouldn't be in this situation. But then why have you stumbled on a field of question marks? Questions like: What is your ex-spouse really like? Will he or she change now? Is that what you want? Does having a pleasant time with your ex-spouse mean you should get back together?

You think you have it figured out, and then as you drive along the highway, fifty-five miles an hour, free and happy, the radio is having a commercial-free hour of music, it's Columbus Day weekend, the sky is clear—maybe you're going to spend the weekend with a new love and then, thud! You get that heavy feeling in your chest.

It's hard to admit it. You've come so far out of your old life. But you still feel ambivalent about the breakup and this causes you a great deal of anxiety.

Ambivalence is another basic stage of Crazy Time. It's the

emotional mother of Doublefeel—having two contradictory feelings at once. It encompasses a wide range of emotions and serves as a psychological switching station as you swing back and forth between guilt, anger, depression and euphoria.

It's important to realize that although ambivalence is very unsettling, this is just the way you *should* feel. It's common sense that you be ambivalent. The essential nature of Crazy Time is that you can't be really sure of anything, including yourself. The one thing you know is that things are going to change. You are going to change and so is your ex-spouse. Perhaps you were continuously berated in the marriage for smoking cigarettes. Now your former spouse smiles and brings you an ashtray when you light up. So where are you?

If only you didn't have such mixed feelings, everything would be easier, you think. Perhaps you try to push out your feelings of ambivalence; you stick to rage and yell at the mere mention of your former mate, or you cover your head and say you're sorry, sorry, sorry, over and over again. The ghosts start dancing, start to boogie again. You jump to a new relationship to protect you from the old one. The ghosts dance faster. You still feel torn.

If you are to face the reality of divorce, you have to confront your own ambivalence over it. This is a crucial moment in the divorce process. If you reject the anxiety of ambivalence by escaping into a new relationship or retreating into an emotional box of pure anger or pure despair, you die a little inside. A big chunk of emotional muscle atrophies. After that you don't feel so much—another form of Divorce Flameout.

There's no question that conflicting feelings make you feel terrible. But anxiety is the most fertile emotion for growth and change, therapists point out. Allowing yourself to feel torn on the rack of ambivalence is a sign you're coming alive, that you're working through the painful emotions triggered by the loss of an important relationship.

Conflicted feelings in Crazy Time are often heightened by logistics. Most people stay in the same community during the separation period. You have to work out legal details together. If there are children to raise, you usually remain in contact with each other indefinitely. You are still parents together and you have to work out living arrangements for the children and visiting schedules. You brush up against each other again and again.

Much of your ambivalence is rooted in positive feelings for your ex-spouse. These feelings are usually buried under hate and shock when you separate, but they persist. A number of studies show that no matter how bad the relationship, most people feel a persistent attachment to the former spouse and the past marriage. In a study on *The Predicament of the Newly Separated*, by Drs. B. L. Bloom and W. S. Hodges at the University of Colorado, half of the individuals separated less than six months reported they wanted to spend time with their estranged spouses. Some 45 percent discussed reconciliation at some point during the separation period. Interestingly enough, warm feelings and discussions of getting back together occurred more frequently among spouses without children than among parents—a further blow to the old-fashioned idea that people stay together or get back together for the sake of the children.

A significant number of couples do, in fact, get back together. Some people get divorced and remarry each other five or ten years later. Many couples who end up getting divorced go through the let's-give-it-one-more-try syndrome before reaching that final point. Maybe you don't really want to get back together, but you don't want to lose each other, either. All in all, researchers find that three fourths of divorcing spouses experience some lingering attachment to their former mates after the separation. For a while, you just feel very ambivalent about splitting up. It's part of the push-me/pull-you process of separating psychologically from the past.

People who do not have second thoughts are usually the ones who have gone through the psychological separation process during the marriage. In the California Children of Divorce Project, for example, one quarter of the men who showed no feeling of attachment five months after breaking up "were the men who decided to divorce their wives, who years earlier had experienced a dwindling sense of attachment and who divorced without any particular internal conflict or anger," explains Joan Kelly. Uncertainty fuels your feelings of ambivalence. In the dark, you admit you don't really understand very well what broke up the marriage.

Perhaps, after mutual revelations of secret desires and double lives, you think you don't really know the person you were married to for so long. You also know that in all likelihood, both of you are going to change in the future. Maybe it could work out if you tried again?

Harry McDonald, forty-one, with his sandy hair, his hazel eyes, is all Irish. Boston Irish. He marries Maureen Fitzgerald, the most beautiful girl at Boston University. Her father is the richest man Harry's ever had dinner with. Harry and Maureen have a big church wedding. Fifteen years after that walk down the aisle, they have four children and a weekend place. Then Harry surprises everybody by moving out of the house. It's no surprise to his drinking buddies; Harry's been talking about splitting for years. Nobody thought he'd ever go through with it, though. He seemed so wrapped up with his wife. She's the dominant one in the relationship. He has a minor administrative job in a Boston bank. He doesn't like his job. His wife berates him for doing low-level work, for not making more money, for getting indigestion, for being rude to her father. He hates her now with all his heart, this shamrock princess who thinks being rich is her divine right, who never has worked in her life and therefore thinks you shouldn't have a job unless it involves interesting, meaningful work. One day he just walks out of the house. Every time he thinks about her, he sees a psychopathic Godzilla. He's glad to be out of it, he thinks. Fifteen years of hell. Spoiled little bitch who never left her parents. She doesn't live in the real world.

Then one Sunday about a year after the breakup, he is taking the kids back to the house. It's raining. She invites him to stay for a drink. They sit down and talk. She tells him she now understands about the money difference between them—how he has to

131

work and she doesn't. She talks about the pressures of having a job, of not liking what you do all day, of trying to find a niche for yourself—how that must have been so difficult for him. She can see that now and she wishes she had realized it earlier.

"When she acknowledged that, it really scared me," he says. "She finally acknowledged something I've been preaching for years. How much I needed her to understand that when we were together. How much I resented her for not ever having to face that."

At first he's pleased to hear this from the woman he's battled with all these years. Then the Deadlock ghosts start dancing in his head. Relief turns to panic. He thought he had pegged his ex-wife away in his memory as a dragon lady and had dealt with that person. Now she's different. Different in a way he had always wanted her to be. What now?

"We both know we'll grow and this fuels the ambivalence," he says. "We both know we'll grow and become better partners."

He looks off into the distance and sighs. How do you know? Know for sure? After a while, you get used to feeling ambivalent. You give up waiting for an external vision to lead the way. Harry acknowledges that he's not good at making decisions. After mulling things over again and again, he's left with his gut instincts. For Harry, that's the way out of the stalemate of ambivalence to the final decision to divorce.

"She still doesn't stir me here," he says, patting his stomach. "I've got to trust that. I've got to go with that."

Sometimes there is a heightened sexual tension between spouses during Crazy Time. You both know the other is on the market. You want to test things out. Maybe you've been thinking more about sex these days. You want to go back and see what it's like. Although studies indicate that sexual intercourse is rare between separating spouses, it may be more frequent than is generally recognized.

In bedroom politics, making love to your ex-spouse is physical testimony to your ambivalence and unresolved feelings. Sometimes sex is an expression of buried guilt or repressed anger. Sometimes you are searching for a physical answer to your emotional confusion. You are desperate for answers and sick of talking about problems in relationships. You think of the poet John Donne: "For God sake hold your tongue, and let me love."

Maybe things will work for the best in bed.

But there is a dark side to sex with your ex-spouse. You can get badly hurt—or can hurt badly—and come away from the experience feeling very bruised. Sex in divorce is often a silk-sheeted Trojan horse. You have intercourse not to make peace but to wage war. It's a way to settle the score once and for all.

Or maybe you're just very drunk and it's too late to resist the temptation to go to bed with the person you had made love with so many times.

A woman, forty-two and now divorced, describes sleeping with her estranged spouse: "We had agreed to separate. It was late in the summer. We went to the beach for two weeks. I said, This is our last family vacation. I took the kids up the first week. He came up the second week.

"It was like rerunning an old movie. We put the kids to bed. Then we went to bed. In retrospect it was unrealistic. We had not been sleeping together for more than a year. But then, there we were. We had one more flight at sex—mostly because I felt sorry for him. ... We'd both had too much to drink. It wasn't very good. Afterward I felt bad about it."

Sometimes you sleep with your ex-spouse out of curiosity. A man, forty-five, who got divorced twenty years ago recalls: "I hadn't seen her for a year. I was in the army. I wanted to see what it would be like. We were still so young—in our twenties. I had gotten her pregnant when she was sixteen. I just had to test it out."

For some people, sex with the ex-spouse is the click experience that leads to a firm decision to divorce. A woman, thirty-eight, explains:

"We did something crazy. We had been separated for almost a year. We decided to spend three or four days in the mountains, just the two of us together. We had a lot of sex. I really wanted to put things together again. I felt we had to give it one more try.

"Afterward he told me it meant nothing. I was a stick compared to the other girls he knew. He said he had plenty of other women he'd rather sleep with. That really finished it for me. I knew I had to get the divorce."

For most people, sleeping with your former spouse does not resolve the anguish of divorce. It's only more proof of how confused you are. You have sexual intercourse because you feel sorry for your ex? That's the ambivalence of guilt at work. You want to see what it's like? That's the ambivalence of curiosity fueled by nostalgia. You want to get back at your ex by having terrible sex? That's the ambivalence of anger.

You soon realize there's no shortcut in Crazy Time to sorting out these conflicting feelings.

Often you don't find out how entwined you are with your spouse until you try to separate. You may have lived together as strangers, but during those years you wrapped emotional tentacles around each other in ways that neither one of you can understand. Even though you are now physically separated from each other in Crazy Time, you have probably not separated yet psychologically. As Washington psychoanalyst Douglass Carmichael says: "You don't know how much you are in a marriage until you try to get out of it."

People often get their legal divorce before they've worked through their ambivalence. Three days before signing divorce papers, a man writes about his estranged wife in his diary: "She was ill last night. I ministered to her, brought her soup and rubbed her back. Her comment was that she wondered what it would be like to be sick and alone. My reply was that she should have thought about that before. A friend at work said to me: 'It's obvious you still love her.' She had no comment when I told her that."

Getting an emotional divorce means you have to separate

psychologically from your spouse. It's a long and complex process. Your ambivalence reflects the attachment you still feel for your spouse as well as your own inner turmoil over making major changes in your life.

One of the tasks of Crazy Time is to work through and accept these contradictory feelings. You also have to lay the emotional groundwork for the future relationship with your ex-spouse. What makes this process so difficult is that you are being pushed from two directions: the behavior of your former mate and your own inner stirrings. You listen to both voices and go a little crazy.

At first it seems much easier to cut the marital umbilical cord if your former mate behaves badly during Crazy Time.

Roger Smith, a fifty-five-year-old graphic designer who left his wife for a much younger woman he fell in love with at work, puts it this way: "If my wife hadn't behaved like a crazy vindictive bitch, I would have felt so much guilt I don't know if I could have gone through with it. Had she been understanding and decent, I would have felt too awful. Even though she made it hell for me for several years—she delayed the divorce, she'd call up my girl friend and shriek at her, she told the children I had beaten her—I was secretly relieved. It took away my guilt."

Melissa Sweet, thirty-five, who runs her own public relations firm, has been separated for three years. The divorce was final last year. "As far as I'm concerned, the man is a raving asshole," she says. "Subconsciously it is to my great delight that every time he comes to the house to pick up the kids, he behaves like an asshole. If he didn't, it would be worse. My God, what if he looked terrific to me?" She pauses, her eyes widen with a look of horror. "I'm really glad he doesn't look good to me anymore," she says, and bursts out laughing.

But there are pitfalls to relying on your former mate to clear up your feelings of ambivalence. Looking for such signals keeps you trapped in the should-you-or-shouldn't-you dilemma of divorce.

* * *

Jim Ware, fifty-one, separated for two years, plays tennis with his former wife. He loves a good game of tennis. It's something he and she used to do a lot. One afternoon, they play two sets. She's an excellent tennis player, with long legs and a vicious forehand. He has a wonderful time batting the ball back and forth.

That night he's sitting in the bar with a friend. He knows he's on edge. He buys a pack of cigarettes even though he hasn't smoked in five years. The feeling burns into his chest. He tells his friend that it was an impossible marriage; she drove him crazy; he just didn't want to be around her, ever. He takes out a cigarette and lights up. But he has to admit that today he had a fabulous time playing tennis with her. He shakes his head and emits a long sigh.

"Maybe we should get back together," he says.

"Do you like tennis?" asks his friend.

"Yes."

"Well, that might be it," says his friend. "That might account for the fact it was fun."

Ware looks at him, startled. His friend continues:

"So what does having fun playing tennis have to do with getting back with your wife?"

They both burst out laughing.

The moral is: Don't look at everything through the prism of whether or not you should get a divorce.

Yet the habit of looking for cues in your former spouse is hard to break. It's evidence that you're still tied to each other emotionally. There comes a time in the divorce process when you have to say: *No matter what is going on with my spouse, this is the way I'm going to lead my life. I can feel tenderness for my spouse and it doesn't mean we have to get back together. I can feel anger and it doesn't mean I have to retaliate.*

This is what therapists mean by emotional separation. Only when you disengage psychologically from your former partner do you gain real freedom from the past. It's a critical process in the divorce experience.

* * *

Bob Dinsmore, thirty-eight, has green eyes, thick brown hair, an athletic build. All his life, he passes tests with top grades and makes the right choices. He gets a job in sales at IBM and works his way up in the international division. In terms of the Robert Frost poem about two roads in the woods, he always takes the right road. The future is clear . . . until his wife has a marriage-breaking affair. After eight years of marriage, with no children and two cats, they decide to split up.

But he is torn by ambivalence. A year and a half after the separation, he breaks off a current relationship to "give it one last shot."

"The hardest part of my separation was the ambivalence I felt," he says. "To make the decision that there was no reasonable hope of getting back together was impossible for a while. I had to make the distinction between the fantasy that I wanted my marriage to succeed and the reality when I looked at the situation, when I looked at the person I was married to. I said no—despite it all, I don't want to be with this person.

"The worst period lasted six months when I agonized whether to go back to the marriage or on to the divorce. I could have decided to stay married and maybe made a go of it. But I realized I didn't want to do it. I had changed. In renegotiating the relationship, we just couldn't do it.

"During the separation I felt in limbo. Ultimately the reason I got divorced was that I was tired of being in limbo. That was the main incentive. I just didn't like where I was anymore," he says.

A main part of accepting your divorce is accepting the ambivalence you feel along with the persistent emotional attachment you have for your spouse. In time, your ambivalence may turn into nostalgia. The horror scenes recede. There were good times, you think. You find you can remember the past without feeling anxious for tomorrow.

This is also good mental health policy. The chances are, especially if children are involved, that you and your ex-spouse will have to establish some kind of divorce relationship—for better or for worse. If you don't work through your ambivalence, you risk keeping old battles of marriage alive. Your divorce relationship may turn out to be just as bad as your marriage was. It's another way to flame out.

9

DEPRESSION

You feel terrible. There are days when you just drag yourself around; nights when you can't sleep. You lose weight. You gain weight. You blame yourself for this mess. It's as if you're a two-time loser: First you fail at being married and now you fail at *not* being married. Your self-esteem is low and your guilt high; as you look at the calendar on the kitchen wall, you wonder how you're going to make it through all the days ahead.

Depression is a common response to breaking up a marriage. Statistics link separation or divorce with major depressive illness and higher than expected rates of suicide for both men and women.

In the California Children of Divorce Project, roughly 30 percent of the men and women were diagnosed as severely or acutely depressed after separating. In addition, one third of the men and three fifths of the women were "mildly to moderately depressed after separation, and this group included both those who had initiated the divorce and those who did not want it," explains Joan Kelly.

You don't need modern science to verify that you feel down in the dumps. Depression is a constant theme in Crazy Time. It is fueled by low esteem and guilt. For Divorce Seekers, the initial relief wears off pretty quickly and you feel overcome by guilt. What have you done? Now you're going to pay. . . . For Divorce Opposers, your disbelief fades as the separation continues and you are forced to deal with the blow to your self-esteem of being "left."

In the turmoil of Crazy Time, depression is often the flip side to anger on the emotional coin. You swing back and forth between despair and rage and achieve an equilibrium of sorts. Depression doesn't make you feel good, but it plays a key role in the divorce process. It forces you to look at yourself and not lay all the blame—and anger—on your spouse. Ultimately, depression is the prelude to sadness and grief as you mourn the death of your marriage.

Therapists point out that in times of stress, depression can be a healthy emotion. It's the psyche's way to cope with loss. In contrast to anger, depression is a numbing response.

"A depressive response to a powerful stress is often a sign of normality, not weakness," says Dr. Frederic F. Flach, associate professor of psychiatry at Cornell University Medical College. "A resilient patient not only quickly recovers but also grows from the experience. In fact, patients who use self-denial, alcohol or some other means to dodge *appropriate depression* are usually only postponing it. What finally arrives may be profound and chronic depression."

What you wonder about as you stare at the late show on television or ask the bartender for one more drink is whether your depression is "appropriate" or you're really going over the edge.

Much depends on how long your depression lasts and how disabling it is. How long have you been wandering around in a daze with a sad-sack look, speaking in a flat tone and sighing all the time?

Divorce-connected depression is different from general

depression. Were you depressed before the breakup? In the California Children of Divorce Project, Judith Wallerstein and Joan Kelly documented a significant amount of depression in people *before* the separation. Their findings mimic national statistics on general depression, with a higher incidence of depressive symptoms seen in women. Roughly 14 percent of the women in the group tried to commit suicide during the marriage and 42 percent suffered chronic depressions lasting more than five years. Only 16 percent of the men experienced such disabling depressions and none of them tried to commit suicide.

The post-separation picture of depression is very different. The people in this study who became acutely depressed in response to the breakup were not the ones who had been severely depressed during the marriage. Most likely they were Divorce Opposers who were totally unprepared psychologically for divorce and living alone.

In contrast to national statistics on depression, an equal number of men and women—30 percent—suffered disabling symptoms of depression as a result of the separation.

For a significant minority of people, moreover, divorce helps their depression. These are usually women who had been seriously depressed in a difficult marriage and who had reached the painful decision to divorce, often with the help of psychotherapy. For them, Kelly and Wallerstein found, the greatest period of stress occurred before the breakup, and after separation, these women were no longer severely depressed. Some people, in fact, seem to glow after the breakup and continue through Crazy Time with feelings of having a second chance at life.

Most people getting a divorce fall in between the two extremes. You feel a tremendous sadness and you're a little scared when you think about the future, but you more or less function at home and on the job. In general, women experience tremendous anxiety over living alone and taking on new responsibilities as head of the household. Anxiety deepens your depression; depression heightens your anxiety. You end up feeling overwhelmed. Yet most of the time, you manage.

"For a year I was frantic," says Jessica Wayland, who was thirty-five when her marriage broke up. "Here I am owning a new house, struggling with children aged three and five, figuring out how to pay bills, how to pay taxes, how to get myself organized and have a meal on the table every night.

"Having the children, I was always conscious that I had to keep this show going. I felt terrible, but I can't think of a day when I stayed in bed and did nothing."

In men, depression is most often triggered by the loss of daily contact with the children. *Do you know what it's like to lose a son/daughter?* is a common refrain. According to most research on divorce, one of the most difficult adjustments during Crazy Time is establishing a new parent role beyond being the weekend sugar daddy.

At the core of divorce depression is low self-esteem. Those years of ego erosion in the marriage have taken their toll. Whether you are the Divorce Seeker or Divorce Opposer, you feel like a failure. You don't like the person you've become. You don't like your life or the world you've created.

You know you are hurting your children and you've "failed" your spouse. When anything goes wrong, you think it's your fault. Your spouse has a minor car accident. Your daughter fails history and dresses like a slob; your son starts sucking his thumb. Would these things happen if you were still married? You blame yourself and sink deeper into depression.

You can't come out of a marriage without feeling rejected by your spouse—proof that you are unloved and unlovable. No matter whether you're the Divorce Seeker or the Divorce Opposer, you feel rejected, humiliated. You wear the big letter *F* on your chest for failure. The past has been taken away from you through betrayal; there seems to be no future. *Where did I go wrong?* you cry in the dark. You blame yourself some more and sink even deeper into depression.

"One of the most important emotional tasks is to try to keep divorce away from your self-esteem," says Suzanne Keller.

All too often, failure becomes a self-fulfilling prophecy: you think you are no good—you are no good. With each setback, your self-esteem drops down another notch. Just at the time when you need confidence, you don't have very much.

Depression is a critical stage in the divorce process. You make a choice. You either live through the sadness and depression and recover or you get stuck in despair and become another victim of Divorce Flameout.

Winton Kennedy, fifty, is a computer specialist in San Francisco. He's what country people call a smart dresser. His body is lean, his eyes twinkle, he has sideburns and graceful limbs. He's a nice man, warm and generous to his friends. They're glad he's over his divorce now. Winton is married again, this time to a dark-haired public interest lawyer who represents indigents. They have two children of their own, a baby boy and a girl of seven. He does most of the child care since his wife usually works late. The main thing for him is his family, he says. Then he pauses for a minute. His first marriage seems so long ago, he muses. His two daughters from that marriage are now nineteen and twenty-one. The worst part of his divorce was leaving the girls.

He grew up in Cincinnati, where his parents were leaders in the Presbyterian Church. It is a time when nice girls are still virgins on their wedding night . . . or are supposed to be. After graduating from college with a major in mathematics, he goes to work in Albany, in the New York State Department of Transporation. Soon he meets Mary, an Atlantic seaboard Protestant from Stanford, Connecticut. "She was cute as a bunny's ear," he says. It's not long before they start sleeping together. "The only way, it seemed, to take care of the Protestant guilt was to get married," he says.

It starts on their honeymoon: Every time they make love, she locks herself in the bathroom afterward and cries. He never asks why, and to this day he doesn't know. They move to Saint Paul, Minnesota, and stay together ten years. In the process they grow to hate each other. He feels she is always scraping at him, putting him down, not caring about him. By the time he moves out into an apartment, the daughters are five and three and he's a broken man.

"The worst was my sense of worthlessness," he says. "I felt I was a failure. Somehow I had failed. I had no self-worth at all." A failure in his personal life, he becomes a failure to the outside world. He wants to leave the company in Saint Paul and has two interviews, one with a Blue Cross–Blue Shield office that is installing a new computer system, the other with an electronics firm in Texas. "I flubbed both interviews totally," he says. "I didn't get any job offers and it all just seemed to confirm my deepest fears that maybe I really wasn't going to make it."

A few months later he has an interview with a major computer company in Los Angeles. "I think the guy I was talking to understood what I was going through," he says. "His marriage was about to blow up. He sympathized with me, saw something good beneath my shadow of despair and hired me."

His confidence begins to rise with new prospects of a new job, a new place, a new life. The despair of low self-esteem turns into the despair of sadness over leaving his daughters.

In a house of hatred, what has held him together during those bitter years of marriage is his love for the girls. Now his former wife makes it difficult for him to see them. He pleads with her. It goes on like this for years. "She used them as tools for revenge," he says. "I'll never forgive her for that."

As he sets off for the West Coast, he wonders how he will be able to keep up his relationship with the girls while living in California. Will they remain close? Will his wife bad-mouth him behind his back? (She does.) When he comes to say goodbye, Mary tells him not to do anything "heavy" because the girls have enough to handle just with the divorce. They stand in the driveway. He hugs each one. They ask him questions: "Where are you going, Daddy?" and "How long, Daddy?" He doesn't know what to say. He just holds them very close and whispers over and over: "I love you . . . I love you." He turns around and walks away.

"I got back in the car and drove halfway down the block and

then I broke down," he says. "I pulled over to the side of the street and bawled." He starts crying now, thinking of that day. "I cried and cried. But after a few minutes, I said to myself: I've got to handle this." He stops crying and sits in the car for a while, letting the silence calm him down. He slaps the steering wheel, steps on the gas and heads for California.

Escape is not that simple, though. It's not over yet, the problem with self-esteem. Once he is settled in L.A., Winton gets into therapy, in group and private sessions. "The therapist was a woman. She'd ask, 'Now, what's happened this week, how do you think you responded?'. . . Slowly I began to build up my self-worth and gain control of my life."

In a few years, the acute pain wears off. He gets a promotion at work and is moved to take over the office in San Franciso. In time, he starts another family with another woman. The sadness over his daughters lingers. He worries about the nineteen-year-old, so beautiful but she doesn't go out much. It's going to be different this time with his new wife and their young children. He smiles. The main thing is having self-esteem. "I know now I don't have to be trapped into certain behaviors by other people or other situations. I can set my own course," he says.

For some people in Crazy Time, depression is a psychological testing ground. It's where you find out how resilient you really are. Unlike anger and ambivalence, depression is an emotion turned inward on yourself. You are alone in your depression and part of the despair is confronting your own loneliness. You realize you are utterly and totally alone.

Helen Atkins is thirty-five when she and her husband separate, after two children and fifteen years of marriage. She has no job, no boyfriend in the wings; only the kids, a mortgage to pay and group therapy twice a week.

"The most difficult thing I ever had to do in the world was separate," she says. "I had no career. I had an instinct for real estate, but it was just an instinct.

"In those first months, I just wandered around," she continues. "I didn't have a ring on my finger. I felt that was indicative. I didn't know who Helen Atkins was. I was scared. There were times when I felt like a grease spot on the floor. I can remember standing at the edge of the kitchen counter and wondering if I was ever going to get through those endless days."

She's a woman who was defined by her husband's name and position as a high school history teacher in Springfield, Illinois. When they separate, she is lost and overwhelmed. Slowly she puts herself together and fends for herself. She takes a course in real estate, learns about points and mortgages, and gets a job selling commercial properties. She buys a car. She gives a dinner party. With each month, she gains more self confidence. Her depression begins to lift, and in time, her despair turns to sadness.

"I think about what we'd done," she says. "We got married, we had children, we brought them into a family, we said this is the American dream—and then we get divoced. It's really unfair to the children. I am so grateful to them for hanging in there while I was so crazy. They were so good and I'm sorry for them. It's a terrible sadness. I feel a real sadness and a real twinge in my gut—I don't know if it's guilt; I don't think I feel guilty, but I feel really sad." She starts to weep. "That's really what's so hard about divorce. Yes, life gets better afterward, but it's just so sad."

Hers is a woman's story of the eighties. Brought up the old way to be a good wife and mother for someone else, Helen is struck down at mid-life when the old way doesn't work anymore. She is forced to change. Her work at the real estate firm goes well. She raises the two children. She becomes self-sufficient economically and emotionally. It's been five years since the marriage ended. Helen is a changed woman today, taking out clients on the expense account, attending PTA meetings, and spending weekends in New York with a man she's not sure she wants to marry.

"For the first time in my life, I can say that I like myself," she says. "I know how strong I am and I trust myself. I know that I can get through it. I feel I've really been tested. I don't feel I have to apologize to anyone for anything—ever.

"But something really bothers me," she continues. "I wonder

if it's possible for women brought up the way we were to get where we are today without a divorce. . . . If that's true, it's so sad."

Once you fall into the pit of despair, it's hard to get out. This is when you make the choice of whether you live through your depression or you get stuck and flame out.

Some people retreat from their turmoil by getting sick. A former nun turned college professor of anthropology gets a bad back when her marriage breaks up. A few months after her separation, she lands in the hospital and spends four weeks in traction. "I couldn't move. It was part of my healing time. My mind didn't confront these traumas; it all came out in my body."

Most people have rescue fantasies. You just want to lie down and be taken care of. A social worker finally gets out of a demeaning marriage after twelve years and four children. She's thirty-one years old. When we separated, I wished I could go into a hospital and just be taken care of. It would be a relief to go crazy and let someone else takeover for me," she says.

"But then I had to think: Who was going to take care of my children? They had a father they couldn't count on; now they were going to have a mother they couldn't count on?"

Today she is a marriage and divorce therapist. "I think there is a place in terms of emotional deterioration where you have a choice, where you say, 'O.K.,' and let it happen, or you say, 'I will not let it happen.'"

But some people give in to despair. They never accept their divorce. They stop living and die bit by bit inside. You read about them in the newspapers:

Boston (AP)—John Adams, 65, once a prominent Massachusetts and New Hampshire politician, died Thursday in a Boston city hospital as a homeless transient.

Adams had no known address, no job, no friend at his side. A slip of paper listed a sister in his hometown of Exeter, N.H., as his next of kin.

"We've known for years that someday this would be how it

would happen," said Joan Simpson, one of the three daughters of the former Republican state senator from Massachusetts and a New Hampshire congressional nominee.

"It began when my mother and he were divorved 20 years ago," Simpson said. ". . . my father never accepted the divorce . . . he lost his footing and he never regained it. . . ."

After making an unsuccessful run for governor in 1964, Adams dropped from political view. He lived at the Soldiers' Home in Chelsea, qualifying as a disabled World War II veteran. His only income was a Navy disability pension.

(May 22, 1981)

A major theme in divorce depression is guilt. You feel guilty about your ex-spouse, your children, your parents, your friends. It's hard to know where so much guilt comes from—but when you sit down alone and think about your divorce, the guilt feelings come flooding in. A little bit of guilt is probably a good thing. You want to do right by the ones you love. You want people to think well of you. The trouble with guilt is that it doesn't come in little bits. Guilt is also a freezing emotion and if it takes over your life, your emotional cells simply freeze to death.

One hazard of feeling guilty during Crazy Time is that it's too easy. Instead of working through your many different and painful emotions, you lump them all together in a bag of guilt. That way you don't have to face them—or reality. Besides, playing the hangdog role may be more socially acceptable, especially to your ex-mother-in-law.

For some people, therapy is a good way to come to terms with this phony guilt, especially if you're in a group with other people in similar situations. You usually get away with one grand siege of guilt pains with the group. But it's not a habit that other people will put up with for very long.

Think about it. You failed? You're to blame for the divorce? What makes you think you have so much power over a relationship between two people? You sit there and snivel. "If only I had . . ." and you're off again. Whine. Whine. At this point, a loud groan is going through the room. The person next to you slouches down. The therapist does a quick eye roll. "Where did I go wrong?" Wail. Wail. Finally you get to the punch line: "Does this mean no one will ever love me again?" For a brief moment you stop sniveling to look pleadingly around the room.

"Well, I think anyone who sounds as awful as you deserves to be divorced," cracks a veteran member of the group.

"Don't you ever get angry?" says another.

Stop for a minute. If you're down in the dumps and feeling worse all the time, if every day you get dragged down a little further into general despair, maybe it's time you started ringing some alarm bells. An essential quality of Crazy Time is switching from one stage to another. You don't want to get stuck in one phase. Getting stuck in a guilt-ridden depression is like drowning. You slip into unconsciousness without knowing it. To get a good emotional divorce you have to stay alert.

The next time you think of how you were rejected, what an awful person you must be, how you deserve to be unloved—you'd better start giving equal time to those other feelings, rage and confusion.

Most people who seek counseling during Crazy Time stay in therapy for about two years. There are many brands of psychotherapy—Freudian analysis, Jungian analysis, behavioral modification, family systems therapy, crisis counseling. You can have individual sessions or join a group. You have to shop around to see which approach seems to work best for you. Therapy is not magic. Getting into therapy won't fix all your problems and make you happy. You still have to face those Deadlock ghosts and build a new life for yourself. What therapy can do is give you road signs along the way to help you through your divorce journey. You can learn some special skills to unravel your special relationship drama. You still have to do the hard work of getting a psychological divorce yourself.

In time, the depression of Crazy Time turns to sadness. You accept the sadness of the divorce in order to mourn the death of the marriage. Mixed with sadness are often warm emotions for your ex-spouse and nostalgia for your your marriage—not so much for what was there but for what might have been. In the end you have to say goodbye to the past and your dreams in order to preserve them.

Margot and Sam Whitman separate after fifteen years of marriage and two children, Sara, eight, and John, five. They are a typical American couple in a typical divorce. After the split, they do therapy together; they scream at each other and have their landmark anger scene; they sleep with each other (only once); they hassle lawyers over child support; they divide up mutual friends and pictures, and fight over the sofa they bought together. Eventually, they gain a stability in their quasi-married/quasi-divorced relationship. They fall in love with others and out of love with others. They both change, they are different people now, they both say. They go to parent meetings at school together and agree on music lessons for the youngest. They get through Thanksgivings and Christmases and make separate lives for themselves.

It's three years after they split up when Margot writes Sam her last letter. Sam has taken the children to the mountains for a two-week vacation; Margot has just gotten back from visiting her parents over the weekend. She writes:

My dear Sam,

Your postcard was waiting for me when I got back from Atlanta, which was nice to find because I had been thinking about you—us—on the plane. I was reading a book. There was a passage in it, the heroine was thinking back on her marriage. She remembers the day when she and her husband and the two sons are picking blueberries. The wind is blowing. They are in a field behind their house in the country. It's all quiet and safe and she says how much she loves her husband and I started to cry.

I feel so sad for us. It was the image of the hill. The peace of sharing a life together—man, woman . . . two children. We replenish the earth with them, with ourselves. The continuity of it.

I still have those expectations and nostalgia of that vision. I ache in my throat and tears come to my eyes as I write of the pain inside me over what we did not hold together. The image on the hill. It's not a scene from our past, it's an expectation, I realize that. But time has dulled my hurt and anger toward you personally. I must grieve for that expectation. And I grieve badly. I am haunted by the thought of whether we could have made it

I wish I could look in your eyes and know the truth with you. What you really wanted with me. Us. What you could really live with. There's a part of me that still wants you, wants to make it with you, wants to keep you as a half-mate, if there is such a word. A timeless friend, an anchor, a part of my life that can never be erased or replaced. I'm scared of losing you . . .

As I read this over, the thought crosses my mind: Why don't you ask him to come back and move into the house and go along with the image of the hill? I guess that's the closest I can come to asking you. I ask you for the image and the expectation of the marriage we shared— I don't know the reality of you and me.

Well, I've rambled on long enough. Nothing is said of the children and your vacation together. I love them very very much as I love you and always will—whatever happens to our "reality."

Love,
Margot

Sam thanks her for the letter and writes back in kind. In the end, they don't lose each other. It's too late for a marriage together, but they keep their dream. They acknowledge their nostalgia for the past and the image on the hill. In the reality between them, they are two strangers who have little in common now. They both recognize the reality. The marriage is finally over and they are divorced emotionally from each other. Somehow, after the exchange of letters, things are easier between them. Despair and ambivalence have been fused into sadness and nostalgia. They both go on in their lives a little richer in their hearts and more confident in their separate paths.

PART THREE

RECOVERY

The world breaks everyone and afterward many are strong at the broken places.

Ernest Hemingway, *A Farewell to Arms*

10

EMERGENCE OF SELF

You are alone. The bed is empty; the nights are quiet. Coming out of a broken marriage, you feel like half a pair of scissors. The edge is sharp, but you can't cut with it.

The key transformation in the divorce process is the emergence of self. Or as theologian Paul Tillich says: "Man is what he makes of himself. And the courage to be as oneself is the courage to make of oneself what one wants to be."

It takes two to get married, but you get divorced by yourself. You already know that severing the legal bond with an ex-spouse is a small part of the divorce experience. Severing the emotional bond with the past and building a new life for yourself is what your divorce is really all about. It's an individual experience. No one else can do it for you. In the end, how it works out is up to you. You write your own script.

Getting divorced places you in a personal struggle between the failure of the past and the possibilities of the future. In the course of the divorce experience, you are forced to deal with a number of specific tasks in your social environment: You must renegotiate your relationship with your ex-spouse, your children, your family and friends. You have to redefine yourself in terms of work and the community. You must reestablish yourself in terms of sex and love and new relationships.

As you face each task, you are torn between the poles of your failed past and the uncertain future. Maneuvering between these two poles is what forces you to change and grow emotionally. It's like learning to ride a bicycle. You learn by doing. You fall off and get hurt. You get back on and try again. Learning how to get a good emotional divorce is a highly dynamic psychological passage. You feel very unsettled. You *are* unsettled. Your life is filled with stops and starts. There are times when you forget that your divorce journey has a destination.

The recovering process from divorce seems to break down into at least three general stages of psychological growth. The way you respond to each task—whether it's dealing with your old boss or a new lover—reflects how far along you are in your divorce journey. To psychologist B. Bradshaw Minturn, a founding director of the Marriage and Family Institute in Washington, D.C., the three phases of divorce echo the three stages of human consciousness envisioned by the philosopher Sören Kierkegaard in *The Courage to Live*.

In this extended analogy, the first level of response to divorce is the Hummingbird Phase—roughly equivalent to Kierkegaard's "aesthetic stage." If it looks good, you like it. If it feels good, you do it. At the first sour taste, you bolt. It's a shallow, empty phase, a dead end, if it goes on too long. Hummingbird people aren't able to reestablish themselves as new entities because they never allow themselves to confront the pain and anxiety of divorce or of a new life. Their wings flutter too fast.

The next psychological level of response to divorce is the Foundering Phase—equivalent to Kierkegaard's "ethical or moral stage." Foundering people allow themselves to confront the pain and anxiety of divorce. You "founder" like a ship and run aground. You lose your job. A new romance suddenly ends. Foundering people acknowledge the damage. Instead of running away like a Hummingbird, you stick with the pain of divorcing. The danger is that some people never get beyond this level of psychological growth. They seem to give up life in despair and cynical resignation. That's why there are so many bitter divorced men and women around—the *never-again* crowd. Once was enough.

Most people go through the first two levels of emotional growth during Crazy Time. What you're aiming for is the third level—the Phoenix Phase, the equivalent of Kierkegaard's "religious stage." A new you rises up out of the ashes of divorce. In this passage, you have literally gotten into the psychological "narrows" of divorce, run aground on the rocks, stuck with the discomfort, and then pushed yourself off the rocks to deep water. The psychiatric buzzword for this is *individuating*. You learn how to negotiate your own way through the rocks. You pass through the final stages of grief and let go of the past. You accept your failure. You are comfortable with yourself and more tolerant of reality. You understand that you are basically alone. As Tillich puts it: "The courage to be is the courage to accept oneself as accepted in spite of being unacceptable."

When you reach the Phoenix level, you have come to the end of your divorce journey. It takes a long time. Most people find that it takes at least five years from the time of separation to reach the Phoenix level of confidence and personal freedom from the past.

A significant number of divorcing people go through a Hummingbird Phase in terms of sex. You sleep around. Mr. Feelgood. Ms. Bedhopper. It's a way to discover your body and find out what feels good. You alight on one sweet flower and as soon as the passion wanes, you're on to the next flame. Some people remain sexual Hummingbirds. You never form lasting relationships. It's another form of Divorce Flameout. And the cost is high. In the era of the AIDS epidemic, if you are promiscuous, you risk exposing yourself to the virus that causes this fatal, sexually transmitted disease.

In general, Hummingbird people refuse to deal with hard issues. You flit from job to job. You balk at dealing with your ex-spouse even though urgent decisions must be made: Who gets the car? the antique chair? the country music CDs? How do you divide the photographs? Since Hummingbird people usually refuse to confront the ex-spouse on any issue, nothing gets settled. When Jack comes to the house to divide up the furniture, Mary tells him she wants to keep the stereo. Instead of fighting it out and reaching an agreement, Jack explodes. "You bitch," he says. "I hate you." Then he stomps off. A Hummingbird. If it doesn't feel good, you move on. That way, though, you never get divorced.

Most people leave the Hummingbird level fairly quickly and get into the Foundering Phase of divorce. This is when you're at the height of Crazy Time. The shock has worn off. Your defenses are down. It's a desperate and confusing passage in the recovery process, but a necessary prelude to building a new life. You have to acknowledge the devastation of divorce to let go of it.

Foundering people are easily recognizable. You sigh a lot. You seem locked into despair and resignation. All around you, life hurts. You expect the worse. You are resigned that your ex-spouse preferred someone richer/brighter/younger and bought a new car. You expect all your mutual friends to side with your former spouse, so you don't call anybody. You go to the beach and it rains. You never meet anyone "suitable," or you meet someone wonderful but you know it's not going to work.

You live, it seems, under a broadening shadow of gloom and doom. But despair is just one aspect of the Foundering Phase. As the rough equivalent to Kierkegaard's moral stage, the Foundering Phase in divorce involves personal choices. In confronting the different tasks of divorce—dealing with your children or looking for a new job—you can decide how you're going to respond. This is how you learn to gain control over your life. When you meet someone wonderful but doubt it's going to work, you can either try to make it work and risk failure or you can decide to back off and take shelter in your despair. If you don't like your job, you can go to your boss and try to change it or you can look for another job.

The danger in the Foundering Phase is that you forget you have choices. You confront the agony of divorce but let it overwhelm you. You grow resigned that life is not going to work out, whether on the job, in bed, or out to dinner. It's easier this way. You become a professional Divorce Victim. After a while, all you do is wallow in your pain and confusion. You expect little, you risk little. When your friends call you up, you notice they don't ask you how you are anymore. They don't have to. You've become a lifetime member of the Foundering Club of Despair—a Divorce Flameout.

A combat soldier's definition of courage is moving from a safe place to an unsafe place (in order to win the battle). For an infantryman under fire, courage is leaving the safety of a foxhole for a new position. In psychological terms, the definition of courage in divorce is moving from the safety of one stage to the uncertainties of the next. Courage in divorce means moving from the safety of shallow feelings in the Hummingbird Phase to the pain and confusion of the Foundering Phase. It means moving from the safety of despair in the Foundering Phase to the making of choices and taking risks for a new life in the Phoenix Phase.

Getting to the Phoenix level sneaks up on you. You get in the habit of making difficult choices. You accept what in the beginning was unacceptable: yourself and your past of failure in marriage. You bring to your new life a survivor's confidence and a tourist's vision that the world offers many different experiences. It's just a question of deciding what you want to do.

You don't have to make love just because someone else wants to. You don't have to cut yourself off from your children because you don't live with them. You don't have to curse your ex-spouse for the rest of your life.

All of a sudden, when Jack, the dreaded ex-husband, comes to pick up the children, Mary finds she doesn't have to yell at him even though he's late as usual. Instead she offers him a cup of coffee. As they sit there in the kitchen, Mary realizes that this man who has dominated her life for twenty years has no effect on her. She's at the Phoenix level in dealing with her ex-spouse.

People can change a great deal in midlife. The prevailing view among therapists today—pioneered by psychiatrist Harry Stack Sullivan—is that your emotional life is not written in cement during childhood. You write each chapter as you go along.

As a Phoenix person, you have written a new script for yourself. You have enough confidence from discovering your own individuality that you don't feel crushed by the past reasserting itself. That makes you less afraid of the future. You gain more control of your life and take greater charge of the present. You change jobs, get married again—or not; you take piano lessons, become a minister. You finally become you.

But you never forget the pain of divorce. This is your strength. Kierkegaard compares the final stage of human consciousness to the shirt in the old fable: "The thread is spun under tears, the cloth bleached with tears, the shirt sewn with tears; but then too it is a better protection than iron and steel. . . . The secret in life is that everyone must sew it for himself. . . . (Then) there is peace and rest and comfort in sorrow."

Although the basic emotional stages of divorce are essentially the same for both men and women, there are practical differences in the recovery period and these differences are mainly rooted in cultural habits. American society has undergone a quiet revolution over the past thirty years. Most important has been the increased economic independence of women. As sociologist Andrew Cherlin explains, in the forties only one out of seven married women worked outside the home. In the "Leave it to Beaver" fifties, middle-class mothers only worked—if they worked at all—once the children were safely in school. All this began to change in the sixties and seventies. Now in the nineties, more than half of all mothers return to work within a year of their child's birth. Many women have no choice but to work; their families depend on two incomes.

Despite these changes, many men still see themselves as primary breadwinners for their family and women still find themselves primarily responsible for raising the children and keeping house. With the birth of a child, suddenly the most modern, egalitarian couples can become very traditional. "Children have a primitive capacity of activating the tapes of what a mother does and what a father does," says Augustus Napier.

At the University of California, Berkeley, researchers Philip and Carolyn Cowan were surprised to find how quickly couples in their study slipped into conventional roles after they had a baby. "We conclude that there is a discrepancy between the ideology of egalitarianism and the reality of the couples' lives," says Philip Cowan of the 96 couples he and his wife studied. "They are different from previous generations, but not much."

As a result, by the time you split up, you and your spouse may be on very different economic planes. In many situations, the husband as chief breadwinner earns more money than his wife. If the family has sufficient economic resources, many married women cut back and work part time, putting their careers on hold while their children are young. Like their mothers in the fifties, they are in charge of running the household and arranging child care. If the marriage breaks up, they are often at an economic disadvantage. While cultural patterns are changing, the label "displaced homemaker" is still a reality for a significant number of divorced women, who, as one employment counselor puts it, "have no skills, no clothes and no confidence."

The bitter fact of breaking up is that divorce makes you poor, especially if you are a woman. According to sociologist Cherlin, women on the average experience a 15 to 30 percent decline in their income after separation. Men, however, may see a 10 to 15 percent increase in their income. Since children usually live with their mother after the breakup, this economic disparity not only affects the suddenly single mom but also the children. More than 40 percent of divorced women are not awarded any child support. Only about half the women awarded support get the full amount from their ex-husbands. Sometimes you have to sell the family house, adding the stress of a move to the trauma of divorce. In a

California study of divorce settlements, the family home had to be sold in one third of the court-ordered divorces.

Economic instability is a constant source of anxiety as you try to rebuild your life. Law reforms are helping women collect owed child support and advances in the workplace will make it easier for women to be single mothers. But when a couple breaks up, there just isn't enough money in the marriage pot for two separate lives. This makes getting through Crazy Time all the more difficult.

For many women, a major task in the recovery period is learning how to take financial responsibility for yourself. You reexamine your job options. If you've been at home, you go out and look for a job. If you've been working part time, you take a full-time job. There's a hellish period you go through of juggling baby-sitters, pounding pavements, doing scut work for low pay, and always feeling bone tired. At first you're a Hummingbird—the first bad day at work and you want to quit. As a Founderer, you see the limits of any job and put up with the drudgery. Eventually you reach the Phoenix level and carve out a niche for yourself in the outside world. In the process, you learn to take control over your life and you gain an independence that in the end is vital to a good emotional divorce. Sitting back and waiting for another Mr. Right to come along to pay the bills—or trying to squeeze more out of your ex-spouse—is like waiting for the tooth fairy to dance on your pillow every night. Besides, it's not good mental health. It means you're still married—to anyone who will pay the bills.

The women's movement has gone a long way to improve working conditions for women. Nevertheless, women earn on the average only two-thirds of what men earn. The older the woman, and the longer she has been out of the job market, the more difficult it is going to be for her to establish herself in the working world. In general, it takes about five years for divorced women and their children to regain their predivorce standard of living.

As you recover from your divorce, it's important to separate the emotional tasks of uncoupling from the economic realities of being a single woman. In the end, you alone are responsible for your recovery. A job, a place in the work force, not only gives you a paycheck, it gives you an identity. Studies show that, in general, women who go to work after a divorce fare better than women who stay at home.

Many women, in fact, flourish in their new role as breadwinner. The divorce gives them "permission" to make the job a priority. They gain confidence in assuming "male" roles. Without a spouse to worry about at home, they can focus their energy on their children and their work.

As researcher Patricia Diedrick concludes in her doctoral study at the University of Georgia: "Women face more stressors due to divorce than do men because of gender differences in income, social activity and single parenthood. This has led [some researchers] to conclude that women suffer more as a result of divorce. Yet there is overwhelming evidence that females actually fare better in terms of divorce adjustment than do males. . . . For females, a sense of growth in self-esteem appears to result from the divorce. The effects of such changes appear long-lasting."

For many men, a major task in the recovery period is learning how to be a parent. Of course, the Absent Father Syndrome is not confined to divorced families. It has been a feature of American families for generations, where the roles between the sexes were divided so that the mother focused on the children and the father—who was out earning money—remained in the background. In many families, the husband deferred to the wife on anything to do with the children; Mom was the gatekeeper who controlled Dad's connection, or lack of it, with the children.

The rise of the men's movement is driven in large part by the anguish caused by the lack of a strong male figure in the family. When a couple splits up, and the children remain with the mother, this problem is exacerbated. Yet divorce can have two completely different effects on fathers: It can push you out of your children's life; or it can bring you into their lives, perhaps for the first time.

In troubled marriages, the father often escapes Deadlock by

staying away from home and living on the job—leaving all the care to the mother. As a divorced father, you have to establish a new and separate relationship with your children. This takes a special effort, especially if the children are living with your ex-wife. You can't depend on her to be a beneficent gatekeeper anymore.

Initially many men say it's better if they go away and never see their children again. It hurts too much, the Hummingbird father says. The first time your child spits at you in a restaurant, you say you're not going to be a Sunday Daddy anymore, and so you stop visits. But if you stick with the turmoil of raising children—despite the strain of dual parenting with your ex-spouse—you get to know your children and you gain a confidence about being a parent that doesn't depend on anyone else's blessing. As one man puts it: "I discovered the woman in me." Just as women discover "the man" in them on the job, men learn to tap their nurturing side with their children. Everybody benefits, especially the children.

Research shows that it's not the divorce per se that affects the children—but the quality of life after the divorce. This in turn depends on the parents' adjustment to the breakup. Most important is the stability and life-style of the custodial parent.

In the last decade, family researchers have become much more aware of the long-lasting impact of divorce on children. The effects vary according to the age and sex of the child when the parents break up. In the immediate separation period, children are likely to show signs of depression and anxiety; they may have behavioral problems at school. As adults, they may have difficulty trusting others and establishing intimate relationships.

But most children can and do adjust to the breakup of their parents. In marriages where there has been a high level of conflict, children may fare better after the divorce—as long as the conflict stops. "It's not the divorce that's the big issue; it's the family relationship problems that are the issue," says psychiatrist Edward W. Beal of Georgetown University Medical School.

To minimize the damage to children in the separation period, researchers recommend that you:

1. Keep the family routines functioning. Keep the same meal-times, bedtimes, be-ready-for-school times so that the kids can lean on the routine—though this is difficult to do as you plunge into Crazy Time and don't know how you're going to pay the telephone bill.

2. Keep the kids out of any conflict with the ex-spouse. Don't use them as weapons; don't use them as messengers—though this is difficult to do when conflict with your ex-spouse often escalates after the separation.

"If you do these two things," says Cherlin, "and the kids were doing well beforehand—then, after a period of adjustment, they will do well again."

Single parenting and marital instability, of course, are nothing new. "The fact that we have this instability is reminiscent of early American life on the frontier when death was the great mixing process, not divorce," explains Jeffrey Evans.

Yet, for children, divorce seems to have a somewhat greater effect than the death of a parent, largely because of the lack of social and economic supports for divorced families. British research on teenagers raised in single-parent families found that children who lost a parent because of death were not more depressed or more disrupted in their schoolwork than their peers in two-parent families. For children who experienced the divorce of their parents, "there was a modest but noticeable impact from the divorce," says Cherlin.

When death strikes a family, survivors are viewed with sympathy and rituals are in place to help people mourn the loss and recover a new life. There are no equivalent rituals when divorce strikes a family. "Death is easier. We've had thousands of years to learn how to deal with death in the family," says Cherlin. "Society is only beginning to learn how to deal with divorce."

Many men and women say they feel closer to their children through divorce. That's because you are sharing a critical period of your life with them. Few pretenses of Happy Family Life are left when a marriage breaks up. In many respects, your children are the ones who bear witness to your divorce. They know what you went through, and for a while, before you get involved in new relationships, your children are the only ones who really know about your divorce. In that honest sharing of daily events, you build a real closeness. Eventually all children grow up and have to establish a separate relationship with each parent—and vice versa. In divorce, you just can't always wait until everyone is grown up to do this.

Then, too, many people find that they have to renegotiate their relationship with their own parents when the marriage ends. Often you get married before you have broken away psychologically from home. During the marriage, your relationship with your family is on hold. When the marriage bursts apart, so does the old bond with your parents. You have to confront the reality of the past with your parents—often a painful confrontation—and build a new relationship with them as fellow adults.

Getting over a divorce is a two-step process: first, the mourning of the loss of the marriage; second, the emergence or reconstruction of the self. As Diedrick explains: "Adjustment has been defined as the development of a separate identity and the ability to function adequately in new roles."

As you recover from your divorce, you are like Paul Bunyan embarking on a personal journey into uncharted emotional territory. You must cut down forests, change the course of rivers. You are tested by your past, challenged by the future. As you successfully complete each task, you pass through the lands of the Hummingbirds, the Founderers, the Phoenixes. It's a near-mystical journey which at times you're not even aware you're making. With a little luck and perseverance, you'll finish the course.

11

PUBLIC DIVORCE

You really get two divorces—a private and a public one. In your private divorce, you face your ex-spouse, your past and yourself. In your public divorce, you confront the community you live in— the network of friends, family and acquaintances that you built up as a married couple.

Both divorces are battles of perceptions. Who are you? Who is your ex-spouse? What kind of marriage did you have? What went wrong? The trouble is you probably don't know yet. Getting separated is like living in a hall of mirrors. It's not clear what is real and what is reflection, what is happening and what *seems* to be happening. Your sense of reality is skewed. It's hard to explain what's really going on, let alone how you feel and what you want.

That's why you go a little crazy getting a divorce—and why you seem a little crazy to your network of family and friends. They may not know about the near-inevitability of Crazy Time, and your behavior is very disturbing to them. *We just don't understand it*, they say like a Greek chorus commenting on your public divorce. *It's her drinking . . . his fooling around . . . she went back to school . . . he lost his job,* the network continues in its search for social buzzwords to help them assimilate the news. *They haven't been getting along for years. . . . It came out of the blue. . . .* Very quickly your public divorce takes on a life of its own and a wall builds up between you and your friends. At times there seems to be little resemblance between your public and your private divorce. In the process, your old network collapses.

One of the traumas of divorce is the loss of friends. It heightens the panic you feel in Crazy Time—maybe you really are "bad," unlovable, crazy. It takes away emotional support just when you need it most; it feeds the feeling that you've been used and abused—first by your ex-spouse, now by the network of people who seem to disappear when the marriage ends.

In some cases, the public divorce overtakes the private divorce. The courtroom becomes the prime stage for battle. There are scenes at network events—school plays, Christmas parties, weddings, funerals. Friends are divided up and then used as arrows to hurt the other spouse. Sometimes a Judas emerges, an old premarriage friend of yours who openly sides with the other spouse, meddling in custody battles and even testifying in court for one spouse against the other.

In the dark hours of Crazy Time, it seems that the betrayal by your ex-spouse in your private divorce is being repeated by the betrayal of "good" friends in your public divorce. You die a little more.

You have to work at it to get through your public divorce. At first you're a Hummingbird. You ricochet from one friend to the next, looking for support. At the first sign of waning interest, you bolt. On to someone else. On the other hand, some Hummingbirds are so convinced they will be scorned and rejected, they simply withdraw and disappear. The network says, *It wasn't that we sided with Bill; it's just that we never heard from Mary again.*

After you reach the Foundering level of awareness, you are able to deal with the pain of losing friends. You have to accept the fact that some people who were in your married orbit simply slip away. There are times when you try to maintain a friendship and your overtures are rejected. The hurt starts all over again. You swing back and forth between reaching out and withdrawing.

It's important to make peace with your network. After a lapse of several years, you run into an old friend and have a drink. Although you don't talk about the divorce, it's a dead subject by now, and you talk about everything else. You can't believe how good you feel afterward.

The rules for dividing up the marriage network of friends and acquaintances are murky. At least, when you divide up the furniture, you talk about who wants what. With friends, the dividing process is often wordless. It's difficult for you, for your ex-spouse—and for your friends. You expect colleagues or family connections of your former spouse to side with your ex. But after ten or twenty years of marriage, who is a friend of whom? Can a person be friends to both spouses in a divorce?

You learn to make choices. You accept the loss of certain close friends. You try to keep the friendship of others in your new status. You make new friends and rebuild a network of people around you. You finally reach the Phoenix level in your public divorce.

One of the most important factors in your public divorce is the Friend Who Stands By You. Sometimes it's a new friend you meet after the marriage is over; sometimes it's a friend from childhood who knew you before you were married; rarely is it a friend who knew you both well. This solid friend is the person who bears witness to your divorce journey. This is the person who knows the pain of your breakup, who sticks with you during Crazy Time and who celebrates your success when you reach the Phoenix level and have a new life for yourself. There is no room for rhetoric or gestures when you're going through a divorce. In that honest sharing of trauma, your friendship deepens.

Few people are prepared for their public divorce. You expect private turmoil, but you are usually unprepared for the public trauma. You think you're having a tough time and you expect your friends to rally around. After all, you're supposedly living in the

Grand Era of Divorce. From television talk shows and how-to-cope magazine articles, you've been hearing that divorce is no longer a stigma, that it happens in almost one out of two marriages, that it's not good to stay in a marriage for the sake of the children and that school systems have special programs for single parents; in short, that divorce is so frequent it has become a "normal" experience in American culture.

The reality is that you find yourself on very shaky ground in your public divorce. Breaking up a family may be common, but it still makes the country's society of couples very uncomfortable. Although legal and religious restrictions on divorce have been largely lifted, social pressure is still strong—and you are very weak.

The outlines of your public divorce are drawn fairly soon after separation—just when you're most distraught and confused. Which story does the network believe? Spouses rarely agree on the causes of the breakup at this point in Crazy Time. Much depends on which one of you gets to the network first. Accepting the point of view of one spouse is the network's first step toward supporting one spouse against the other. Ideally the network, like Solomon, should hear both sides so that the public divorce can reflect a synthesis of two people's private traumas. But breaking up a marriage is rarely so orderly.

Usually you are so disoriented you're not sure what your case is. Confusion and ambivalence lead to panic, especially if you feel the network closing in against you. It's no wonder that the network gets a fuzzy picture of your divorce. At first one of you reacts to the breakup with a mixture of relief and guilt; you mumble how terrible the marriage was. The other responds with disbelief and anger; you say that the marriage was basically good. It's hard on friends. With two perceptions of the breakup so different, the network wonders if you are both getting the same divorce.

In the weeks following the breakup, there is often a frantic search for the "good case." Who's to blame? In the manners of divorce, one spouse usually ends up taking public responsibility for initiating the marriage crisis. From now on, one of you has in the eyes of your friends the role of Divorce Seeker, the other of Divorce Opposer—although in private it almost never is that clear-cut. Yet this distinction made in the immediate post-separation period usually sets the moral tone of your public divorce.

Says Suzanne Keller: "In our culture, the person who declares for a divorce carries the burden of that decision forever."

When you start feeling your network of friends slip away, let your paranoia subside. You are not being singled out. Recent studies on divorce document the collapse of couples' social networks. Men and women both report that they are treated differently because of their separated or divorced status. "Shared friends from the disrupted marriage seemed conflicted about which spouse to call and often quietly terminated the friendship," says Joan Kelly. "Separated women in particular were more likely to let the social relationship collapse, feeling unwanted, vulnerable and therefore tentative about expressing their strong need for continued support and friendship."

In a 1979 study of fifty divorced adults, nearly half of the men and women reported growing more distant from their close friends after separation; the people getting divorced seemed to be as responsible for the estrangement as their friends. But nothing prepares you for some of the bizarre reactions from people you thought you knew well.

Sue Casey is thirty, with four small children and a fear of going to hell just as the nuns said she would if she was a bad girl. Now she and her husband are breaking up after ten years of marriage. Tom is a navy pilot and they live in a subdivision near the base at Patuxent, Maryland, a pilots' ghetto of other young couples with small children and husbands away much of the time.

Her Best Friend comes by. "We were like sisters," Sue begins. "I am her child's godmother; she is my child's godmother. When she found out that Tom and I were splitting up, that was it. She turned against me. 'You can't do this,' she said. 'It's not right for you, for your friends, for your family.' She was furious. She couldn't stand my divorce. I've never seen or spoken to her again."

Sue is stunned. She sits alone in the same old house in the same old subdivision, coping with blown fuses, broken tricycles and overwhelming loneliness. Soon the Sudden Male Friends come by. They are husbands of her women friends in the neighborhood and colleagues of her ex-husband.

"They were very interested in me," she says. "They were extra nice to me. They'd drop by and play around with the children. They'd help in the yard. Looking back, I had probably been leading them on. They all wanted a little piece. It was shocking. They were all close friends when we were married."

About a year after the breakup, Sue is invited to spend a weekend with old friends. The man is her ex-husband's closest buddy. They went to school together, worked together at the base. They went on fishing trips together. "The man took me aside and said, 'Well, you know, we wondered how you stayed in that marriage so long. You had nothing in common. We've been waiting for this to happen.'" Sue is shocked. She thought everybody saw them as a perfect couple. All those times they spent together as couples? This man is her ex-husband's best friend? The shocks get worse. "Then the wife took me aside and said, 'How did you ever have the nerve to do it? I've been miserable for years. I've had an affair. But I don't dare to leave him. It would hurt too much.'"

Sue can't believe what she's hearing. It's not just her own world that is turned upside down—her whole universe has gone crazy.

You find that when you are getting divorced, people tell you things. They know you are suffering and think you will understand. Their private miseries and secret longings will be safe with you. You're an open target. They also look at you and see a reflection of their own lives. Sometimes they respond with rage to your divorce and cut you off. *How could you do such a thing?* they mutter. You are stunned. Very quickly, you discover how shallow and shaky this whole married world is. It's as though a curtain has been raised on a backstage drama. The play has been going on all these years. In getting a divorce, you see backstage for the first time.

Sue survives her divorce and remarries. Twenty years later, she observes: "I think the people who fight your divorce most vehemently are having problems in their own marriage. They are jealous—or feel threatened—that you're breaking out. Divorce brings out their own misery—especially if it happens to a—quote—happy couple."

It's easy to forget that your divorce presents a crisis for your friends too. Not only are they threatened in their own marriages but they get trapped in the hall of mirrors of your divorce. They don't know what to believe, how to comfort you, or whom to ask to dinner. You don't give them much guidance. Crushed by Crazy Time, you retreat into your own guilt and despair and withdraw from your old friends. Or you give vent to your rage and wash the dirty linen of your marriage in public. Your friends don't know how to respond.

"It helps if both spouses are clear and decisive about getting divorced," says Becky Rust, a married woman who lives in Dallas. "Then it's a relief for everybody. But few couples are clear and decisive."

At first most of your network friends try to be friends with both of you. They don't want to take sides. But it's almost impossible. Whom do they invite to their annual Christmas party? "With some divorced couples, we thought we could be friends with both," says Becky. "But we always end up with one person or the other. It's usually due more to their behavior than our picking one over the other," she continues. "One friend stays closer to us, or the other moves away. Sometimes it's simple—in one case, the wife was my friend from childhood, so we naturally stayed close to the wife. In another case, we were close friends of both the man and the wife. We were with them when they decided to break up. We've kept up with the wife, but the husband has drifted off. We were always the ones to call him. It never went the other way. We finally stopped calling."

Can a person be a real friend to both spouses? How can you listen to the horror stories of marriage from one spouse and remain loyal to the other spouse? "Just hearing the side of one spouse is an act of betrayal," says Becky. "By listening, you're sympathetic to one side. Yet if you say you don't want to hear, you're not being a friend."

You have an impulse to say your public divorce doesn't matter; to hell with the fair-weather drones of the past. But you soon find you can't escape your public divorce. It's an essential part of the emotional divorce experience. You have to confront your network and come to terms with its judgment of you. What is right and what wrong? Is there justice? When? Your public divorce becomes a morality play of your private divorce.

Some people are destroyed by their public divorce. You are swept away by the network's initial verdict. Something in you wants to believe the worst. Your greatest fears of rejection are substantiated. You don't fight back. Instead you live out the damning judgment of your public divorce. That way you never let go of the past. You never have to rebuild your network. You keep your old network instead.

Nancy Abbot, fifty-five, is an example of a Public Divorce Flameout. When her marriage breaks up after twenty-two years, everybody turns against her—family, friends, neighbors. Partly she is a victim of her husband's manipulation of the network. But most of all, her flameout is due to her own behavior.

In the mid-sixties, Nancy is living in Palo Alto, California. She's a cum laude graduate from Bryn Mawr College, with gray-blond frizzy hair and bright blue eyes. Her husband, Joe Romano, is a vice-president of a medical supply company in San Francisco. They have three overly bright children. Joe, a self-made man from Indianapolis who smokes a pipe, is very understanding of Nancy and helps the kids with their homework. He has a winning smile and tells funny stories about such things as taking his Italian grandparents to the Grand Canyon. He is slightly shorter than Nancy and is several years older. They meet when she is a college freshman, he a science teacher at Haverford. He tells her she has to study three hours for every hour of class if she wants to gradu-ate with honors. It's clear to Nancy that there's no other way to graduate if she wants to keep his approval. She becomes a grind. He is pleased with her. That's how it starts. Nancy simply does what Joe tells her to do. In their Deadlock, he is dominant. She is passive-submissive.

Her grand old (but sliding) Midwestern family says how lucky she is to be married to such a terrific man and have three terrific children. Every Christmas, she sends out a family picture with a calendar of triumphs: Joe gets a promotion and is put in charge of West Coast sales; Deedee, twelve, wins a debating trophy in sev-enth grade; the boys, Joe junior, nine, and Larry, eight, are on the lower school football team. There's nothing on the Christmas card about her.

The days Nancy gets up, she wears shaggy sweaters, A-line skirts and loafers. Other days, she stays in bed and reads. There are no curtains in the bedrooms. She just hasn't gotten around to it. It's hard to believe they moved to Palo Alto eight years ago. She would die if she couldn't read. Sometimes she works at Stan-ford University, translating French, which had been her major in college. The living room looks like a secondhand bookstore that takes in laundry on the side. The children eat a lot of frozen pot pies for dinner.

As Joe rises on the corporate ladder, he looks younger, more at ease with himself. Nancy looks older, is grayer in her moods, more tentative in her movements, like a sick bird. She goes to a psychiatrist and is told she's depressed. That's it? she thinks. Now what happens? She keeps going to the shrink. He keeps telling her she's depressed. After a while, Nancy starts hitting the sauce. At least she has more fun at those company cocktail parties. The network watches her closely. Her hair gets frizzier; she starts smoking cigarillos and talking politics like a Black Panther. No one knows quite what to make of her. A colleague of Joe's points out to the network that her great-aunt was like this—a little queer. It runs in the family. Joe has told him so. "I just wish she wouldn't drink so much," says another voice in the network.

Meanwhile Nancy keeps up those Christmas bulletins about her family, happy-sounding letters to her parents saying how successful her husband is, how well the children are doing, how nice it is at Stanford. Back in the living room, she glares at her husband. But he doesn't notice her.

Nancy is going down, down, down. She knows her husband is leading a double life. For five years, Joe has been having an affair with a tennis coach at a local health club. Nancy had studied three hours for every one hour of class and graduated cum laude. She put herself in his hands. She followed the rules. Now Joe betrays her with a lesser brain. She looks at her books: *Chanson de Roland* . . . *À la Recherche du Temps Perdu.* "That woman has the kind of brain that puts name tags on athletic shorts," says Nancy many years after the divorce.

But that's all she ever says about her rival and Joe's betrayal. She never tells anybody—not her family, not her friends—about her private hell. The husband promises to end the relationship and keep up the marriage dream: successful tycoon, cum laude wife, three successful children.

But it doesn't work. Joe keeps up his affair with the tennis coach while maintaining the pretense of the new start with Nancy. She knows something is wrong. Out of Deadlock habit, she looks to Joe to tell her what's going on. He denies there's anything wrong. So Nancy becomes paralyzed between what she senses and what she is told. Her feelings have no legitimate basis, she tells herself. Gradually her hold on reality—and herself—slips away.

Meanwhile the grapevine gets to work: *Nancy's looped again. . . . It's too much for him. . . . She never paid attention to the children. . . . He takes them to buy clothes. . . . She never cleans the house. . . . She never cooks.* And so the battle of perceptions begins: No-good wife vs. poor long-suffering husband.

The leaves turn gold in California and Nancy tries to fight back by being a good wife. Thanksgiving is the time for family solidarity. She decides to put on a grand family Thanksgiving dinner. What better way to establish herself as a good wife and mother? She'll do it all: stuffing, gravy, homemade cranberry sauce. She invites some second cousins who live nearby. "How nice you're doing this, Nancy," they say. "We haven't seen you in so long." She invites two students from Pakistan who have nowhere to go. The show is to start at noon.

That morning, Nancy gets up early. The table in the dining room is set with family silver. The living room looks spotless. The books are put away and an afghan rug is thrown over the sofa, covering up and old wine stain. The children dress up. A roll of toilet paper is put in the downstairs bathroom. The wine is cooling in the refrigerator. Nancy wears a silk dress and stockings.

And then at about eleven-thirty, the children discover that Nancy has put the fourteen-pound turkey in the coat closet instead of the oven.

It's all over after that.

Her husband takes the role of aggrieved spouse. His wife must be mad—stark, raving mad. The children shake their heads. Just like crazy old Mom to do something like that. Nancy goes to bed. In desperation, Joe telephones Nancy's sister in Chicago, his voice shaking: "Nancy's put the turkey in the closet." Her sister gasps.

The network is shocked. So is Nancy. A turkey in the coat closet? Raw and dripping blood on boots and rubbers? She didn't know the difference between an oven and a coat closet? The heavies shake their heads: mother, father, sister, brother, three children. *She must be crazy to do a thing like that.* Her husband shakes his head. Common wisdom says they can't go on like this. It's best that the marriage end.

Now the network gets on Nancy's case: *They are getting a divorce because she's crazy.* The poor husband. He's suffered so. She goes to the psychiatric institute. He has custody of the children. *She really must be crazy.* It's best for everyone this way. Isn't it nice he's found a girl friend? You know the family like her too.

Within a year, the network neatly wraps up her public divorce. Everybody agrees she's crazy. No one suggests that Nancy is acting a little crazy *because* her marriage is crumbling.

Most "normal" people go a little crazy when a marriage breaks up. Well, then, is Nancy crazy-normal or crazy-sick? In the end no one knows, because at this point in the divorce process, Nancy flames out. A passive victim in the marriage, Nancy becomes the passive victim in the divorce. She accepts the verdict of her public divorce. She never tells the network of family and friends her side of the breakup. In fact, when the marriage ends, Nancy has no close friends. Nobody seems to know who Nancy is, what she feels or what she wants.

"We all thought that Nancy was crazy and that's why she got divorced and had a mess of a life," says her sister. "She had no support at all. I admit I went against her. So did everybody. There was no women's movement she could turn to. The disapproval was total: She wasn't a good wife, she was unstable, she was drinking too much. We were all much more loyal to him.

"It turned out he was the worst bastard in the world," Nancy's sister continues. "We found that out later from our own dealings with him. But Nancy never told us anything. We didn't know about the affair with the tennis coach. We didn't know how she suffered. One day Nancy had a black eye; she never said her husband hit her. All her letters talked about her husband's success. There was no mention of problems. So after the turkey episode, everybody thought she had gone crazy."

The tragedy is that Nancy spends the rest of her life in Crazy Time. After the separation, Nancy is hospitalized for three months. Then she gets a little house on the fringes of the crime zone in Los Angeles and bolts the door. She thinks her husband is after her money, so she buries her grandmother's pearl necklace in the yard and puts all her furniture in storage. "She really is crazy," the network whispers. "Imagine burying your grandmother's pearls in the yard!"

It turns out Nancy is right. Her husband *is* trying to siphon off her family money as part of the divorce settlement, but that's not apparent to her family until much later. Meanwhile Nancy goes downhill. Stuck at the Hummingbird level of awareness, she never confronts her husband's betrayal with the tennis coach or the network's betrayal of her at the time of the breakup. She doesn't question the verdict of her public divorce. Instead she moves into a permanent emotional stalemate of despair. She expects the worst to happen and accepts it when it does. Drifting into the Foundering level of awareness, she only feels the pain. She makes no choices about her life. *C'est la guerre!* she sneers. She doesn't take any risks or try to set the record straight with those people she cares about.

Five years after the marriage breaks up, Nancy is a messy eccentric. Her eyes get more vacant, her hair frizzier and her tongue sharper. Most of her money is gone. Meanwhile Joe marries the tennis coach and supposedly lives happily ever after, the successful businessman, with a much nicer wife this time, the network says. The children grow up and never visit their mean and nutty mother.

Nancy doesn't show her hurt. She doesn't begin to work through the anger buried in her. Instead, at family parties bitchy remarks leak out of her mouth as she reaches for another drink.

"Nancy's life was ruined by the divorce," her sister says. "She was never the woman she could have been."

It is tempting early in the separation period to use your public divorce to take care of the painful emotions you have in Crazy Time. As the Divorce Seeker paralyzed with guilt, for example, you let your friends turn against you because you feel like a superworm. You feel that you deserve to be punished. So you don't call anyone. *Why, why are you breaking up?* the network wants to know. The words don't come out easily. *Well . . . I thought I was going to die. . . . I had no choice. . . . It was over a long time ago. . . . We were destroying each other. . . . I failed. . . . You lower your head.*

If you follow the most common pattern of the Divorce Seeker, you start out in the marriage in the submissive role. It's not your style to be the initiator in relationships. Yet you are usually the one who takes the route of deception in Deadlock. You learn to be an activist outside the marriage. Now, in the eyes of your public divorce, you are branded as the one who broke up the marriage. But there's a part of you that is still passive and dependent, the old you. You aren't really that comfortable in the activist role. It's too new. You no longer have the protection of subterfuge. It's all you can do to hold your own vis-à-vis your estranged spouse. You can't deal with the network. In your public divorce, you retreat for a while. You become the child again. You've made the gods very angry. Now they're going to get you. You wait for blows to strike. Guilt enters the bloodstream and infects every cell in your body.

Or you are the Divorce Opposer, consumed with rage at the time of the breakup. Your departing spouse is a witch, a rotter, a big shit, a raving asshole.

In Deadlock, you are usually the dominant one. You are used to being the initiator, the leader, the controller. In the relationship, you take the route of denial. After the breakup, you turn to the network to affirm your view of the marriage. You may be deposed from your dominant position in Deadlock, but it's still your style to take charge. You don't feel the guilt—not yet—so you're not shy about getting in touch with friends.

Sometimes you take the soft line: *All I want to do is get back together. . . . We had a good marriage. . . . I don't understand what's come over him/her. . . . This is so awful I could die.*

In the normal course of the separation process, it's not long before your public divorce escalates. Now even the Divorce Seeker begins to take the hard line. *He/she beat me . . . cheated on me . . . stole the cookie money . . . had an affair with my sister/brother. . . . I couldn't stand to see what he/she was doing to the children.* The Divorce Seeker tries to justify the breakup. The Divorce Opposer could kill the Divorce Seeker for causing all this trouble.

Very quickly your public divorce can be reduced to several basic clichés: *She's crazy. He's crazy. She's a bitch. He's a bastard.*

As you work your way through Crazy Time, you realize that divorce is never that simple. Beware of the person with the "good case." A favorable public divorce can't substitute for a good private divorce. You can't expect the network to get angry for you, to feel sorry for you, to pick you up and put your life together for you. It's a fine line in your public divorce between getting support from friends and letting others do your emotional dirty work.

The distinction between seekers and opposers quickly fades. Perceptions of the marriage change and so do the battle issues between divorcing mates. The marriage itself fades. Both of you are confronted with the same basic tasks in rebuilding your life. In time, you realize that there is no standard of emotional justice to be handed down in your public divorce. As Paul Tillich says: "There is no norm, no criterion for what is right and wrong. . . . Resoluteness makes right what shall be right."

One danger is that you may try to settle your public divorce too soon. On a practical level, you may lock yourself into a legal settlement that you can't live with five years later. On an emotional level, you prevent yourself from working through the conflicting feelings of Crazy Time. You get a quickie public divorce to take care of your guilt or your rage. Sealed in the I'm-to-blame category, you don't come to terms with your anger and disappointment that the marriage didn't work out; or bursting with rage, you won't confront your own guilt, your own responsibility in the divorce. Eventually these emotions come back to haunt you.

John Hampshire, sixty-two, is condemned by the network when he leaves his wife after thirty years to marry a woman twenty years younger. Certainly his case looks bad. Because of his terrible guilt feelings, he completely accepts the network's verdict—for a while.

John works for Xerox Corporation in Stamford, Connecticut. At the time of his divorce five years ago, his wife is fifty-five, a classic case of the displaced homemaker with no husband, no confidence, no job and no recent work experience.

John's public divorce is simple and quick. John is cast in the role of divorce rat.

"My friends, almost in unison, turned against me," he says. "Ninety percent of them made moral judgments. My friends condemned me not so much for the third party but in breaking up a marriage that lasted so long. My wife said the same thing to me:

'Why didn't we do this ten years ago? Why did you wait until I was in old age?'

"How do I answer that?" he continues. "I don't know how to explain it. I stuck it out and at some point I couldn't go on any longer."

But if John is labeled immoral in his public divorce, he has been emotionally predictable in his private divorce, an example of the submissive spouse in a marriage programmed for divorce. From the beginning, he's not too sure he wants to walk up the aisle, but she insists on it. The Deadlock lasts three decades. He takes the predictable route of deception and has a number of intense affairs. Meanwhile their sex life crumbles and they have no sex together for the last eight years of the marriage. "She always had something planned for every night in the week—on the eighth night we were supposed to have sex," he says.

With each affair, the emotional gap between them widens. She snaps at him and tells him not to monopolize the conversation at cocktail parties. He talks mostly to women at cocktail parties. The inevitable happens: he falls in love with a woman who looks up to him. Deadlock is broken.

His relief at getting out of the marriage is overtaken by guilt. "I feel very deeply for my wife's plight," he says. "I just didn't see any other way. I had to do what I did."

The network comes down hard on him and he tries to buy off his guilt. He pays his wife's lawyer's fees and pays her more alimony than his lawyer advises. He leaves everything in the house to her—even some of the pictures on the wall she never liked. He lets the old friends drop away. He assumes that they are all on his wife's side and she needs the network's support more than he does. Besides, he is about to get married and have a new life.

This tactic works at first. After a few years, John rebuilds a new network with his second wife. The guilt he felt during Crazy Time starts to subside, his depression lifts and he finally discovers a reservoir of anger aimed at his first wife.

He now resents being cast in the role of divorce rat. He resents even more the blood money he pays in the form of alimony and property. The rage wells up in him. He's still not finished with his emotional divorce.

"My wife said she loved me—even after we were divorced—which made me feel so guilty," he says. "But why did she say that if she didn't mean it—and if she meant it, why did she take so much substance away in terms of alimony? When I retire I'm going to have to read the riot act to her, and that's not going to be easy. I'm going to have to pay the attorneys a lot of money to get off the hook."

John is still working through his private divorce. He still has to settle who is right, who is wrong? Where is justice? John finds himself still tied to the past, stuck at the Foundering level and awash in anguish and growing bitterness. He has yet to finish the battle of perceptions with his dominant ex-wife and write the last chapter of his public divorce.

Negotiating a new relationship with your ex-spouse and dealing with the emotions of guilt and anger are essential tasks in the divorce process. If you shift these important psychological passages to your public divorce, you just make your private divorce experience more complicated—and longer.

It takes time to get a good public divorce. Don't rush it. Don't rely on the network to rescue you. But don't turn your back on the network, either. In the end, you are responsible for the kind of public divorce you get.

Candace Maloney, forty-one, gets her public divorce when she remarries and has a big wedding. She is three months pregnant and wearing a soft Indian print dress. The room is crowded. The judge is late. Her mother is straightening her daughter's collar; her father is talking to one of the guests. Her sister is smiling. Her bridesmaid from the first wedding is best woman. The champagne is ready.

Six years earlier, Candace almost flamed out. She and her husband, Jim Olney, are splitting up after ten years of marriage and three children. During the marriage, Jim has an affair. Candace gets depressed and joins the women's movement. Jim has another affair. Candace gets more depressed, more frantic. They finally break up in great anger. The battle centers on the children and they fight over custody. In the end, they go to court. *Who is the better parent?* the Deadlock ghosts are asking. *Who is the better person?*

It's a closed-in company town in Ohio where Jim works for a steel company. It turns out, however, that Candace's childhood friend lives nearby. She and Candace go way back as friends: elementary school, high school and college. She and her husband become good friends of Candace and Jim's. Then when Candace and Jim split up and are fighting over custody, this friend of Candace's stands up in court and testifies in favor of Jim. "He's a good father," the friend tells the court. Candace breaks down. First her husband betrays her privately in the marriage and now her childhood friend betrays her publicly in the divorce. She feels demolished, as far as the network goes: first as a woman, then as a parent and as a friend. It's a small town—his town, not hers. She moves back to Philadelphia, where she grew up. The children stay in Ohio with their father. Why does she always look so grim and fierce? the network asks.

But Candace fights back. She hires lawyers and goes into therapy. "I had to make the decision of whether to end it all right there or accept the fact that I would probably spend the rest of my life alone," she says. She passes through that critical moment and starts to rebuild her life. She visits some of her old premarriage friends in Washington and New York and realizes that they stand behind her. She goes back to school in Philadelphia and gets a degree in social work.

One day a man telephones her. He's the friend of the husband of an old college friend, and he plays the flute in the Philadelphia Symphony Orchestra. They have dinner. His name is Richard and he says he'll call again. She goes to court one more time to get her children back. Maybe someday, when you're settled, the judge says.

Richard calls her again. "He was the one who sought me out," she says. Now she laughs when they go to dinner. He likes Greek restaurants. In time, they decide to live together in his apartment in the heart of the city. Her children come to visit. Then her parents come to visit.

After a few years, Candace and Richard buy an old town house and restore it so that there are rooms for the children and a little garden. She has a job as a social worker in the public school system, and counsels pregnant teenagers. She goes back to the judge and says she is settled. The judge agrees. When she goes to pick up the children, her ex-husband seems shrunken to her, the community looks vacant. She takes the children back to the city. They are a family again; they go to the zoo, to the movies. Candace begins to enjoy her new life.

The school year has barely started when Candace finds herself pregnant. After the usual cracks about a sex counselor getting pregnant, they decide to get married. Richard has never married, never had a child. They plan a big wedding. The children are excited. Richard chooses his groomsmen. "This is Richard's wedding," Candace says laughing. "He's the bride."

Her face glows. There are flowers everywhere. Around three o'clock, the people start pouring in: her family, his family, her old college friends, his old college friends, friends they've made together in Philadelphia, her friends from work, his colleagues. She looks out at her new network. The judge arrives. Candace stands with her children and looks at Richard. The ceremony begins. "Do you, Candace, take this man..." Richard looks at her the whole time the familiar words are said. Candace smiles. "I now pronounce you man and wife," says the judge. With that, a cheer roars up from the crowd. Friends start clapping and shouting. They hoist glasses of champagne and yell hooray. There's laughing and dancing and hugging. The best man, who's a woman—the widow of Richard's brother—kisses the bride. The children are cheering and patting Mom's belly. The champagne is flowing. It seems more like a New Year's party than a wedding.

Candace's old friends smile. They take off their shoes and have another glass of champagne. Maybe there is justice, they say. You just have to wait it out.

One thing to remember in your public divorce is that you can take a long time to make your peace with the network. Candace's friends are right: Things can work out. The main thing is not to give up. It often takes as long to get your public divorce as your private divorce. In the end, living well is the best revenge.

12

SEX

Coming out of a broken marriage, you wonder how you are going to deal with sex. You're alone, but your sexual appetite remains. Often the marital change has heightened your sexual cravings. Now's your chance. What do you do?

You start by making friends with your body, accepting your bumps and soft spots. Then, through trial and error, you find out what makes you feel good. On the outside, you may lose fifteen pounds, buy new clothes, take up jogging. On the inside, you think about sex a lot. You separate sex from marriage. You assess your experience and fantasize about the future.

The sexual revolution that began in the sixties with the Pill has changed the rules for men and women in search of sex. The I'm O.K.–You're O.K. approach to life moved into the bedroom with women eager to catch up with men in the pursuit of quality and quantity of sex—with no strings attached.

But now in the nineties, The Wow! Pow! Just-say-yes! era of Free Love is waning. With the emergence of AIDS, the price of promiscuity can be fatal. Researchers first noticed the strange wasting-away disease in homosexuals in San Francisco in 1981. A decade into the epidemic, more than 200,000 cases have been reported to the federal Centers for Disease Control. An estimated one million Americans are infected with the virus. AIDS has emerged as a leading cause of death for young adults. Roughly three-quarters of the cases have occurred in people between the ages of 25 and 44. The pace of the epidemic is also accelerating. The first 100,000 cases occurred over an eight-year period; the next 100,00 cases over a two-year period.

What puts men and women at risk for AIDS, according to federal health officials, is having many sex partners and being infected with other sexually transmitted diseases. So far in the U.S., AIDS has infected mostly homosexual and bisexual men, and intravenous drug users and their partners. But in Africa and other countries, AIDS is predominantly a heterosexual disease. Now in the U.S., the most rapid spread of the disease is occurring among people who are exposed to the virus through heterosexual intercourse.

The number of Americans who develop AIDS from heterosexual sex is still relatively low—accounting for less than 10 percent of all cases. But the rate is rising among women with AIDS, with nearly 35 percent of the cases attributed to heterosexual sex. Overall, the disease strikes blacks and Hispanics disproportionately. In addition, the rate for men is about seven times higher than that for women.

All this is having a chilling effect on the public culture of sex. "People worry about AIDS. It is really making a dent in sexual behavior," says Florence P. Haseltine, director of the Center for Population Research at the National Institutes of Health. "It's affecting the married lifestyle, too. Married people are not having as many affairs."

The manners of sex are changing, too. You go to a party. You're on the prowl. ISO (In Search Of) Alert! You see someone. You think, maybe this could be Antony and Cleopatra: for one night. You know there is a blood test that can detect the presence of the virus. So do you say: *Have you been tested for the AIDS virus? When?*

Even if you're willing to ask the question, you should know that the test is not perfect. (There are false-negative and false-positive results.) People who are infected can go for ten years before they show severe symptoms. You can't tell by looking at someone.

You've heard all about "safe" sex practices. Do you never leave home without a condom? Do you always use a condom when you have sex? At least in the first six months or so of a relationship? Or until both of you are assured that neither one is infected—or is at risk of being exposed to the virus by having other partners? Using a condom reduces the risk of AIDS, but doesn't eliminate it because condoms can break. Still, apart from not having sex at all, a latex condom is the most effective protection against potential exposure to the virus in semen.

In the new etiquette of sexual romance, the redefinition of a gentleman is one who uses a condom. With those men who aren't yet gentlemen, Haseltine advises: "Women have to realize they can't let the male do the whole thing. They have to learn how to put a condom on a man." In the era of AIDS, assuming the role of passive innocence can be deadly. "Women," continues Haseltine, "have to be assertive about using a condom, and sophisticated about using lubricants. It means sex is no longer as spontaneous. There's less unplanned sex—but also less infectious diseases."

As the AIDS epidemic grows, some people may shun sex, at least for a while. The culture may shift to a new code of safe sex— a kind of cautious chastity that encourages abstinence and monogamous sexual relationships. Yet despite these changing attitudes, the need for sexual satisfaction is primal. "You have to have sex," points out Haseltine.

For many people who get divorced, heightened sexual activity is a part of building a new life. Knowing yourself and knowing the risks are the first steps to discovering how to fulfill your own sexuality. In time, you realize that most Americans are *not* infected with the AIDS virus. That means you may look for a sexual partner, even if you end up just saying no. You don't take extreme chances. You learn how to make careful choices.

After a marriage ends, you are free to have sex without making a long-term commitment. Even with AIDS in the shadows of your social life, you may go through a sexual experimentation phase. It's part of the challenge of being single. In the pre-AIDS era, many men and women eagerly sought a variety of sexual experiences. As one woman says of that period: "It was amazing. I did the singles bar scene. I'd usually go with a girl friend who was married. I think she was jealous. Inevitably I got some terrific hunk of guy." Says one man looking back: "I did a lot of prowling. Two different women in one day, having sex in weird places—in a public park when it was raining, on a train late at night. . . ."

For many people, such experimentation is an essential passage in the recovery process. You feel the need to prove to yourself that you are good in bed. You want someone to hold you and care for you, to ease the pain of Crazy Time. It's a way of writing your message of revolt against society. On the negative side, there's an element of self-loathing in frantic sleeping around that matches your depression. You are filled with anger.

As Joan Kelly explains: "Separated men and women approached the post-separation period with intense longing and cautious hope for gratifying social and sexual experiences. The majority moved very quickly to establish an active heterosexual social life."

In the first part of Crazy Time, you are usually in no shape to make a long-term commitment to someone. It's all you can do to go from one day to the next. Your life is complicated enough: trying to keep the children on an even keel, working out living arrangements, making sure you still function on the job. You may also be intensely involved with your ex-spouse as you let loose your rage and disappointment at each other. This is not the time to try another exclusive relationship, you tell yourself.

But what about sex? There seem to be some cultural differences between men and women when it comes to sex and divorce. Although both sexes tend to go through an experimentation phase, women usually face a more significant emotional challenge as well as greater physical risks. This is especially true for women who were traditional housewives and stayed at home taking care of children during the marriage. The chances are you haven't had too much opportunity to experiment sexually with numerous partners. Many women discover sex after they get divorced.

Men, on the other hand—particularly those in white-collar jobs who travel on the expense account—have ample opportunity to sleep around if they want to. If you're suffering in a miserable marriage, you've probably had several outside sexual relationships in the years preceding the breakup. In the California Children of Divorce Project study, for example, 71 percent of the men had sexual affairs during the marriage, compared to less than 20 percent of the women. So as a man, you have probably had more sexual experiences than your wife when you split up.

For a woman, getting divorced often heralds a personal sexual revolution. This makes you very exciting—and threatening. One of the reasons you find yourself excluded by the network is the heightened sexual aura around you. You're on the market. Everybody knows it. Nervous wives are threatened. Unhappily married men are attracted to you.

As more women work, and more married women with children stay in the job market, the premarriage differences in sexual experience between husband and wife diminish. A working woman has just as much opportunity to meet people as men, and if she travels on the expense account, she can also take advantage of anonymous hotels and convention centers to gain sexual experience.

You soon learn that logistics and opportunity play a major role in your sexual recovery process. If as a woman you are raising small children, it's going to be more difficult to organize an environment in which you can experiment with sex. Since most divorced men do not have the daily responsibility for children, opportunity is not usually a problem.

Everybody needs some luck in this phase of the divorce journey. Sometimes the circumstances of your breakup give you a head start on your recovery process. This is the time to take that assignment to Australia for six weeks or help open a new office for the company in Chicago. You get away from the restrictions of your daily routine. Other times, you find out that you just happen to be in the right place at the right time to start your single life.

Ann Wilder and her husband, Jerry, split up while they are stationed in Jerusalem for the State Department. He leaves her to finish out the school term with the children and immediately goes back to the U.S. This gives Ann a six-month suspension time, an enforced period of separation before she has to face the reality of divorce.

Ann, thirty-eight, grew up in Vermont. She has always attracted men, but she doesn't realize it. It's in her eyes, the look of sex, her gray-green eyes that turn brown in the dark. All during her eighteen-year marriage, she has been a good foreign-service wife. But her husband has fallen in love with someone else.

In Jerusalem, she lives in a nice house and has a servant. As a member of the diplomatic community, she is invited to all the parties. "There were lots of visiting dignitaries coming through. They were all very bright. I like bright people. I'd find myself sitting at dinner with the under secretary of something or a White House something. They'd ask me to show them around. They were attractive and were attracted to me and it was very heady. I got to thinking: There are other people in the world besides Jerry."

It's during this time that she goes through a phase of multiple affairs. "I had such a strong need to be considered attractive that I did a lot of sleeping around," she says. "With all these people coming through, if there was an occasion to hop into bed, I'd do it. It was a crazy period. There must have been half a dozen or more just in the first few weeks." Sometimes Ann goes back to their hotel room, sometimes they come to the house, to the "guest room." "I found out that I loved sex and that I'd never really had it before. I found that I was sexy. I never thought I was. With Jerry I felt so mean and ugly."

There is one man in particular, a big man from Los Angeles who works in the White House. "He represented power and authority and he liked me a lot," she says. "He was big in stature and in mind. He was extremely open and very funny. His name was always in the papers." They spend a night, a day and a night together. He calls her just before he flies out from Tel Aviv. Ann is lying in the bathtub when she picks up the telephone. He says to her, "You're a hell of a broad and don't you forget it."

Ann's period in Jerusalem helps her get started on her recovery process. She comes back to the States and starts a new life as a teacher in Kansas City. For the next few years, whenever Ann feels depressed or overwhelmed by her divorce, she remembers the words of the man who worked in the White House. Then she smiles.

Most people who get divorced have been badly bruised when it comes to sex. You can cover up a lot in a bad marriage, but it's hard to cover up a bad sex life. For a long time, you silently agree to sexual separation within the marriage.

Recent studies reveal a shocking degree of sexual starvation in marriages that end in divorce. The California Children of Divorce Project discovered that more than one third of both men and women rank sexual deprivation as the major cause of the breakup. A significant number of couples had not had sexual intercourse for three to five years.

If you've been living in Deadlock, it's no surprise that sex went to hell. Therapists point out that an unequal power balance between partners is often a source of sexual problems. Intercourse becomes a battle for control. Lack of sexual satisfaction is a way to strike at your spouse and in the process you prevent the possibility of closeness or intimacy.

According to a joint paper, "Intrapsychic Factors in Sexual Dysfunction," by Drs. Alexander N. Levay and Josef H. Weissberg of Columbia University and Dr. Sherwyn M. Woods of University of Southern California: "People who are power-driven tend to dominate their partners as a defense against intimacy. . . . Many of these people are fearful of being exploited and overwhelmed by their partners, and are reassured by their ability to seduce and thus control them. This way of making threatening figures innocuous may succeed in preventing intimacy; if there is an additional threat from the partner, then a further defense, such as impotence or sexual unresponsiveness, may be created. Also a dominating person's partner may react with resentful passive resistance, i.e., 'withholding' sexual functioning. The partner seems to go along with the other's need to dominate, but unconsciously resists by becoming 'unable' to respond."

Whether you were passive or dominant in the marriage, you end up with similar sex scars. A period of sexual experimentation allows you to heal those scars. You learn how to break your Deadlock habits in sex. If you were the submissive one, you learn to be the seducer, the initiator in sex. You walk into a party, pick out someone you'd like to spend the night with and then make your move. There are times you won't succeed. But learning to lose and be "rejected" is as important as learning to win and follow through. You find out that the world doesn't come to an end if you stand up for yourself—even though you don't get what you want.

If you were the dominant one, who always had to stay in control, it's time to let yourself be seduced, let yourself be taken. You go along with the other person's wishes for a while. You meet someone at a party who says come back to my place and listen to bird-call records; you're not interested in birds, but you go along to see what will happen. There are times when you wish you'd never let yourself get taken. Then you learn how to get yourself out of sticky situations. You learn to navigate with the opposite sex. That way you don't have to be afraid of getting close in the first place.

Where do you begin? Here you are in Crazy Time. The marriage is over. You look at your ex-spouse. That's all you need to remind you that someone who knew you well found you inadequate in lovemaking. At first you can hardly wait to have an affair; no more guilt about sex, you say to yourself. You figure a good seduction scene will make you feel alive, staving off those feelings of abandonment and emptiness, of being half a person, of being nothing.

"Promiscuity, like amphetamines, promotes a short-term high," says science writer Maggie Scarf in *Psychology Today* (July 1980). "It surely won't cure feelings of despair, grief and depression (neither will amphetamines), but it may keep them at bay, keep them contained for a while."

If all goes well during your sex phase, you exorcise some of the ghosts from the past and prove to yourself that you are normal. Then the sex phase ends.

For Mary Altman, sleeping around for a while is her salvation after her marriage breaks up. That was five years ago. She is forty now and more relaxed. She was the dominant one in the marriage. Her husband had a series of affairs and quickly remarried when the divorce came through.

Mary has short red hair and loves to do gymnastics and aerobic dancing. She always suspected she was a secret sex fiend, but she is brought up to be a "good girl" and with her strong will, she makes sure she remains good, even during the dark years when she knew her husband was coming home to her after midnight, exhausted from another woman. She had twelve long years of marriage, with no sex during the last two years.

For the first few months after her husband leaves her, Mary wanders around the house like a zombie, sobbing, always with a wad of Kleenex stuck in her hand. She's got to get hold of herself. She starts going to self-improvement classes. She studies interior decorating, banking laws, Spanish. She starts therapy twice a week. Her life becomes a blur of baby-sitters and parking tickets. After a few months, she decides to test out her new sexual freedom.

"Did I ever go through a promiscuous phase?" she says, and bursts out laughing. "Right after the marriage, I did a lot of sleeping around. Maybe I'm promiscuous by nature. Even when I was going with someone, if things weren't going well we'd break up and I'd go off with other people. I had a capacity to have affairs with two or three people at the same time. I slept with people I didn't give a shit about, people I wasn't even attracted to. I was curious.

"I learned a lot about what I wanted and didn't want," she continues. "I learned a lot about what men feel. I learned I was good at sex. I learned that men were very different—not because of me but because of them.

"I began to define what a good relationship was, what a good friend was, what intimacy was. I began to like myself better. My standards got higher," she says.

Mary's self-confidence begins to go up. The more she gets to like herself, the less afraid she is of intimacy. She no longer feels powerless and inadequate in a relationship, the way she did in the marriage.

"When something good came along, I could recognize it and enjoy the sexual intimacy," she says. "When someone was just using me, I could sense it. I had enough faith in myself to say this guy is not treating me right and I could let him know it. If he then disappeared, so what? If things don't work out, I don't automatically feel there's something wrong with me," she says.

"I started out feeling that if a man looked at me, that was just wonderful: he was giving me his blessing. I was an O.K. person. If a man didn't look at me, I felt that it was my fault. I was no good." She pauses, smiles. "I don't feel that way now."

It takes Mary about two years to make this transition. Then, abruptly, her sex phase ends in a supermarket.

Mary is wearing her gymnastics tunic. Her legs are long and tan. She has an athlete's build—no bust, firm thighs. There's a guy standing at the frozen vegetable counter. He looks her up and down. He must be working on a construction project, she figures. Brown eyes, black hair, big hands. His face is smeared with dirt, his green shirt unbuttoned halfway down his chest, his khaki pants stained with grease. A sex object for nice suburban ladies. She smiles and stops in front of the frozen peas and orange juice. It's an easy mark. He comes over to her and they talk about frozen pizza. "How about having a drink?" he says. She agrees to meet him in half an hour, after she's gone home and put away the groceries.

Halfway through unloading the bags, she stops. What in

God's name am I doing? she says to herself. Going to bed with that creep? I could be killed. This is crazy. She finishes putting away the groceries. Then she stays at home for the rest of the day. She looks back on that moment as the end of her experimentation phase.

"I learned that promiscuity just made me feel empty. It was an important phase, but I'd learned everything I could from it."

Mary is lucky. She only gets one mild case of venereal disease—not pleasant—and doesn't fall victim to Mr. Goodbar violence. She also goes through this phase before the AIDS epidemic emerges. Meanwhile she starts a new job and ends up with her own decorating firm. She raises her children and goes to parent-teacher conferences. She starts a steady relationship with an attorney and eventually tries marriage again.

At the most elementary level of sexual activity, promiscuity is Hummingbird sex. It's essentially solo sex. The other person is quite irrelevant. Nothing heavy. Nothing emotional. This way, you hope to break your dependence on any partner to give you pleasure or make you feel like a failure. You break out of Deadlock from the ghosts of your ex-spouse and the failed marriage.

The next stage—the Foundering level—is to have sex with meaning but not necessarily commitment. You put into practice what you have learned and start defining your standards for a good intimate relationship. You take some risks and allow yourself to get hurt. You develop new habits. You learn to keep your eye on equality in the relationship. You catch yourself when you start making the same mistakes you made in marriage. You find out what you can live with, what your limits are. You get wiser.

In the last stage—at the Phoenix level—your goal is to have sex with meaning and commitment, and at the same time have a lot of fun. You don't fall back into your old patterns of self-destruction just because the drums are rolling for an exclusive relationship. You're not so afraid of intimacy. You learn to navigate in a relationship. After a while, you realize that sexual adventures are part of a broader search. You are looking for something—first it's self-confidence in bed. But that's a prelude to finding emotional support, affection, companionship. In time, your encounters are more like Flash Affairs.

Most people look back to one Flash Affair that holds a special niche in the divorce experience. Usually these encounters have a slightly antiestablishment quality to them—getting a divorce, after all, is a rebellious act. There's a certain satisfaction in playing boudoir Robin Hood and thumbing your nose at society.

Tim Mahoney, forty-one, covers sports for a national newsmagazine. He begins his career on his hometown newspaper in Wyoming, where he ends up covering the state capital for a year and marrying his high school sweetheart, Mary Lou. In Kansas, he works for a wire service. Six years later, he has three children and a prize-winning series on drugs in sports. He starts stringing for the newsmagazine. It's not long before he is hired for the Chicago bureau. Two years later he's brought to New York.

He looks Western, with his easy manner. He's six-foot-two and there's no extra fat on him. He hates New York: the traffic, the noise, the dirt, the staggering expenses. "My family had to live out in Long Island," he says. "We couldn't afford a place in Manhattan despite my higher salary." He doesn't see his wife and children very much, and if he has to be honest, he doesn't really miss them at all. He starts spending most of the week in town. He hasn't much choice, with those endless days on Thursday and Friday when the hard core of editors, writers, researchers and assistants put out the magazine.

Tim feels very alone. He has nothing in common with most of the other writers, who all seem to come from Greenwich, Connecticut, or Oyster Bay, Long Island. He doesn't play racquetball or belong to the Harvard Club. He brings to the magazine an outsider's contempt for the insiders.

But it's not as though he feels at home back in Wyoming or with Mary Lou. She's not a bad woman. She's just a dull one.

They talk less and less. His style is to keep quiet, do his job and drink. He also starts sleeping around a little, mostly with researchers and editorial assistants at the magazine, who all seem to have gone to Vassar or Sarah Lawrence. He finds East Coast girls awfully bony, which isn't as bad as he'd thought. He goes home less and less. Before long, he and Mary Lou officially separate. "I didn't feel bad about leaving her," he says. "We had nothing for years. But I missed the kids. I couldn't get over how bad I felt when we split up."

Tim plunges into Crazy Time and sets up a routine for himself: long lunches Monday and Tuesday; nighttime in the bars; work immersion at the end of the week; Sundays with the kids. Word gets out at the magazine that Tim's available. One day as he walks by the office of the president of the corporation, he notices a woman with pale skin and dark hair and a funny nameplate. The next time he's up on her floor, he points to her nameplate and asks her what it means. *"Volia Ukrayjenie,"* she shouts, raising her fist.

"What's that—a new kind of Swedish car?" he says to her.

"Freedom for the Ukraine," she shouts, raising her fist again.

Her name is Natalka Petrenko. She comes from Cleveland and has a degree from Columbia's journalism school. She thinks a job in the president's office will lead to a reporting assignment. It's been five years since she joined the magazine and she hasn't left the mahogany desk in the front office. The only change in her life is that the shadows under her eyes have gotten a bluish tinge and she's beginning to wonder if a life alone in a dead-end job is her destiny.

He asks her out for dinner.

"We went to a Mexican place for dinner," he says. "It was early in the week; the magazine was dead. We got into the margaritas. We started laughing."

Natalka likes this Western maverick with his obvious cheek and open disdain for the-way-things-are-done-around-here. He likes her large breasts and her belly laugh. They swap more office stories and both laugh so hard they can hardly speak. Her eyes sparkle. They order another round of margaritas. Tim feels good for the first time in months. They are fellow rebels on a Tuesday night in Manhattan: both bored, depressed and angry with life.

Natalka has to go back to the office to pick up her raincoat, she says. It's now one in the morning and they're both floating on a margarita high. They sign in and go up to her floor. All is quiet except for her giggles. Tim kisses her in the elevator.

"When we got up there, she asked me if I'd ever seen the boardroom," he says. "Of course I hadn't. She had a key and it was just one of those crazy things. We went into this very grand room—walls of beige raw silk, a view over the city, landmark covers on the wall—the election of FDR in 1932, the landing on the moon in 1969, a portrait of the founder at one end. At the other end was a statue of George Washington, a gift from the founder's wife.

"We were both laughing and full of margaritas. We made toasts to the Pope, Sister Kenny, Secretary of State Kissinger. Natalka would do a little dance and say, 'Here's looking at you, Winston Churchill.' I pretended to be General MacArthur. We ended up making love on the rug."

The years pass. Tim and Natalka go their separate ways. She lands a job on a newspaper in Texas. He goes overseas. In time, each gets married to another and has a busy life. But every now and then when summer comes and it's time for margaritas, each one thinks back for a moment to the night they spent together in the boardroom. It was only one night, one crazy, wonderful night, but after that, things started to go better for both of them.

A fabulous sex experience helps you get through a divorce. You carry it around like a trump card. A Flash Affair can make you believe in life again.

Sometimes you're very unlucky and you have a bad experience with sex, so bad it diminishes you even more than you were in the marriage. It's not just the risk of physical violence or exposure to disease that is always there in sexual experimentation. Psychological violence can be destructive too.

Perhaps you jump into an active sex life too soon. You hear all these good things about the singles scene and you want to make up for what you've been missing. Besides, you're very lonely and hurt. The need for sex may be there, but not the wanting of it. Psychologically you're not ready and you set yourself up for failure.

Kitsy Bonheim, thirty-eight, of New Orleans, has her first sexual encounter six weeks after the separation. For the last three years with her marriage, she and her husband haven't touched each other. The sex used to be good, she says. Now her self-esteem in bed is gone. She enters the separation period determined to put her sex life back together.

"I went to a party and immediately this guy latched on to me," she says. "He was bright, never married and had a good career. After all those years of sexual frustration, I thought: Well, now everybody screws around, so that's what I want to do. I picked up this guy, got involved sexually and then I found out I was terrified about any possible relationship," she says.

She sees him only twice. After that, he doesn't call. She freaks out. Why doesn't he call? "I think at first he was more serious about me. All I wanted was sex. He wanted something more." Yet she feels that he rejected her by not calling her again. What does Kitsy really want at this point?

"In retrospect, it was very destructive, especially with my nontrusting nature. I set myself up to convince myself that it wouldn't work out," she says. "Then I manipulated the situation to prove my fears were right. After that experience, I just did not want to get involved." For a long time she doesn't.

You have to listen to your body talk. You can't force satisfaction in a low-rent rendezvous the same way you couldn't force sexual satisfaction in marriage. Sometimes you heal better by taking your nights alone for a while. You need a quiet time. But at some point in your divorce journey you have to come to terms with sex—for better or for worse.

One of the main dangers in divorce is that your sex phase goes on too long. That's a sign of major emotional problems. Chronic promiscuity, therapists say, is often associated with severe depression and barely controlled hostility. Maggie Scarf points out that promiscuity may also reflect a childish search for the Unobtainable Perfect Parent to make the world right for you. Perhaps divorce has pushed an inner panic button set in place during childhood. The rejection and betrayal of your spouse triggers much older feelings of rejection and betrayal, felt when you were a child—"horrible, untenable feelings of having been unnurtured and uncared for," says Scarf.

"The promiscuous female and the Don Juan are engaged in a similar—and similarly desperate—quest," explains Scarf. "Their search is for a Caring Parent and it is a search fueled by great fear and great rage."

Sleeping around can also be a form of avoidance strategy. If you don't have time to be alone, you can't confront the painful emotions of depression, sadness, anger, anxiety. You remain a Hummingbird both in sex and in the process of mourning the loss of your marriage.

This is why some people are subconsciously attracted to the physical dangers of promiscuity. As Scarf explains: "The psychic risk then changes from an inner one—that one may be an unattractive, desperate, deserted individual—to an outer one . . . real risk . . . of possibly being caught by someone's wife or by another lover, and/or beaten up by a partner, or perhaps even contracting venereal disease."

In the end, promiscuity can enslave you in a neurotic fairyland where you preserve your unwanted bond with your ex-spouse and the myth wish from childhood of being rescued. Meanwhile you keep eroding away your sense of self through nameless encounters. If you don't stop, promiscuity can be a form of sexual suicide. Psychiatrists call it "depersonalization"—the destruction of an individual's personality. In the police station, it's called murder, manslaughter and other labels of physical violence. In the doctor's office, it's called AIDS, gonorrhea or syphilis. It's another way to be a Divorce Flameout.

You don't have to be caught in a compromising position to suffer that dirty-shirt feeling about sleeping around. A child hears strange noises in the night. "I thought you were having an asthma attack," says the child. Or you go to a cocktail party and you realize you've slept with four of the twelve people there of the opposite sex. How many times do you pray you never hear from the one you went out with last Thursday night? Your life begins to sound very sordid.

Perhaps you don't realize what you're doing. You've gotten into the habit of sleeping around and shunning any involvement. Sometimes it takes an outside event to force you to confront your promiscuity. You need to be shaken out of yourself.

For David Devreaux, forty-five, an aerospace engineer from Houston, the moment of truth comes to him in Thailand when he's riding a bus in the black of night through the countryside.

The space program is over for him. So is his marriage. He was the dominant one and he was devastated when his wife took the kids and walked out the door. That was five years ago. She told him one of the things that made her want a divorce was his screwing around. She knew it was going on. All those trips to the Cape in Florida, to the space center in Huntsville, Alabama. He told her over and over again that the other women didn't mean anything to him. She still wanted to get a divorce.

Now that his marriage is over, he has freedom to travel. It's a nice life; he's an attractive bachelor around town with a good job and more women than he knows what to do with. He's always liked sleeping with women. But there's an emptiness in his life. Perhaps it's just age. The midlife passage. He takes three months of accumulated leave and buys a round-the-world airline ticket. Now he'll have plenty of time to think things through.

He arrives in Thailand toward the end of his trip, after having a series of adventures in France, Greece, Lebanon and India.

Everywhere he goes, he likes to travel around the country by bus at night.

As the bus barrels through the gentle hills of Thailand, he looks at the window and sees his reflection in the glass. All the people around him are Thai. He looks at himself outlined in the blackened windowpane, alone and isolated against a background of Asian faces. Then he looks at his reflection in the glass again and watches as the dark silhouetted landscape behind the window goes by. He thinks about all the women he's slept with in the past year. He tries to remember the names, the places, the details.

Inside the bus, the sharp lights on the foreign faces around him seem to accent his isolation and loneliness. Each time the bus goes over a bump, his reflection fractures in the windowpane. He realizes he can't begin to remember all the different women. He can't conjure up the names or the faces. They become one huge collage in his mind. The reflection of his face in the window fractures again. He realizes he can't remember them because there have been so many. Endless, nameless, faceless encounters.

"I realized that there was no love in my life," he says. "Never again will I feel for a woman what I felt for my wife." The bus roars on through the night, his lonely face cracking apart in the window.

For David, his image in the glass is a significant landmark on his divorce journey. After he returns home, he goes into therapy. He finds he's not so interested anymore in hit-and-run sex. It's as though by sleeping with faceless partners he was keeping the space for love open to his ex-wife. After a while, he begins to accept the fact that his wife is gone and his marriage is over. Now it's up to him to put some love into his life.

For most people, a post-divorce phase of promiscuity is a stepping-stone to more meaningful relationships. The critical element in this phase of the recovery process is that it's a short-term period. You have to be careful. You have to learn the new rules of conduct and practice safe sex and use a condom. You need a little luck. But then you "graduate" to sexual involvements that carry some measure of commitment. Otherwise you are a Humming-bird long after you have stopped fluttering your wings so fast. And if you are a Hummingbird in sex, the chances are you are a Hummingbird in other areas of your divorce. Listen to your body talk. It's often the most honest voice to tell you how far along you are in your divorce journey.

13

LOVE

A central passage in the divorce experience is falling in love. In the midst of pain and doubt—you're not clear how it happens—just when you least expect it, you fall desperately in love. It's the classic *coup de foudre*—bolt of lightning—romance, and you are swept away. It's like being a teenager again. Just touching each other, looking at each other; you feel you've known each other forever. You stay up late, talking and talking, and then you make love as you've never known it could be.

The physical symptoms are familiar—the pull in your stomach, the speedup of your metabolism, the flip of your heartbeat. You seem to have more energy. Your esteem shoots up—you're better-looking, sexier, brighter, funnier. How the tension builds up in your chest when you know you'll be together in a few hours; then the creeping terror you feel when the telephone doesn't ring or answer.

You've been dead so long in marriage, it's time to be alive again, to be born again. Falling in love is your emotional midwife.

Therapists call this phase in the divorce process the search for the romantic solution. It usually happens early in the separation period—within the first six months. Sometimes the *coup de foudre* takes place just before the actual separation, when you're foundering on the rocks of a broken marriage, and evolves into the grand passion in the early phase of your single life.

In some ways, falling in love is part of your retreat into adolescence, an attempt to get back to the Garden of Eden. It echoes your flight into promiscuity in that you are swept away, you are not yourself, you have the feeling that "it's bigger than both of us" and you're not really responsible. You just lose yourself for a while.

A *coup de foudre* is also a commonsense avoidance strategy. You are exhausted by the trauma of breaking up. Your psyche needs a rest. Passion for the New Person is a temporary way to put your depression, anger and ambivalence on emotional ice—not to mention the welcome break you feel from mortgage payments, college tuitions and sticky Christmas plans.

Sometimes your *coup de foudre* lasts two weeks. Sometimes you live together for a year or so and the grand passion is the start of a significant affair. Sometimes it's the springboard to your second marriage . . . and if you don't learn a few things in the process, falling in love again becomes the trigger for your third, fourth and fifth marriages.

Whatever happens, the essential characteristic of a *coup de foudre* is that it is temporary. Chemistry is the way most relationships start. The trouble is, say therapists, that the only way to maintain chemistry beyond the natural life of a *coup de foudre* is through denial and living in fantasy. That way you can preserve the dream of falling in love and living happily ever after.

The high of being swept away eventually peters out. You crash. The affair ends and you have to come to terms with the loss of love. Even if you stay together after the crash, you still have to renegotiate the relationship on a new basis. In other words, you are back to reality and your old struggles in forming intimate relationships.

Says Erich Fromm: "(Love) is often confused with the explosive experience of 'falling' in love, the sudden collapse of barriers which existed until that moment between two strangers. But . . . this experience of sudden intimacy is by its very nature short-lived."

For battered veterans of a broken marriage, having a *coup de foudre* is like finding water in the desert. To begin with, it affirms the existence and importance of romantic love—which is at the base of our culture. The temporary nature of passion also helps you along your divorce journey. When the *coup de foudre* ends, it forces you to mourn the loss of love and let go of your fantasies about relationships. You give up your subconscious wish to be rescued by the Knight of Love.

You find out that when two people fall in love, this happy state doesn't automatically cure all your woes. You learn to love the hard way, and it's what you do with your bolt-of-lightning passion that matters most to your recovery in the long run.

For Jessica Baine, her two-week *coup de foudre* in midlife is the central passage in her divorce experience. Jessica, thirty-four, looks like an Indian princess, but when she smiles, you think her face might crack. She's not used to smiling, she explains; it's new for her. In fact, everything is new for her.

It's been three years since she left her husband. They aren't anywhere near a divorce yet; they are still fighting over custody and child support and who's a better parent—who's a better person.

Her husband scares her. She thinks he must be crazy. She's been through hell, her eyes say. He seems a mild sort of man to their friends. They don't know what he's really like, she says. If she hadn't fallen in love, she wouldn't have made it, she says.

She grew up in a small town in Utah. Her father is a nuclear scientist and works at the government facility nearby. Her mother, a kindergarten teacher from Pittsburgh who had eloped with her father during the Depression, drinks. It's done quietly upstairs in their bedroom and no one talks about it. In fact, Jessica doesn't know that her mother is an alcoholic until she's twelve and visits her grandmother in Pittsburgh, who asks her about the bad smells in the upstairs bedroom. Even today, when she thinks of her mother, she sees a woman in bed reading a book and chewing Juicy Fruit gum.

Jessica is not popular in school. Her parents were in their forties when she was born. She grows up feeling she's odd one out. During high school, when her schoolmates are going steady and losing their virginity, she is reading books and feeling empty. She never has a crush on the captain of the football team; she never dreams of kissing Paul Newman.

Instead she gets good marks and pleases her father. She goes to the University of Colorado and in her freshman year she meets Peter, who plans to major in chemistry and be a scientist like her father. Three months before graduation, they get married. She is submissive, he is dominant. They live out the marriage Deadlock for nine years and have two children. Peter becomes a high school science teacher. They move from Colorado to Texas and then to Boston, where Peter takes an administrative job in a private boarding school.

Jessica has her books. They live outside the city in Concord, near the school. Jessica joins a women's group in Cambridge and starts writing short stories, vignettes about growing up in Colorado and being bored at football games, about being pregnant and working in an abortion clinic in Cambridge, about women who lie in bed reading and chewing sticks of Juicy Fruit. The other women in the group cheer her on. She sends a story to *Harper's* and it gets published. She writes every day now. Meanwhile, housekeeping slides and the house becomes a mess. "Jesus, Jessica, what do you do all day?" yells Peter when he comes home from the school.

She wins a fellowship to go to a writers' workshop for two weeks in the summer. Peter is against it. Somehow he knows all along that going to this workshop is going to lead to no good. He's watching her very carefully these days. There's no good reason why she shouldn't go, he has to admit. He just doesn't like it.

He says he'll come with the kids and pick her up at the end of the conference. Jessica goes off.

Then it happens. For the first time in her life, Jessica, thirty-one, falls in love. The love object is Harold, a writer who teaches at the University of Massachusetts.

"About the second day, I noticed him and I thought he was attractive. It was late one night and a group was getting together to read poems and short stories. We sat next to each other," she begins her reminiscence of that star-struck night.

"I don't know, you just feel it. He got up to get something to read and for some reason I left. I'm not sure why. It must have been some sort of avoidance. The next day I ran into him and said, 'I want to apologize. I didn't leave because you were going to read.' 'Oh,' he said, 'I thought you did.' We started talking." She remembers every detail of it, every conversation they have, each step of self-revelation.

"It was just one of those things," she continues. "I don't know how to explain it. He was someone you'd known forever even though you just met him. It was really romantic stuff. It makes you believe in another life. You know the person so well. . . . I never experienced anything like that before. I had never known what that felt like."

They talk and talk. He takes her to his room and they make love and talk some more. The two weeks fly by.

"I was a virgin when I got married," she says. "I believed in all that stuff, how important it was to be intact and how great it was going to be. Then suddenly you're married. In my marriage sex was never very passionate. I was always sort of playacting. Oh, yes, I could be stimulated, but there was no passion.

"With Harold it was different. That was an incredible experience with me. I hadn't had anything like it. I learned about pleasure. It took the taboo out of it. I discovered sex. I discovered myself as a woman."

What's so crazy is that they are so alike—emotional clones. "We both grew up in small towns and had similar backgrounds, similar craziness in our families. He's a middle child and I think he always felt like I did—the odd man out, never quite understood by anybody, never fitting in."

He says to her one night, "Sometimes I want to know someone so well that I disappear into them."

For the whole conference, they lose themselves in each other. It's total fusion—an essential characteristic of *coup de foudre* romance. The sharp corners of your individualities are blurred as you melt into each other.

The affair ends with the workshop. He is married and has children. She knows in her head that he is not going to leave his wife, that their grand passion is not going to last. But her heart clings to the passion that has brought her to life. After the conference, they keep in touch; deep inside her, she thinks there's a chance things might work out. "When you fall in love like that, you think it just has to work out," she says.

It doesn't work out. It takes her three years to let go. Meanwhile the *coup de foudre* triggers a psychological revolution inside her. It gives her a whole new view of herself. She breaks down the armor of the depression she had wrapped herself in during the marriage to protect herself from Peter—just as she had protected herself from her mother and father. For the first time, she likes herself.

"For two weeks I was a totally different person," she says. "I didn't have someone standing over me saying do this or do that, complaining that I wasn't keeping the house neat enough, that I was immature. I felt free. I felt newborn in some way. I don't know how to explain it. I felt free to be myself, to be spontaneous, to react to things. I was so numb in the marriage.

"I was very disassociated from my body, so it was important to get that part of myself back. To discover my sexuality. It was wonderful. I feel very lucky for having Harold. I'll always love him— I'll always be a little bit in love with him because of what he meant to my life," she says.

She uses the new freedom and power she gains from falling in love to confront the marriage. She gets support from an unexpected source, her mother, who says, "I understand. I knew you would have died if you stayed in that marriage."

For the first months of Crazy Time what sustains her is the feeling in her groin for Harold; every time she thinks about him, she knows she's alive. Every time she remembers those two weeks, she is reassured that love exists out there. She knows you don't have to spend the rest of your life in misery. There is also a part of her that wants Harold to rescue her and make all these bad ghosts in the night go away.

"It would have been much easier if I could have gone from this unhappy marriage to a white knight. There was a part of me that had to realize that he wasn't a white knight. He wasn't perfect at all," she says.

"I realized it intellectually very early on, but it was a long time before I accepted it emotionally.

"Two years after our first meeting, I drove across the state to meet him at a conference and we spent one day together. Driving there to meet him, I still had that sinking feeling in my stomach and some hope that somehow it was going to work out. When I saw him, I realized I had to accept that it wasn't going to work out. It just wasn't there. Another year passed before I saw him again. It was at a reading in Cambridge. He was there with someone else. Then I knew I had accepted it; when I could see him and see he's my friend and I'm his friend and that's the way it's going to be forever. It's not going to turn into something else and I'm not going to die because it didn't work out." She stops for a moment and smiles.

Getting over her *coup de foudre* with Harold helps her get over her divorce. Not only is her affair with Harold her first experience with passion; her acceptance of the end of the affair is her first experience with mourning the loss of love.

In Crazy Time, Jessica is too conflicted and angry at her ex-husband to feel any grief over that relationship. And yet there's the sense that something has died in her with the breakup of the marriage. In her affair with Harold, she is able to work through her grief for the past. By falling in love, she finds out what she was missing in her marriage—and in her childhood. When it ends and she grieves over losing Harold, she also grieves for the other losses in her life: her mother and father, her husband, her children. Most of all, she lets go of her fantasy of perfect love and her subconscious search for the romantic solution.

"If you love somebody that much and it's not going to work, at first you can't believe it. I mean, if you love like that, you have to live happily ever after. Right?" She looks up and smiles. Then her eyes drift off and she shows her sadness.

"This was the first mourning I had ever done in my life. It was the first real grief. I really felt so awful. It's a truism—when somebody says their heart is broken, I know what it feels like. I never knew that before. I had never mourned anything before.

"I learned a lot. It was really painful. I also learned you can go through pain and survive. I've had to relearn that lesson in therapy, but it was an important period for me to illustrate how you get through pain and trauma and make a new life."

Jessica starts writing about her affair with Harold. It turns into her first book. "Harold was essential to my emotional growth and to my growth as a writer. In every way, that relationship was crucial to me. I was reborn in a way and I'll always be grateful to him for that. The fact that I had to go through this mourning was also the best thing that happened to me. Falling in love for the first time at eighteen is one thing," she says. "Falling in love for the first time when you're thirty-one is pretty extraordinary."

For most people, the Crazy Time *coup de foudre* is not the first time you fall in love. You remember this kind of craziness when you were a teenager, the mad crushes you had on people. But you're older and wiser now. Although you have vivid memories of falling in love, you realize how hard it is to describe what the objects of these passions were really like. That's an important point. Falling in love has a lot more to do with you than the magic attributes of the other person. You've been on this seesaw before, with fantasy on one end and reality on the other.

Your thoughts turn to your ex-spouse and the first time you met—standing in line for an airplane, the weekend when you were both with someone else, the night you discovered your common passion for Louis Armstrong. You remember the chemistry. "We immediately fell in love," one divorced man says of meeting his ex-spouse when they were both twenty. "We adored each other." Most couples begin marriage with their own version of *Love Story.*

The key feature of falling in love is losing yourself in the other person. It's part of the mystique of marriage: Becoming One. The wedding ceremony: *That Two Shall Become One.* It's also one of the biggest myths of marriage.

"That 'two shall become one' is nuts," says Ann Leahy. "I don't like the symbol. When the priest says to the groom your job in life is to know what she's thinking, and to the bride, your job in life is to know what he's thinking, I almost scream. A marriage is created by two people who will talk to each other, who will grow, who will be respectful of each other."

Losing yourself in another person may be an experience of great passion but if you don't find yourself pretty soon in the relationship, you end up in Deadlock. It's what happens in a lot of marriages that run amok. As Bradshaw Minturn explains: "The extent to which each person can define him- or herself is critical. The degree of self-esteem of each partner is critical. A marriage is made up of two separate people, not one. If you don't get separateness, you get separation."

So here you are a decade or two later, in Crazy Time. No one really needs to tell you that falling in love is not any guarantee of happiness. You bring a certain caution to midlife passion. But then, in the emotional twilight zone of your groin, it happens. You recognize all the signs. You fall under passion's spell. The restraints of social convention don't apply anymore. You don't have to fight it. You take the plunge and try loving again. Therapists point out that one way to bring reality into passion is to spend a lot of time with the other person. That's how you learn how to reconcile fantasy and experience. It's a little like that Zen mystery of the clapping of one hand sound. You have to give in to passion to gain freedom from it.

* * *

214

That's the route lawyer Tom Meyers takes with paralegal Angela Brown. Tom is a partner in one of the largest and most prestigious law firms in San Francisco. After twenty years, he has built up quite a reputation around the office; no one is a better trial lawyer—and no one is worse to fall in love with. Good-looking and funny, he has a lawyer's instinct for people's secrets. That's why women fall in love with him. He seems so warm and understanding, but there's always a part of him that remains hidden and distant. All his love affairs have been stormy. At this point, he and his wife have separated and the marriage is officially over.

Angela has tight blond curls and speaks softly with a New England accent. Her skin is pale, her lips thin. She has never married. It's as though there is a veil around her: you can look, you can touch, you can spend time with her, but you can't ever have her, really have her. All her life, men fall in love with her, because she's the Unobtainable She.

After college in New Hampshire, she goes west and eventually lands a job with Tom's firm. It's not long before she is assigned to work on one of his cases. There is a lot of staying late at the office, getting a bite to eat at midnight and making sure she gets home all right. Early on, they start sleeping together. He is fifty, a little battered, and drinking too much. She is thirty-two, a little bitchy and coming out of an affair with a man who wanted to marry her. There's something about her he doesn't like, doesn't trust. But he falls in love with her anyway. He's surprised. It's a real *coup de foudre*.

They move in together. He looks forward to the end of the day when they go out to dinner. Her lovely face, her turn of phrase, her hands. Sometimes she seems childlike, other times like his fifth-grade teacher trying to control the class. Alone, he goes crazy wondering if she isn't deceiving him, with her long lunches and her constant flirting when they go to parties.

There are other things that bother him. She doesn't read, she sounds like Herbert Hoover when she talks about politics and she's rude to his cleaning woman of ten years. As he gets to know her better, he is bothered by a shifting-sands quality of their relationship.

Most of all, he realizes he is losing his temper more often, drinking a great deal and turning on the television to avoid conversation.

The affair lasts several years. His track record has not been good. How available is he for an intimate relationship? It's not as though he's a young turk anymore. He wants to make a commitment. Tom and Angela break up and get back together. They fight and make love and grow to care for each other more—and like each other less. The affair runs its course. Tom realizes he doesn't want to continue the relationship any longer and finally breaks up with her.

In the process, he learns not to be so afraid to love anymore. He knows if he lets himself go, he won't be swallowed up by a lady dragon in passion's clothing. He trusts himself to know when to say yes to a woman, and more important, when to say no. It's a new freedom he finds in his own struggle with women. By learning to trust himself in love, he learns to trust others. The next time with a woman, it's easier.

You gain a tremendous self-confidence when you ride the big *coup de foudre* wave to shore. You learn to fall in love, make a commitment, fall out of love and let go—often all in a relatively short space of time. You learn to balance ideology with reality in intimate relationships. In many ways, the *coup de foudre* affair is a psychological microcosm of marriage and divorce. Learning how to survive and thrive through the affair helps you come to terms with your divorce.

But there is also a dark side to falling in love during Crazy Time: you can make *coups de foudre* a lifelong habit. All you do is fall in love; you don't get any further. You don't stay around long enough to develop a relationship. You don't allow yourself to grieve when it's over. You only taste the high. It's basic body magic—a chemistry thing: you're turned on, you have all the symptoms of love. Soon you become an addict for passion. You find you can't survive too long without a romantic fix and it happens again and again.

You're at risk of becoming a Passion Repeater and being stuck at the Hummingbird level of love, which is another form of Divorce Flameout. The key element is that you feel you are not responsible for what you do. It's always "bigger than both of us." You don't make any decisions. You just drift from one *coup de foudre* to the next.

In many ways, Passion Repeaters are the cousins of promiscuous people. Both are in a sense Hummingbirds, going from one flesh fix to another. The big difference is that Passion Repeaters are constantly falling in love. But after a while, as one passionate affair fades into the next, the distinction gets blurred. Is a weekend of passion a *coup de foudre* or a fabulous sex experience?

In general, Passion Repeaters tend to be passive-submissive people. You are groomed to find someone to make the world right for you, to wave the magic wand over you. You are having a hard time accepting your divorce and think that since it didn't work out with your ex-spouse, the problem is with your mate selection. Maybe it's just a question of finding a better partner, someone who makes you feel good, someone who really loves you. So you send out signals. Let's fly to the moon. You fall in love. It seems like such a logical solution in Crazy Time. That's the trap of the *coup de foudre* syndrome.

For a long time, Caroline Chapman is a Passion Repeater . . . until it almost drives her crazy.

In her late thirties, Caroline is a first-family Californian from Los Angeles. Her father is a vice president of a utility company. Her mother is a "typical wife," who does not work outside the home. As a child, Caroline has things done for her: sailing lessons, dancing class. She goes East to college.

In her twenties, the pattern is set when she marries the perfect person, John Holcomb, twenty-seven. "I was just getting out of college and thought he would sort of form me," she says. "He'd give me books to read, he'd direct my interests in art, poetry. We had this charmed life. We went skiing a lot and bought a place in Aspen."

At this point, Caroline is a superpassive in what she thinks should be the golden marriage. After all, she is a pliant *tabula rasa* on which her husband is to write "happily ever after."

Then why aren't things working out? She and John are having some problems; not enormous problems, she tries to explain, but she knows things aren't right. Finally she says, "I was the one who had the symptoms." She pauses. "The symptom was getting attracted to other people; just fleeting flirtations, not affairs, but I felt so guilty. I thought when I got married all my sexuality would be with my husband and I wouldn't feel like that anymore. I felt very confused by these feelings. People would come on to me and I'd say, But I'm married. They said they didn't care. I was so shocked. I couldn't handle it and decided to seek professional help."

Caroline is basically a very down-to-earth woman but the upbringing that was supposed to give her so much has also been her cage. She is so used to having things done for her that she is paralyzed in her confusion. It's as though she has no control of what happens in her life. "I didn't understand why we were having problems," she says. "We did everything right. Why weren't we happy?"

Caroline goes to one of the most famous psychiatrists in town, who made his reputation thirty years ago doing breakthrough work with autistic children and manic-depressives. In his sixties now, he looks like Colonel Sanders.

"The first session, I burst into tears," she says. "He patted me on the back and said, 'There, there.' The second session, I said, 'You know, when you patted me on the shoulder I admit I had feelings of attraction for you.' He said, 'Don't worry about such feelings; they're perfectly normal.'

"The third session, he said, 'Take off all your clothes.'"

She is so submissive, so brainwashed with the idea that teacher knows best, that she goes along with him.

"I remember asking the psychiatrist how much my sessions were going to cost. I knew he would be very expensive because he treated movie stars and politicians. He said that as a favor to my family he would treat me for nothing, and after we started having sex, I kept thinking: Well, when is he going to get to the analysis part? Incredibly, I thought this was part of the treatment. That shows you how passive or sick I was. I gave him carte blanche. I thought this was his magical treatment and I really wanted magic. I wanted someone to make everything right."

Very soon, her world crashes. Her husband discovers her affair with the psychiatrist and explodes like a nuclear bomb. He is outraged—with her, with her therapist, with her family. He divorces her immediately (he's got a good case against her) and never speaks to her again. The marriage lasted eight years.

Caroline is left very alone, devastated and confused. What did she do wrong? Very slowly, she makes the difficult psychological journey from lying back and waiting to be rescued to standing up on her own and making decisions. It would take her about ten years. As she points out, "What I didn't realize was that I had to start thinking for myself. I was a very passive little creature."

When she comes out of her marriage, she finds it's a crazy world. Everywhere she turns, she gets involved: the next therapist, the teacher at the art workshop, the guy next door. She lives with a photographer, but at the same time she starts having an affair with an old teacher. "It was a repetition of this compulsion I have," she says. "I was so angry and I felt very down on myself. I had so little confidence.

"I finally met this guy who was so good-looking I couldn't believe it. My emotions got worked up. He was in his forties, lean, curly hair, a real twinkle in the eye—the eternal little-boy type. We had five incredible days together in his house in Malibu. It was just before he was leaving to spend the summer in Greece. He made me feel I was the woman I wanted to be. I think I touched something in him that no one had touched; he certainly did in me. Lying together, we'd talk about the future. After he left for the summer, I had this fantasy that love was going to work out for us. I had planned this romantic weekend for his return." She pauses. "He came back, all right—and started calling up his old girl friends." She stops.

It's the *coup de foudre* that hurts. But unlike the other compulsive romances, it triggers a major change in her. For the first time, Caroline sees that falling in love is not a solution. She starts taking some responsibility for her life. A few months later, she makes two important decisions on her own: she enrolls in graduate school and starts analysis with a female therapist. It's a significant beginning.

Meanwhile the affairs continue, all beginning with the chemistry: a quasi-married quasi-alcoholic, who tells her about his German mistress, who infiltrated terrorist groups for the government; a Jewish veterinarian, who raises rabbits and reads the poetry of Heinrich Heine; a blond, good-looking stockbroker, who rushes her off to Hawaii for the weekend.

The passion circus goes on for several years. "It was so annoying to get these crushes," she says. "Here I was this middle-aged person and I kept getting crushes on people. It was awful. What was I doing?"

At times, Caroline is a gay Hummingbird with her crushes; then she's a Founderer—depressed and angry at herself. She knows she doesn't want to live like this. Meanwhile she gets her master's degree and begins teaching Latin American affairs at the university. Beginning research on her doctoral thesis, she plans a trip to Guatemala. She gets used to making decisions on the job and this feeds over to her emotional life; she gets stronger.

Several years later, at a Christmas party, she meets a man with granny glasses and gray hair, a physicist at UCLA who plays the guitar and writes music. "Talk about your *coup de foudre*," she says with a smile. But in fact they begin slowly and test it out. They break up and get back together. She goes on another trip by herself, to Syria. He is absorbed by his job and often works late in the lab. He expects her to go her own way and she does. Every time she retreats into her little-girl make-me-happy mode, he refuses to play her game.

It's a new kind of relationship for her. She sees she can love him, be attached to him, without her individuality being swept away. She is able to break her passion habit. She doesn't lose herself in her crush on him and then have to go find herself again through another *coup de foudre*. They live together for several years before they get married. She has finally broken the mold.

Some people never get out of the *coup de foudre* syndrome. Life seems bound by bouts of passion and long stretches of passivity. You don't get out and make things happen; everything along the way, from your job to your children, just seems to happen to you. You go along with it all for a while. Then you fall in love. Your life changes—you leave your spouse, you change jobs, you move from New York to California. You go along in your new mode for a while, five years or so, and then you fall in love again. Your life changes again. You use passion to shape your destiny. You don't consciously make the changes in your life; instead you let passion make the hard decisions for you. Whenever the going gets tough and you're not content with your destiny, you fall in love and move on. You're a Hummingbird. A chronic Passion Repeater.

Gerald Hansen, sixty, almost destroys his life this way. There's something of the little boy in Gerald that makes women want to take care of him. Wives of his colleagues always have him out to dinner and worry over him. Is he getting enough to eat in that apartment all alone? What about introducing him to a nice girl? they say.

Gerald marries when he is seventeen years old and gets a job in the mayor's office in Indianapolis. His wife is living in the suburbs with their child. He pours himself into his work. Every day, he rides in a car pool to the office. One of the riders is a woman with whom he falls desperately in love. "After about three or four months, it just exploded," he says. "Just thinking about her, I ached for her." They have a passionate affair. He expects her to leave her husband. There's no question but that he's going to leave his wife, who is a mere shadow to him now.

In the end, his lady love doesn't leave her spouse, but the

affair is enough to catapult Gerald out of his high school marriage. He moves into an apartment in Indianapolis.

Soon he meets another woman, a schoolteacher. "The first time I kissed her, it was electric," he says. Her sensuality draws him on and sex becomes their glue. They are both twenty-eight. "She was a mother to me," he says. They get married but it doesn't follow that they're happy forever after. Gradually he gets bored with her and the old deadness seeps up in him. He begins to withdraw into his work just like before.

And just like before, it happens again. He falls in love with a woman at work who is married to a policeman. She and Gerald have a very public and very messy affair. Gerald starts drinking too much and snipes at his wife. They rarely talk. After a while, they get divorced; he gets a new job in Cleveland in the state's transportation department.

He repeats this pattern two more times. At the age of fifty-five, he bottoms out. He's an alcoholic with no job and four ex-wives, women who shake their heads, like mother, and say how much they loved him.

Gerald gets into treatment for alcoholism. He has nothing to drink for five years, not even a glass of wine. He keeps up with his ex-wives and is friends with a number of women. You can't avoid being fond of Gerald. He's such a warm man. Women see the dreamer in him; he's not of this world exactly, but he's kind and he loves to talk to women about things that matter to them, such as the nature of passion.

Falling in love is a more difficult habit for Gerald to break than drinking. He's still looking for passion, but he's also learned a few things. He's not going to be swept away by drinking ever again, he says. He feels he has control over his life and continues to attend AA meetings. Eventually, he finds a job with a bus company. The next time, he says, it's going to be different when he falls in love.

There is nothing more glorious than falling in love. It's a key experience in recovering from divorce. You have to test yourself against passion. You have to learn how to be comfortable with the *coup de foudre;* you also have to find out what the limits of passion are. That's the paradox of modern marriage. When you base marriage solely on love, you raise the possibility that a new love can always tempt you out of marriage. Learning through experience how to separate fantasy from reality makes you not only wiser in love—but also stronger in marriage.

14

REMARRIAGE/REDIVORCE

You marry again. The guests gather, the children laugh, the champagne cools and the words are familiar: "To love, honor, cherish . . . till death do us part." At that moment, shivers go up your spine.

For many people, being divorced is a transition period between marriages. Statistics show that three out of four divorced men and women eventually remarry. Most remarriages take place within two to three years of the divorce date. Many others who are separated or divorced live together without the legal seal of marriage. Men between the ages of forty and forty-four are twice as likely to remarry as women of the same age. As people get older, remarriage rates drop; this is especially true for women.

The dark side of remarriage is redivorce. Remarriage does not automatically mean that the emotional process of divorce is complete—quite the opposite. The depressing statistical fact is that the redivorce rate for people who have been married and divorced before is significantly higher than the divorce rate for people in a first marriage. About a quarter of all second marriages break up within five years. Even more depressing is the fact that with each remarriage, the risk of redivorce increases. You can't help but echo the sentiment that remarriage is the triumph of hope over experience.

Successful remarriages are built on successful psychological divorces. One problem is that many people enter a second marriage before they have time to recover psychologically from the first relationship. About 20 percent of remarriages, for example, occur the same year as the divorce. Unfortunately, that may mean you are programmed to repeat the patterns of the past. All too often, after the honeymoon is over, you get that déjà vu feeling. You don't realize it, but you are still locked into the past and your old marriage Deadlock.

"Most often I see people doing the same thing again and again and again," says Robert Kirsch. "One way to stay married even though you divorce your spouse is to repeat the relationship over and over again."

It doesn't seem possible. Here you are with a new mate—a different head, a different body, a different past—and you find yourself back in the same box you were in with the last marriage.

At this point, you have to make some significant changes and finish the divorce process within the context of the new marriage. Or you risk becoming a Remarriage Recidivist, doomed to repeat the same drama of love you played out in the last relationship. It's another form of Divorce Flameout in the revolving door of marriage.

It's an astonishing thing you notice about other people getting remarried: More often than not, they keep marrying versions of their former mates. It's obvious to their friends, but they don't recognize it. You go to dinner for the first time with an old friend who has just remarried. The man is smiling, laughing, telling stories. You knew his first wife: a square face, long brown hair, too much money. She was the dominant one, constructing their married life and masterminding his glamorous corporate career. In the end, he said she made him feel like shit, and then he fell in love with the new woman. You look at her: a square face, long brown hair, too much prestige. She's the daughter of the chairman of the board, and fifteen years younger than the first woman. On the outside, it looks like a whole new life for him. He left his wife after eighteen years of marriage for a younger woman, whispers the network. But in his private divorce, not much has changed. The new woman tells him how good he is and then she tells him to start the steaks on the barbecue and get out the wine. He smiles and does what he is told. Remember how the first woman used to build him up in the old days?

You think: The new woman looks the same, thinks the same, acts the same. The only difference is that the man is smiling. What's going on here?

Even more astonishing is that the man doesn't seem to see the similarities in his two marriages. At least not for a while.

It's hard to break your emotional habits of the past—especially if you don't recognize what your habits are. Most people are unaware of the psychological drama that they subconsciously play out in intimate relationships. Often you have to form a new relationship to find out about your own special drama. You can't do it in a vacuum.

Sometimes, if you are lucky, you are able to break your old patterns before you marry again. You have practice relationships—love affairs that start out with the emotional investment of a marriage—and you uncover your special drama. In other cases, you need the legal commitment of marriage to force you into a confrontation with yourself.

People who are Remarriage Recidivists keep their old emotional habits intact in the new relationship. Usually, it is not quite as simple as marrying a carbon copy of the old spouse. More often, what stays the same is your own psychological drama. Your inner struggle with intimacy is never resolved. You just pick a familiar prop in your new spouse, who allows you to follow your old script. The scenes are different in your new relationship, but the basic plot is the same. Most important, you are not aware of what you're doing.

* * *

Peter Welford is a Remarriage Recidivist. He plays out one plot in five different marriages. Each new marriage becomes an exaggerated replay of the last.

Peter looks like a yachting captain, has a slight British accent and speaks several languages. He's dined with university presidents and ambassadors, spent weekends with corporate power brokers.

Born to an old and decaying British family, he inherits pride but no money and in 1937 he wins a scholarship to Brown University in Rhode Island. With his high-rent accent and European manners, he becomes the social catch of the Eastern Seaboard. He's invited to parties, to poetry readings, to polo matches, to Sunday lunches.

But there's another side to Peter, which he keeps buried: the vulnerability of the poor foreign boy with no money and a faded past who is at the mercy of his hosts. He needs to please the teacher to get the debating prize. Otherwise he'll lose his scholarship. He never acknowledges these orphan feelings. Instead he blusters his way to the top of the class as the dominant one.

That's the first act of his special drama: the dominant winner. In the second act, he has to take care of his orphan feelings.

In his junior year at Brown, he falls in love with Cassandra Graves, a rich and beautiful blond from Providence, Rhode Island. Peter escorts her to coming-out parties and talks to her of the medieval lovers Héloïse and Abelard. He describes with authority London's Victoria and Albert Museum. She thinks he's dashing, poetic and worldly. Peter, now an American citizen, gets married to her when he graduates.

In their marriage Deadlock, he is the teacher, the wise one; she is the innocent student. He is dominant; she is submissive.

Within the first year, they have a daughter. But late in the summer of 1944, just when the cup races usually take place in Newport, Peter is crossing the Meuse River into Germany as part of the U.S. infantry. Of the five hundred riflemen in his company, only fifty-nine make it across. Peter continues on to Berlin. Back at home, his wife, driving to Newport, has a head-on collision and is killed instantly.

Peter is a shattered man. It was a happy marriage for him though it lasted only two years. He thought everything was going to be all right after he married Cassandra. He can't believe it. Now his wife and his dreams are gone. After the war, he works with a foreign policy think tank in New York. The grandparents suggest they bring up the daughter and give Peter an allowance. "New York City was no place to bring up children," is the way Peter puts it. He continues to go to Newport in the summer, with his blue blazer, his slightly graying hair. He reads *The New Yorker* and *The Economist* and talks to his father-in-law about the impact of the Marshall Plan. But his wise mother-in-law gets a glimpse of the orphan in him, his inability to take responsibility. "There's something of the little boy in Peter," she remarks to her husband. After all, they are the ones raising the child.

The tragic death of his first wife cements the first act of his psychological drama. He always starts out a relationship as the dominant one, the teacher, the prince. The woman looks up to him, his wisdom, his worldliness. It worked so well the first time—he was so happy with Cassandra—that he never changes his act. He never allows a flicker of vulnerability to show. It never occurs to him that this inflexibility in his first act—made sacred by the death of Cassandra—leads inevitably to the second act. In 1950, Peter marries again. Gwen comes from Short Hills, New Jersey, and is the same genre of woman as Cassandra. She has just graduated from Radcliffe. Peter is quite swept off his feet. To fall in love again after Cassandra . . . maybe everything will be all right now. He tells Gwen about postwar politics in Europe, about cubism, about the lovely restaurant he knows just outside Florence. She thinks she'd like to be a reporter, maybe a foreign correspondent. Peter represents experience and knowledge to her. To him, she is innocence and youth, a chance to continue the old dream.

The first act of Peter's drama goes well, just the way it did with Cassandra. He is the pursuer, the worldly prince. Then without either one of them realizing it, Peter slips into the second act.

To take care of those buried orphan feelings, he does the Deadlock Switch. He becomes the dependent little boy looking for mother. In the first act, he sets himself up in a very unequal relationship that cannot be maintained. Instead of renegotiating Deadlock, he reverses roles—leaving the imbalance between them intact. After he wins the prize—a new wife—in the first act, he tries to manipulate his partner from being the wide-eyed submissive learner into the all-powerful mother to take care of him, love him no matter what, make things go right for him.

After ten years of marriage, they get divorced. In the end, Gwen thinks Peter is a total asshole; he drove her crazy, she says. He says, "I really don't know what happened. She changed. When we first met she was so sweet. Then she turned into a shrew. We'd sit down for a drink before dinner and I'd start to talk and she'd say, Oh, Jesus, and find an excuse to run out of the room. It was terrible. Then she'd get mad if I came home late or had too much fun at a party. Thank God I got out of that one."

Peter never figures out what happened.

The last scene of Peter's two-act play is predictable. Like all little boys, Peter tries to escape from big mama and hook up with a new woman. Or big mama gets fed up with this rotten kid and throws him out. It's no mystery, given Peter's special drama, how his second wife went from a sweet young thing to a contemptuous shrew in ten years of marriage.

Peter continues to repeat his behavior, again and again. His third marriage, in the late sixties, to an antiwar radical from Grosse Point, Michigan, lasts only five years. Then he lives with a Hungarian economist at the World Bank for several years. Each time, the age difference widens and the length of the relationship shortens. Peter becomes a caricature of his former self: an old-world prince who likes to be a naughty little boy.

In his fourth marriage, Ellen is twenty years younger and comes from nowhere, in Peter's terms. She grows up in a small town in Nebraska; she gets a Ph.D. in economics from the University of Chicago and goes to work in a New York City bank in 1975.

In the beginning, Peter transports her with his worldliness and knowledge. He tells her of Baudelaire, castles in Salzburg, protective tariffs and OPEC. She loves his stories and is a quick learner. The wide difference in age and experience assures them of a good first act in Peter's drama. But as the plot continues, the tables turn. Ellen is very ambitious and does quite well at the bank. She ends up earning more money than Peter in his research job. She begins to find his theories about Common Market economics a little thin. She also reads *The New Yorker* and *The Economist* and can order the right wine in restaurants.

Meanwhile Peter follows his inner script and becomes more dependent on her. She doesn't like it. After all, she was attracted to him in the first place because he was so strong, so independent, so experienced. Now the roles are reversed. To get mama's attention, he starts acting more like a bad little boy. He knows the all-night places in New York. He stays out late, he starts drinking Black Russians and smoking dope. He leaves pornographic magazines on the coffee table. He gets into cocaine. He tells her she is a know-nothing square. What would she do if he told her he had a young boy last night? Ellen is at the end of her wits. She doesn't know what to do. Peter becomes very debauched with his drugs and all-night places. In the end, he leaves Ellen and takes a trip with a Danish stripper he met three days earlier. Ellen files for divorce. After a while, the stripper goes on to other things and Peter is back in town.

"Ellen was a nice, but limited, woman," is the way Peter describes his fourth wife and the collapse of his fourth marriage. "She was so ambitious, so career-oriented," he says. "Her job came first."

Today Peter is sixty-five years old and three months into his fifth marriage. His wife, Maria, is forty years younger. She was born on the wrong side of the Mexican border and at the age of fifteen she started working as a whore in El Paso, Texas. She moves on to Houston and five years later she gets to New York City. The city is good to this young, beautiful and ambitious woman, who becomes a very successful, very exclusive hooker.

She meets Peter in an all-night place. He talks to her about the little boîtes in Paris, the fountains in Rome. You look so Mediterranean, he says to her. They have a little cocaine together and Maria, like the others, is captivated by his old-world charm.

Peter wants to take her to Europe. Technically, Maria is an illegal alien. There's an obvious solution: they get married on her twenty-fifth birthday. As the wife of an American citizen, she has no trouble getting a passport. Besides, she likes being Mrs. Welford and Peter is very happy. He gives her *The New Yorker* to read. She plays the roles: she dresses up for him, she makes special dinners. A friend of Peter's offers them an apartment for two months in Salzburg at the height of the Mozart festival, and two days later they leave for Austria.

At the end of two months, Peter is bringing breakfast to Maria in bed. "Maria insists on a big breakfast," he says to a visitor. "Coffee *mit schlag*, fresh orange juice, a boiled egg and these wonderful rolls. Isn't she marvelous? Maria has such good taste. . . . Let me go see if she wants some more coffee."

From being the worldly-wise dominant husband, Peter has become prime puppy dog. That's Maria's cue to switch from tabula rasa baby to big mama. Maria says, "Peter, you should get the tickets to the theater this morning so we don't have to stand in line this evening." He replies, "You're so right, *Liebchen*."

Maria is now in charge of their schedule: the drive to Schloss Leopoldskron, a drink in the old part of town, the fortress one day, the churches the next. Peter talks of Héloïse and Abelard, the socialist governments in Europe, the impact of composer Richard Wagner. Maria says, "Peter, the movie begins in thirty minutes. We must leave now."

In the restaurant for dinner, Peter tells stories about the bishop of Salzburg who was so mean to Mozart, he explains the French influence in the court in Vienna, he describes the sad death of poet Guillaume Apollinaire in Paris on the eve of World War I. "*À bas Guillaume!*" the people shouted, referring to the German king. But lying on his deathbed, poor Apollinaire took it personally. Peter smiles as he tells his story. Maria doesn't get it.

Peter says, "This restaurant is the only place in Europe where you can get a real American martini." And then he orders another one. Maria says, "Oh, no, Peter, don't have anything more to drink. It's not good for you." Peter says, "Just one more, *Liebchen.*" His eyes sparkle. He's getting drunk. This is so much fun, he thinks; he's an adorable, wicked little boy. Maria pouts. By the time Maria gives the dinner order to the waiter, Peter is very drunk and makes no sense at all with his stories. Maria says nothing. It's not as though she doesn't know how to handle a drunk.

As they get on a plane to go back to New York, Maria tells him, "*Liebchen,* why don't you go to Rhode Island to see your old friends for a while and I'll stay here in New York by myself?" She has on a new dress, her eyes smolder; Peter knows that men are always looking at her. Leave her all by herself in New York City? The sense of doom wells up in him. Maybe it's really going to happen: He's going to end up abandoned and an orphan. For Maria, it's a long way from El Paso. For Peter, it's getting to the end of the second act.

To be a recidivist like Peter is to be asleep psychologically. You never wake up to yourself or to others. You remain at the Hummingbird level of awareness. You never confront your inner dreams or work through the pain of loving—and losing love. You never unravel what your special drama is in intimate relationships. In short, you never get emotionally divorced. You are trapped in nostalgia. Peter, for example, keeps trying to get his first wife back by playing the same old song with all his other wives.

Most of us are creatures of habit. We get up and take our coffee with sugar and a little bit of milk. On Thanksgiving, we eat too much turkey. We remember the time long ago when an uncle got drunk at the table and was thrown out of the house. We drive a Ford and wear mostly blue. We subscribe to the *National Geographic;* we drink Scotch and water at cocktail parties. A photograph of the grandparents is always kept in the living room.

It is a mixed bag of habits and memories that gives shape to your daily life.

On a subconscious level, you have another mixed bag of emotional patterns and experiences that gives shape to your relationships. In a successful psychological divorce, you become aware of the emotional baggage you carry around with you. If that doesn't happen, you become a recidivist and remain a pawn of your past.

Some people have to go through several marriages to get a good emotional divorce. You marry on the rebound. You marry to save face, to be rescued, to erase the past, to ease the pain. You need a remarriage to get over the loss of the old marriage—and a redivorce to force yourself to build a new life. Sometimes you don't even begin your divorce journey until after the second marriage ends. Or you start Crazy Time and as soon as you have your first *coup de foudre*, you get married again. When that marriage collapses, you pick up where you left off in the middle of Crazy Time.

It takes Catherine Cunningham Hailey two marriages and two divorces before she can start the emotional process of getting divorced from the past. Now, at age fifty, she works in Sacramento for the state government, putting out consumer brochures.

Catherine is tall and very attractive. The first time around, she marries Ted Cunningham, the boy next door in Cincinnati, Ohio. Together they play golf and go to dances. Ted wants to get into politics. "I thought he'd bring me adventure and excitement," she says. "I'd see the world and get out of Ohio."

She marries what she wants to become: adventurous, exciting, confident. The Deadlock is simple: Ted's dominant and perfect; Catherine's dependent and inadequate. They quickly have two children, and during the Nixon administration, Ted is asked to come to Washington to work in the White House. As members of the young Republican jet set, Ted and Catherine are asked out constantly: to cocktail parties, dinner parties, weekends at Annapolis. It's a golden life, except that Catherine is going crazy.

"I felt like an onion," she says. "You could peel and peel and peel, and there would be nothing in the end. When I started looking at myself, I was terrified that I'd find nothing when I got down to the last onion peel." The pain comes out in her body, as so often happens with marital stress, and Catherine starts getting terrible headaches. She goes to a neurologist and has spinal x-rays and brain scans. Perhaps she has a brain tumor and is going to die. "If you've ever been in real panic, you know how terrible it is," she says. "Your skin crawls. You don't know what to do with yourself. You think about death."

It never occurs to Catherine or to her doctors that something is wrong in her marriage. That's often a mystery solved only after divorce. You don't recognize how unhappy the marriage is for years. Instead you find all kinds of excuses for feeling bad.

"I was not thinking that there was anything wrong with the marriage," says Catherine. "It wasn't part of what one was allowed to think. I was tremendously dependent on Ted. I thought that all the problems, all the emptiness, was in me."

In the midst of Catherine's deepening misery, she seems to get a reprieve. They meet another nice young Republican couple: Jim and Ann Hailey. The four of them hit it off immediately; they have children the same age and are soon doing everything together. They go on family picnics; they go the zoo; they take day-long trips to the mountains. Usually they take two cars and swap mates: Ted and Ann and her children in one car, Jim and Catherine and her children in the other car. Catherine finds she's happier and healthier these days. The big questions are deciding whether to have dinner at the Cunninghams' or the Haileys'. "It was very titillating," says Catherine. "Looking back, we were walking on the edge of a precipice."

Ted and Catherine, Jim and Ann. Ted and Ann. Jim and Catherine. They start sounding like a lot of couples playing games in the wasteland of marriage. For many couples, it's socially acceptable and guilt-free to flirt. You feel alive again. But it's not long before Catherine's script resembles an afternoon soap opera.

When Catherine, married to Ted, needs to have her appendix removed, Jim, married to Ann, visits her in the hospital every day. That's when he says he fell in love with her; seeing her there lying back on the pillow, looking pale and frightened. Every day Jim goes to the hospital, draws the curtains around her bed and, enclosed, they hold hands and talk and talk and talk.

During Catherine's hospital stay, Ted and Ann take all the children to the movies and out for pizza. They also start sleeping with each other. After a week, Catherine gets out of the hospital. The two couples decide to spend a weekend in New York, celebrating her recovery. It's routine now that Catherine rides with Jim and Ted rides with Ann. As they drive up the highway, Jim suddenly asks Catherine when she last slept with her husband. Catherine is startled. "A couple of weeks ago," she says. "How could you?" says Jim. It's clear to her that she is supposed to be in love with Jim.

Their first night in New York, the spouses sleep together. The second night, they don't. They sit around drinking and the two husbands get into an argument. All right, says Jim, Ted and Ann have been sleeping together, why should we keep up the pretense? And so Catherine goes off to bed with Jim.

Two stormy months later, Ann leaves Jim to marry Ted. Catherine files for divorce and Ted calls her a harlot for sleeping with Jim. "I thought: this is madness," says Catherine. They make housing switches. Jim helps Catherine load up her china and antique chairs to put in his house. There's no doubt about her marrying Jim now. It seems inevitable. "At that point I didn't think I had any other options," she says. "I felt terrible. I felt deserted. Ted was getting what he wanted—everybody was getting what they wanted. Why was I feeling so bad? It didn't occur to me not to be married."

Catherine doesn't even breathe between marriages. She doesn't figure out what went wrong with Ted. Very early in her second marriage, she finds that the bad feelings she had in her first marriage don't go away. She still feels desperate. Slowly, with Jim, she takes the first steps to changing her psychological style. It was never a great passion, she says. They were just there for each other. He doesn't hold the power over her that Ted did. She's less dependent on him and stands up to him more. It's not long before they start fighting, long angry fights into the night. "We got more and more accusatory with each other," she says. "Probably what we were voicing was how terribly disappointed we were in the marriage and in what we had done."

Meanwhile Catherine grows more confident. She gets a public relations job in a Ralph Nader consumer group and goes on television to publicize the cause. Jim says, "I hate that damn do-good organization you work for. You're not the same person you were when we met." In the final breakup scene, he yells at her, "You remind me of your mother!" The Deadlock roles are switched. No longer is Catherine lying flat on her back in the hospital looking up to a rescuer. She's a celebrity now, a competitor; bitchy, bossy, pushy.

Several months later, Jim comes home and tells Catherine he's fallen in love with his secretary.

This time, Catherine goes through her psychological divorce process. There is no one to rescue her. She has to confront both marriages. Eventually she rebuilds her own life. She moves to California and gets a consumer job with the government. She raises her children. She passes through a mildly promiscuous phase and has a number of affairs before she starts living with Joe, a widower. After three years together, they break up and Catherine is on her own again. "In my first marriage, it was all *my* fault," she says. "In my second marriage, it was all *his* fault. This time it's the relationship that's at fault. It just didn't work." She smiles. Catherine is much happier now than when she was married. "It takes time to realize that not being married is O.K.," she says. "I'm only just getting there now." Several years later, she marries again.

You want it to work. The *William Tell* overture is playing in the background. From out of the past come the thundering hoofbeats of the great Dream Marriage. Return now to those thrilling days of yesteryear: The White Knight—or White Lady—rides again. You fall in love and get married once more.

And then comes the crash.

Even though the remarriage doesn't work out, you can benefit from it. Some people need a really bad remarriage to push them into growing up and confronting the Deadlock ghosts of the first marriage.

Pat Riston is a good example of someone pushed into confronting her Deadlock ghost. She falls in love, when she is forty-four, two years after the breakup of her first marriage. The remarriage lasts three years. "The second marriage never should have happened," she says. "It was like a love affair taken too far. But I learned a lot in that marriage."

Pat had grown up poor on a farm in Missouri and got married when she was seventeen. "I really got married because I wanted to," she begins. "I was not particularly ambitious at that age to do anything but get married. I was dating this young man whom I liked—whom I was in love with. Getting married seemed like what you're supposed to do."

The marriage lasts twenty-five years. In the Deadlock, her husband is dominant; she is submissive. Then about four years before the divorce, a change in their lives upsets the balance of power. Their two children are in high school and Pat gets an offer of a full-time job in a local clothing store. "We needed the extra money," she explains. "I took the job. I think that's when the marriage started to fall apart, because he couldn't handle it. I never said anything."

Pat, despite her confidence on the job and her new-found ambition, is still very submissive to her husband and torn by guilt feelings as she feels the marriage crumbling beneath her. The evenings are silent; they never say anything to each other. Both of them have grown up in this closed farming community. You just know what you're supposed to do. Nobody gets a divorce here. Her husband starts staying out late. "I had problems talking about what upset me," she says. "I let things go. I wanted to say: Hey, if this is all there is, let's get divorced. But I couldn't say that."

In the end, he suggests a divorce and she blames herself. "All of a sudden you wake up and it's over. We didn't fight. We didn't argue. We just weren't there for each other."

Pat plunges into Crazy Time and for the first time in her life she has a real challenge. Her son, eighteen, gets a girl pregnant and then is sent to Vietnam with the army, leaving his bride with Pat. The younger daughter, sixteen, unmarried, also gets pregnant and decides to keep the baby. For the next two years, they are three women alone, trying to make ends meet and take care of two babies. The network starts whispering. It's all Pat can do to survive. "Heaven knows what the people around here thought of us," she says.

The moment Pat comes up for air, she falls in love. "He liked to dance," she says. "It had been so long since I'd been anywhere or done anything." Pat and John get married very quickly. The Deadlock is the same as in her first marriage. But this time, Pat and her new husband are intensely involved with each other and the battle for control is much better defined. In the open conflict of the second marriage, Pat is forced to grow. She sees how difficult it is for her to be independent and take responsibility for herself in intimate relationships. The recognition is her first step to maturity.

"John had a very dominant personality and he needed to control things," she says. "With him I learned to fight."

In the battle for control, they play the game of symbols and tokens: If you love me, you'll do so-and-so. If you don't do this, it means you don't love me. For John and Pat, the battle royal of their marriage centers on making tea. "John believed in conservation," Pat begins. "When I went to make a cup of tea, he wanted me to measure out a cup of water before I went to boil it—you know, so as not to waste water or electricity.

"I solved the problem by getting a teakettle, so he couldn't see how much water was inside."

Then one day late in the marriage, they are sitting on the porch after supper, and John asks for some tea. Pat goes into the kitchen and starts heating the water in a saucepan because it's sitting there on the stove and the teakettle had been put away. "I forgot to measure out the cup," she says.

After a few minutes, John goes into the kitchen to make the

tea. Instead he comes out with the pan in his hand. He is angry.

"Pat, you put too much water in here!"

Pat explodes: "Why are you hollering about a little bit of water? At least I didn't fill up the whole pan with water."

"It's not just the water," he says. "It's a symbol of everything you do."

Now they really fight: *You talk too much on the phone. . . . But it's my money, I pay for it. . . . You waste paper towels. . . . You don't get along with my sister. . . . I don't like the way you bring up your children.*

Pat can't stand him anymore. This time, she's the Divorce Seeker. John, the typical Divorce Opposer, explodes with rage and threatens to kill her. "I was petrified," she says. "He was ranting and raving: 'How could you do this to me' and on and on." She locks all the doors.

She also gets rid of a lot of guilt—over John, her first marriage, her family, the network. "The night he threatened me was the night I stopped feeling guilty," she says. "I stopped thinking that everything was my fault and that I had failed."

She goes through the building stages of her psychological divorce. She learns how to live alone and is promoted to buyer in the clothing store. She has new friends and a number of relationships. In time, she begins to feel attractive and proud of herself. "Maybe it's not more sex after getting divorced, but it's better sex," she says. She's invited now to network Christmas parties. Maybe she'd like to try marriage again, but there aren't that many unattached older men coming through this part of Missouri, she says. Then she laughs.

"I'm pretty happy now," she says. "I know I'm going to make it. I feel I can go anywhere I want to. I've gotten to the point where I don't mind being alone.

"One thing I've learned," she continues. "Before, with men, I always tried to please them to the extent of changing myself if I could.

"I don't do that anymore," she says. "I'm me."

Pat, in retrospect, needed the drama and conflict of her second marriage to grow up. Her first marriage was a Rip Van Winkle relationship: Both of them were asleep emotionally for twenty-five years. It took the first divorce to wake Pat up, the second marriage to make her come alive, and the second divorce to help her finish growing up. In the end, she reaches the Phoenix level in her divorce journey. Life at present is rich and rewarding for Pat. The future is hopeful.

We never should have gotten married is a frequent refrain. But whether you have a significant marriage-like affair that ends or a remarriage that ends, the psychological goals are the same. You discover your own special drama in intimate relationships and, ideally, you change the patterns of the past that cause you trouble.

Often you need the legal commitment of marriage to force you into a situation where intimacy is possible. Otherwise, it's too easy to retreat when you sense trouble. Getting married is playing for real. You usually enter into remarriage with the same hopes you had for the first: Till death do you part.

The danger with remarriage in lieu of a marriage-like affair is that the stakes of divorce get higher. It's bad enough being a one-time loser—but a three-time loser or a six-time loser? What about the effects on your children? You risk getting very distraught and very bitter. Marriage never works, you say. So you just devalue the whole institution of marriage and the possibility of successful relationships as well. It can be another form of Divorce Flameout.

15

MARRIED FOR GOOD

You want it to work this time. You think you've changed and learned from your divorce. You are older and wiser. Having endured the hell of a destructive marriage and the chaos of divorce, you know more about relationships. You also know the odds of getting divorced from a second marriage are higher than from a first marriage.

But statistics don't tell the whole story. That's because age is a key factor in marriage success rates. The older the bride and groom, the more stable the relationship. Men and women in their thirties have a better chance of a successful remarriage than teenagers in a first marriage. "The fact that people are older when they remarry is a big plus for the stability of the remarriage," says demographer Barbara Foley Wilson at the National Center for Health Statistics.

Remarriages tend to go through an initial high-risk period because people who have been divorced once are usually less likely to put up with a bad relationship a second time. If the remarriage makes it past the first few years, the chances for success are good. As psychiatrist Harry Stack Sullivan—who never married— told a colleague: "Second marriages can usually be more successful. It's like raising dogs; you know more the second time around."

Sometimes the changes people make in remarriage are very small, a fine-tuning of their emotional style that's scarcely noticeable to old friends and colleagues. In other remarriages, the changes are dramatic. Just about everybody is determined to be different so that the marriage will work this time. But no matter what the style, a successful remarriage depends on a successful divorce from the old marriage and the successful emergence of self.

What seem to distinguish successful remarriages are the twin themes of equality and sharing. You know the dangers of Deadlock and you make sure to keep the balance of emotional power constantly shifting between you. You also know that equality in a relationship can be maintained only if you have a strong sense of your own individuality. You have to have passed through the Hummingbird and Foundering phases of growth and reached the Phoenix stage with yourself.

At the same time, you learn to share your life with your mate. People in a destructive marriage don't usually share very much. You are closed in and cut off. Sharing is a new emotional skill. You learn to share your dreams along with the details of the day: what the taxicab driver told you about Northern Ireland, a child getting on the baseball team, the traffic, the weather, the threat of nuclear war, the line at the supermarket. You also share your moods; that's the more difficult part of sharing. You think: What if I tell my spouse how depressed I am or how angry; maybe I'll drive my partner away. It takes courage to remarry and expose yourself to another person. Always, in a relationship, you have to take some risks and there's usually a shakedown period in every marriage. You hold your breath. How strong are you? The more confidence you have, the more willing you are to take risks and share your life with another person.

Chemistry is a vital part of remarriage. You listen to your body and pay attention to your sex life. If your Deadlock ghosts are still dancing, they'll probably come out first in the bedroom. As Robert Kirsch says: "I don't think two people can have a good sex life if the marriage is unequal. Sex is the second language of behavior and it's important to pay attention to its message."

After a greening period, two people get comfortable with each other. Equality and sharing in the marriage grow into mutual respect and tenderness. You reach that Golden Pond moment of accepting each other in spite of being unacceptable in many obvious respects. Over the lifetime of the marriage, you see how you both change and develop in different ways. Yet you remain intensely involved with each other. A successful remarriage seems to be a mixture of individuality and closeness. As Erich Fromm states: "There is only one proof for the existence of love; the depth of the relationship and the aliveness and strength of each person concerned."

Many veterans of divorce are Remarriage Renewers. That means you get remarried before you're psychologically divorced and are then forced to make major changes in the new relationship. You have to *renew* the remarriage contract. It's a painful process—and a number of people end up in redivorce. But the future is hopeful for people who make it through this critical greening period in remarriage. In a sense, you get really divorced and really married all at once.

At the time you walk down the aisle again, you think you are doing everything right. You don't think you're rushing into anything. Your friends are pleased. Your children are well-behaved. You're happy for the first time in so long. Getting married again feels right.

It doesn't take too long before you find you're just as miserable in the marriage as you were before. This is a devastating blow—and for many people the crisis in remarriage is even more shocking than the first divorce. But out of the ashes of your remarriage crisis, you can end up building a much stronger relationship. Many people are more willing to work on a second marriage. It's not so easy to blame the other partner for failure. You are more alert to danger signs. You get to the confrontation scene quicker—and may be more likely to address the problems before that final point of no return is reached in the marriage.

Jim Lincoln, fifty-three, is headmaster of a high school in Minneapolis. He's very good with people, a warm man with a good sense of humor, and he really listens to the problems of students and parents. His first marriage, to Ann, ends after seventeen years.

"My first wife was a very sweet and very passive person," he begins. "I got the message that it was my job on the globe to take care of her. My needs weren't terribly important and they were being continually denied. For her part, Ann always felt like she'd been left out because she had nothing going for herself. I was the center of her life. That led to her feeling disappointed and dissatisfied, to her complaining all the time.

"I was feeling claustrophobic. I felt I was breathing for two of us. There was never enough air. I was drowning. Sex with her was a drag. I'd look at her and think: She's such a dumb bitch."

To break out of Deadlock, Jim and Ann get divorced and she takes the children to San Francisco, where she grew up. After a year and a half, Jim marries again—much to the relief of everyone at the school. Isn't it nice the headmaster is settled again, says the network. His bride, Kate, works for a public interest conservation organization. She has two boys, Roger and David, and has been working full time since her divorce three years earlier. After a short courtship, Jim and Kate have a traditional church wedding and go on a honeymoon to Mexico.

Six months later, they are at the point of splitting up. How could this be? "I began to feel that I had married the wrong woman," says Jim. "Different woman, different figure, different face, different voice, different equipment—same old feelings.

"All I wanted to do was head out the door. I felt the way I did as a child on Saturday morning when I'd finally done the math problems my mother had given me before I could go out with the boys; that was the exhilaration I'd feel when I'd make it out the door and be free from this female crocodile."

Jim's two-act drama begins to emerge. In the first act, he is the pursuer, the "good boy," Mr. Right, the one who anticipates the other person's needs and makes things go right. The only thing he worries about is not being good enough and losing out on his pursuit. In the second act, he is no longer in pursuit. He passes the test and is accepted. As his second wife becomes more enthusiastic about him, he begins to see her enthusiasm not as approval but as demands. He feels trapped into taking care of her. That's what he had to do with his mother after his father died when he was twelve. It was his job then to make mother happy; it was his job to make his first wife happy, and now it's his job to make Kate happy. What happens to *his* needs? Who looks after him in this relationship?

He starts to withdraw to protect himself. In response, Kate becomes frantic. Where are you? she seems to be saying. He withdraws more, tiptoeing out the back door, so to speak, when "mother" isn't looking. She starts grabbing for him, testing him, wanting to nail him down; but all he can think of is escape. Buried anger seeps out of his pores.

They get locked into each other. In times of stress, he closes up; she becomes aggressive and irritable. Psychologically, they play a perfect duet of mutual self-destruction. "I'd say to myself, Well, I guess I've made another mistake," he says.

Jim hits bottom. He feels desperate—about his divorce and now about his remarriage. He questions himself on the job. He misses his children. He is angry at his new wife and resentful of her children. Meanwhile Kate is on the edge of hysteria. They fight about who pays for repairing the roof, the car insurance, summer camp for the other one's kids. It's not long before they reach the crisis point.

"Both of us were on the verge of saying to hell with this and calling it quits," he says, and pauses. "At the same time, I'm glad to say we didn't. We'd both been through a divorce and we knew it probably wasn't just a question of marrying the wrong person again."

For the next two years, Jim and Kate undergo intensive psychotherapy. As miserable as they are together and as devastated by the prospects of double failure in marriage, they both want to find out why they are in so much trouble. They make a commitment to each other to unscramble the dynamics of their relationship. Then they'll talk about whether they want to stay married or not.

Gradually, in therapy, they uncover their personal dramas. Jim, who takes the dominant role in the marriage at first, buries the side of him that is very dependent and needy. As long as he's in pursuit, he doesn't have to face his own needs. Then when he wins his prize and his wife turns to him with a smile, a panic button goes off. "I realized that a very warm woman with arms extended can look like an octopus to me," he explains. "I think that I have to block out my needs in deference to what I assume she needs. Very quickly I turn her into a demanding dragon lady and my eye is on the door."

In therapy, Jim learns how to show his vulnerability. He starts to reveal his fears and tell Kate what makes him anxious and what his needs are. He practices telling her things that up until now have been unspeakable. One day Jim and Kate are walking down the hall to the elevator.

"You know, when you're going down the hall in front of me and you're not talking, I get scared," he says to her. "I feel scared. There's something about your walking down the hall and my not knowing what is going on with you that pushes my panic button. I start assuming all kinds of things. I wonder what you want of me. I wonder if I've done all the things you expected of me. I wonder if you're mad at me."

His wife is shocked. "What?" she replies. "You're frightened?" This is a man who is six feet two and a woman who is five feet four. He's scared of her?

"My wife got a different picture of me," Jim says, "one that I have a hard time showing. She saw how scared and uneasy I can be in a relationship with a woman. She found someone very dif-

ferent from the solid, dominating, always giving, support'
that I was when I was in pursuit of her."

Meanwhile Jim gets a different view of Kate. Here is a woman
who has been on her own for a number of years; she has a full-
time job and pulls her weight as far as the household finances are
concerned. "I found that my wife, instead of being an empty pail
to be filled, has many resources of her own. I saw that the warm
and nurturing side of her was not part of being dependent on me
but a result of being independent. Once I was able to show her
what my needs were, she was able to take care of them—and vice
versa."

For Jim and Kate, it takes a major course of psychotherapy to
bring these fundamental changes into their relationship. After a
while, their remarriage begins to work as they learn how to negotiate with each other better. Instead of withdrawing from the marriage, Jim gets in deeper.

"In my first wife, I picked a woman who could serve as the
reason why I was not having a good time in bed and was not
involved with the marriage. It's a different ball game this time. My
current wife is tough. We fight like bastards. The lovemaking is
very different, very good. Kate gives me a good run for my
money. There's no messing around with anyone else. That's a
strong part of the relationship. It's true there's a lot more uneasi-
ness with Kate—I experience more anxiety with her. But for the
first time, I can say I'm really married; I'm really involved with
another person on an equal basis. We both give and get a lot from
each other."

After five years of remarriage, life starts to look better to Jim.
He finds he likes his job better, he likes being with her kids better,
he likes having his kids for vacations better; most of all, he likes
himself better. He even gets along better with his first wife.
"We're very friendly now. We do business about the children,
schooling, arrangements for vacations. We stopped hanging up
on each other about four years ago. The last time I went to San
Francisco to pick up the children, she gave me a bowl she'd made
at a pottery studio she's working in now."

Jim has reached the Phoenix level in both his divorce and his remarriage. At the first twinges he feels of being swallowed up by his wife and wanting to bolt for the door, he stops. He knows his ghosts now. Just because the old ghosts are dancing doesn't mean he has to follow the old script. Go ahead and dance, he says to them. Then he looks at his wife again. She's furious at the increases in the defense budget and her hair is a mess. He smiles.

"I realize that my psychological struggle is going to be the same struggle until I die. The only difference between my current marriage and my past one is how I handle it. If I can let my wife in on who I am and she doesn't have to get sucked into my struggle—and vice versa—then we can keep the marriage alive. We remain separate but equal. That means I have to expose who I am and Kate has to do the same. That never occurred in my first marriage." Jim pauses: This time the marriage is going to last, he says.

Many people can renew their remarriage contract without therapy. But your personal psychological struggle is often so subtle that you may need guidance in sorting it out. You not only bring your first marriage into your second marriage, you also bring your parents' marriage and the emotional habits you learned in childhood. "We tend to marry someone who presents dilemmas for us that replicate the dilemmas we had in the original family," says Augustus Napier. "What was your mother like? What was your father like? If couples are going to come to grips with these issues, they have to recognize what their families were like."

You don't have to spend the next fifty years in therapy to gain some knowledge of yourself, but you need to know your early script to help you understand your current pattern of behavior. As Martha Gross explains: "You repeat the early script. You do what is familiar. If children are treated in such a way that they learn not to trust the person they depend on, their world is shattered.

"You may be a senator or a president, but if you're afraid of being alone or unloved, you replay that in your marriage. You're on your hands and knees groveling for love. Your self-esteem is so low you cannot renegotiate what you need from your spouse."

Trust is often a casualty in conflict-ridden families—and the reality is that many intact families have a high amount of conflict. "These feelings come back when someone pushes too hard or withdraws," says Gross. "People who have too many wounds early can't figure out how to protect themselves [in intimate relationships]. We work with them in therapy to find ways to protect themselves."

In getting married, you are welding your struggle onto your partner's struggle. What is your spouse's special drama in the relationship? How do you fit in with your partner's script? In other words, you marry each other's ghosts who will all come to live with you in the new marriage.

You also marry a family. The second time around, that may include three teenagers, several cats and an ex-grandmother-in-law who lives next door. A major part of getting married is getting to know your spouse's family. In remarriage, the task is much more complex than in a first marriage. There are usually stepchildren, former in-laws, old lovers and ex-baby-sitters along with the traditional array of relatives.

For many people, one of the most difficult and explosive areas in remarriage involves the children. "It's a package deal," says the child of divorce to a prospective parent. Also in the package is the past life of the family unit, the pain and abuse as well as the hopes and good times. It's important to remember that you both bring a string of old ghosts as well as children into the new marriage. Part of the glue in remarriage is helping each other deal with the divorce-extended network of old ghosts and new family members.

Package Deal families go through a period of adjustment. You may be ecstatic over getting married again, but children see recoupling in a different light. A decade of research has shown that remarriage does not necessarily change the well-being of children (although it may improve their economic status). In fact, children often experience the remarriage of their parents as additional stress on a family already dislocated by divorce. "It looks as though adding a stepparent is adding another transition for children," says Andrew Cherlin. "Stepparents can disrupt the way the single family was working."

In the long run, Package Deal families fare well. The added risk to children growing up in a stepfamily or single-parent family versus a traditional nuclear family is small, says Cherlin. It's just that no one knows which children and what kinds of families are likely to have the most problems.

Researchers know that what really helps children develop is a happy marriage of their parents. They also know that children of divorce do well if the parent they live with is leading a satisfying life. With remarriage, you are trying to put the two pieces together: a happy marriage that provides a satisfying relationship for you and your spouse—and that provides a strong, nurturing home for your children.

Some people deal with the ghosts of their old marriage by making sure their remarriage is the exact opposite. Perhaps you don't rush into anything right now. You are very cautious. You don't want to get remarried on the rebound or when you have your first *coup de foudre*. Maybe that's the way your first marriage started out, and you know what happens when passion wears off. Or, this time, you get married because you fall madly in love. In your first marriage, you thought you were marrying your best friend. It wasn't real love, you say. Perhaps you reverse your mating style—you are the seducer this time, or you let the other person do the courting. Whatever your script in your old marriage, you are determined to reverse the plot in your new marriage. You are a Remarriage Reversalist.

Joan Billings spends six years working through her divorce before she remarries. She's now been remarried for three years and has a year-old son. Her first marriage lasted fifteen years and she had three children. When it ended, Joan was devastated. She knew she had to fundamentally change the course of her life as a result and she entered the second marriage very cautiously. "I was very determined that this marriage would not be like my first one," she says, and then she smiles. It's been three years. They've just bought a new house in Atlanta. Finally, at forty-one, she feels at peace with herself and secure in her life.

"You can only find emotional security in yourself," she says. "That's the only place it's going to be. I guess that's what everyone is searching for in all this jumping around between marriage and divorce. You want a focal point in your life: you need understanding and support. You look for it in your parents and in your marriage. It took me a long time to realize that the only place I could find emotional security was in myself."

Joan grew up in Atlanta, the oldest child of a mother who was an invalid with Parkinson's disease. Her father traveled most of the time on business and Joan became the substitute parent to her younger sisters and brothers. At seventeen, she had a *coup de foudre* and eloped. "It was an escape," she says, to find the emotional security she didn't have from her family.

In her first marriage, she continued to play the mama role and poured all her energies into making her doctor husband a Great Man. In the end, he fell in love with another woman and left her.

Her world crashes. She is thirty-two years old, with two sons, eleven and nine, and a daughter, eight. Joan goes through a couple of low-paid clerical jobs, rents out part of the house and spends most of her spare time on the phone arranging baby-sitters. The most important thing she does, she says, is to get into therapy.

"I had this need to go into a very deep period of reassessment of myself to understand how I got into this predicament," she says.

Slowly she unravels her own special drama: She is both very strong and very insecure. From childhood she is groomed to take the dominant role in relationships, and at the same time to look for a white knight to rescue her from the feeling of being abandoned by her parents. In the first act, she has a *coup de foudre* to get herself rescued and into a marriage. In the second act, she assumes the dominant position and is trapped in the mother role again, bled of her sense of self. In the last scene, she is rejected and abandoned, a replay of her childhood fear.

Joan makes two very deliberate decisions. She won't get married on a *coup de foudre* and she won't take the dominant role in a relationship.

About six months after the separation, a dentist, Rusty Billings, who is five years younger, comes into her life. They meet in group therapy. Immediately, the Deadlock ghosts start dancing. She's older and knows more. It's only natural that she be the initiator, the pursuer, the dominant one.

But Joan refuses to follow the script. She is very cautious. To begin with, it's no *coup de foudre*. They just like being with each other. She doesn't go into the relationship with great expectations. "I didn't believe in the reality of it," she says. "I thought: This person is not going to last. I was glad to have someone around who cared about me, but I didn't take it seriously. It was more a friendship than a romance."

Joan also makes sure there's no rescue element in the relationship: Rusty is not there to rescue her and she's not there to prop up Rusty. "Neither one of us relied on the other for psychological support because basically we were not capable of it. All I could do was take care of myself and the kids. Since Rusty had never been married, he was used to taking care of himself. He didn't expect that kind of support."

As the relationship deepens, Rusty, the younger one, the less experienced one, learns how to take the dominant role at times so that the balance between them begins to seesaw back and forth. Finally, when it comes to the first major decision in the relationship, Rusty emerges as the leader. It is Rusty who forces the issue to get married. "Rusty decided it," she says. "He finally said, 'Look, this relationship has been going on for six years. I would like to make a commitment, but I'm not sure about you. I've reached the point that either we're going to get married or we're going to break up.'" It doesn't take Joan long to say yes. It feels right to her. "Finally someone came along who said, 'Let's do this,' she says. "Always in the past I had to make all the decisions. It was such a relief to have someone take charge."

But the Deadlock ghosts are still singing softly in the background. Joan realizes how easy it would be to slip into her old mama role. Rusty is so young and so in love with her. At the same time, she knows the destructive power of her ghosts. She's determined never to be the dominant mother again. "I think if I were married to a man where I'd have to be a mother again, I would die," she says. "I would get a terrible illness and die—that would be the only way to turn the situation around and get someone to take care of you."

Joan feels she has to go that extra step. It's not just that Rusty has never been married before; he's never had a child before. That final extra step takes shape. Rusty tells Joan he would like to have a child.

It's not going to be easy. A baby at age forty? To stretch your body like that, to ache for nine months? To go through the diapers and the crying again? It's a difficult moment. "I knew I loved Rusty and I wanted the marriage to work, but oh, my God." In the end, she gets pregnant. For Joan it's a psychological humbling she has to go through to free herself from being dominant. She has the baby for Rusty and that way she puts the old ghosts of her marriage to rest.

Meanwhile Rusty is forced to take charge of the household during her pregnancy. It's a testing of both of them. Rusty is good to her while she is pregnant and he likes taking care of her. "My first husband couldn't have dealt with that," she says. "He would have said, This person is insane, and walked out the door. I really was insane those first three months; I was very depressed and I had no energy at all. But Rusty could handle it. By the time the baby came, everything was fine. Having the baby cemented the relationship."

In addition to therapy, Joan carves out a career for herself in social work. She gets a master's degree in psychology. She is still heavily involved in therapy. It's something she and Rusty share and they both discuss their dreams as part of the routine detail in their married life. Joan begins to publish articles. "One of the things I learned after the divorce is that I am totally capable of having a career," she says. "I couldn't have possibly done that in my first marriage. I was too closed in, too scared to say what I thought."

With Rusty, Joan feels she has let the real Joan out of her Deadlock cage. "From being a helpmate in trouble, Rusty became the person I really wanted to be with. It was a comfortable sexual companionship. In my first marriage, I always had to struggle to talk to my husband. Here comes this person to whom I could say what I felt. If I was in a bad mood, I could say so. If I didn't want to go out, I could say no. He wouldn't say, You bitch, and walk out the door. There was a communication and trust that was there from the beginning. It goes both ways. If Rusty has a rough day at work, he will come home and we'll talk about it instead of pretending that everything is just fine."

Joan is now back at work full time. She and Rusty share domestic chores and child care. The key, Joan is convinced, is the equality they've achieved in the marriage.

"For a relationship to work," she says, "there must be equality. Sometimes I'll make the decisions, other times Rusty makes the decisions. That's the way it should be. I guess it's a mixture of temperament and luck. Equality comes from two people being in harmony and knowing each other's limits. You have to learn to be yourself and not play a role." She pauses and smiles. "You spend a whole lifetime learning to be yourself."

Reversalists are usually very determined, very strong people. You take life seriously and work hard at relationships. The only danger is that by totally reversing the past, Reversalists run the risk of throwing out the proverbial baby with the bathwater. If you are too earnest about doing exactly the opposite from the last time around, you also risk making the Deadlock Switch without even realizing it. There's also the trap of not seeing beyond the superficial details of a new relationship. You think you are involved in a totally different scene—but are you? It's easy to do a little window dressing but live in the same emotional house. The key is knowledge. How much do you know about yourself and your personal drama? How aware are you of the changes you are making? In the end, you can only gain freedom from the past by confronting your ghosts and learning to outgrow them.

Another pattern the next time around is the Revisionist Remarriage. Unlike Reversalists, whose changes are very obvious, people who are Remarriage Revisionists make revisions in their emotional script that are barely perceptible. They seem to follow the same basic psychological pattern of the previous marriage, but with a few notable revisions which make all the difference.

Revisionists in relationships can be very misleading. Since the changes are barely noticeable, it looks as if these people are doing the same thing all over again. Then a major issue comes up in the new relationship: whether to have a second family, where to live and work, what the limits of the relationship are. That's when the changes the Revisionist has made come into full view. It's a different approach but the goals are the same: to achieve balance in the marriage while identifying the individual's limits and resources. The formula is the same: equality, strong sense of self and involved sharing of a common life.

Dan Woodruff, fifty-five, vice-president of an international construction company, is a Remarriage Revisionist. He was submissive in his first marriage and for the most part he's submissive in his second marriage—with a dramatic exception. As a result, his two marriages are as different as night and day.

Wearing a Harris tweed jacket and baggy trousers, Dan looks a little bit like a twenties baseball player—even though he went to Saint Paul's school in Concord, New Hampshire, before going to Yale. He's a street preppie, as he puts it. Everybody knows Dan likes the raw life: the Caravel bar in Saigon, by the pool at the Hilton in Athens, the Admiral Codrington in London. As one of the brightest construction engineers in the company, he's spent his life all over the world. He's built airfields in Southeast Asia, hospitals in Saudi Arabia, hotels in Belgium. He has been shot at and has made love in more places than he can remember. He's now trying to cut down on cigarettes. "Life has been very good to me," he says. He pauses. "Getting a divorce was the worst thing I ever went through. But I knew if I didn't get divorced I could never do what I had to do with my life."

Throughout his life, Dan maintains a submissive, non-assertive role with women. Usually he's the one who is seduced. It suits him fine. "I can't stand to be alone," he says. "I'm a very dependent kind of guy. I work hard all day and at the end of it, I just like to have somebody hold me and play with my little thing." Dan's always liked women; he likes to touch them, drink with them, laugh with them. They can't help but be attracted to him. So for the most part he lets things happen in relationships—in and out of marriage.

But there's another side to Dan that comes out in his work. No one is more assertive or more focused when the job has to be done. Through his divorce, he finally brings the two sides together, but it's a long, tortuous journey.

Dan's family are proper puritans from Albany, New York. His father works in a trust company. As the youngest boy, Dan's the rebel in the family and studies engineering. At age twenty-two, he marries Sheila, a large-boned woman with blond hair from Dedham, Massachusetts. He gets a job at the construction company's headquarters in New York City. His wife orders their married life: a mortgage in the suburbs, four children, two dogs, six bicycles and an hour's commute into the city.

He hates the predictability of the scene with the children and the dogs and the neighbors, and escapes more and more into his work. He goes to Saigon and builds an air base for the military; to Dubai to build a medical clinic; he leaves for Argentina on an hour's notice when a fifty-five-story building collapses. He tries to break the Deadlock of his marriage by not being there. It goes on like this for more than a decade.

After a while, women start coming into his life. It begins in Los Angeles when he has lunch with a woman who is a lawyer for the company.

"You know," she says, looking him straight in the eye, "next week I'm going on vacation." She smiles. "And the whole time, I'm going to think about you."

Dan drops his fork on the plate. "What did you say?" he asks.

She squeezes his hand. "What do you say we leave for Mexico next Thursday?" she says.

Dan's ears are ringing. He's not doing anything too interesting next week, and Jesus, this woman is gorgeous.

After lunch they go back to his hotel room. "I was scared," he says. "Here I'd been married for twelve years. This was the first time I'd been to bed with a woman who wasn't my wife. It turns out she'd slept with every senior officer in the company, but I didn't know it. She went in the bathroom to take off her clothes and dab on the perfume. I lay there in bed, petrified."

It's not long before Dan falls in love with her and their affair explodes over the company grapevine. Dan's supervisor suggests he get away and take an assignment in Brazil for several months. His wife looks the other way. A pattern to his life sets in: he's always on the road; she always looks the other way. He sends his whole paycheck home and lives on the expense account.

After the affair with the lawyer dies down, Dan gets seduced again. This time he's at a convention in Houston, and the public relations officer for the National Association of Home Builders asks him to lunch. "Before this afternoon is out," she says to him, "we're going to make love." They go back to his hotel room. He's not so petrified anymore.

People around the office start to talk. Dan's supervisor sits him down and tells him he's ruining his life. He gets an assignment to be in charge of building projects in North Africa. Dan makes Paris his base. His wife and children stay in the U.S. The separation is more or less official, but the dread of getting a divorce paralyzes him. "Divorce was unheard of in my family," he says. To keep guilt at bay, he keeps sending home his whole paycheck.

In Paris, his life gets very debauched. He drinks and works, and he beds everything he can find. He misses his kids dreadfully and he feels guilty about his wife. That just makes him drink and play around more.

Mostly he's seduced. But one time he changes his style and becomes the aggressor. It happens in the Crazy Horse Saloon, where Dan and a colleague are having drinks. Dan can't stand the guy, whom he finds a pompous Brit. The bar starts to fill up. "See that girl over there?" says the Brit. "I'm going to get her to bed with me tonight." Dan looks over. The young woman looks like a character out of Balzac: sunken eyes, a long thin nose, thick lips and long blond stringy hair. The Brit gets up to go to the men's room and tells Dan to order another round of drinks. Dan's competitive streak takes over and the rage wells up in him. For the first time, Dan decides to seduce the woman himself. While the pompous Brit is in the men's room, Dan goes over to her table and talks very slowly in English: "You know, I think you're such a nice-looking lady," he says. "I'd like to take you to our office next door for a brandy." She looks up at him and bursts out laughing. "Hey, baby, you're speaking my language. I'm from Chicago." They link arms and go out the door before the Brit gets back to the table.

Dan doesn't make too much of the incident, but without realizing it, the change of style starts something in him. He learns that it's possible to transfer some of his assertiveness on the job to the bedroom. He finds out he can stand up and take over—when he wants to.

But for the most part, he lets this new skill lie dormant; it's easier to let women take the initiative. After a year in Paris, Dan is still very lonely and he misses his kids, especially during the holidays. He goes to a party and notices a black-haired woman. She takes one look at him and says, "You look so depraved, I know I'm going to end up with you." Oh? he thinks, and moves on. Around midnight, what's left of the party shifts to his apartment for omelets. At two in the morning, the guests leave. He looks around and sees the woman with the black hair.

"Don't you think you should be going?" he asks.

"No," she says.

"Where do you think you're going to sleep?" he asks.

"In there with you," she says, nodding to the bedroom.

Oh, well, he thinks. It's not the first time it's happened this way.

The next morning, they agree to meet for a drink in the afternoon. When he shows up at the café, she has her hair pulled back from her eyes and at first he doesn't recognize her. He discovers she's very pretty. He likes her impish grin. They have a pair of Campari and sodas. The woman's name is Maggie. She's Irish and has just quit her job at the British Embassy. She hates the Pommy bastards.

"Are you traveling light?" she asks. He nods. By the end of the day, she tells him to bring his stuff over to her place.

"I found I really liked living with Maggie," he says. "I never knew what was going to happen next. She's kind of crazy, like me. She loves to travel and that made working so much more enjoyable. When I'd go to Algeria on a job, she'd come too. She was ready to go at a moment's notice. We were like two orphans who finally got placed in a good home together. Life settled down for me."

But after a year, Dan is seized with guilt. It's not right he should be so "bad" and be so happy at the same time. Four children. A good wife. There's never been a divorce in the family before, chant the ghosts. In a fit of guilt, he tells Maggie he's leaving her and is going back to New York to try for a reconciliation with his wife. "I just had to try one more time, if I was going to live with myself," he says.

Dan goes back to the U.S. and moves the family into a bigger house in Oyster Bay, Long Island, with a swimming pool. He commutes again into the city, plays with the kids on weekends—and never sleeps with his wife. It goes on like this for almost a year. Then one Saturday, he gets an unexpected call from Maggie. "She was in Penn Station and she told me she was about to get on a train out to Long Island and could I meet her." Dan, true to form, meets Maggie at the train. She tells him that she loves him and wants to be with him. "I knew I really loved Maggie," he says. "I just didn't know what to do."

For the next six months, Dan lives in the house in Oyster Bay with his wife and sleeps in an apartment in nearby Bethpage with Maggie. The confrontation scene is inevitable. One night in November, Dan's wife follows him in the car to Maggie's apartment. His wife, the denier, is outraged. Dan tries to explain to her about Maggie. He goes back to the house, but finds himself locked out. He bangs on the door. It starts to snow. His wife tells him he can never come into the house again. So Dan gets back in the car and goes to Maggie.

The legal divorce comes through a year later and by this time Dan and Maggie are very much a couple. "As soon as the divorce was final, we flew to Juárez and got married," he says.

To the outside world, the dynamics of the new relationship are the same. Maggie is the dominant one: She picks him out at the party; she seduces him; she starts the live-in relationship; she follows him to New York. But Dan has become a Revisionist and even Maggie is unaware of just how strong and dominating he can be.

For the next three years, Dan and Maggie travel everywhere together. There is much laughter and many good times in bed. "We were really happy," he says. "Maggie has a comedian streak and she makes me laugh and laugh. We spent two years in Hong Kong and she started a little business buying silk for friends back in the States. She's the only person I've seen outbargain a Chinese silk dealer." And he laughs.

Then his world shatters. The crisis in their marriage comes when Maggie announces she wants to have a baby. "She was nearing forty and her biological clock was running out. She said to me, What if you die and I'm left all alone?"

But this time Dan refuses to go along with her. He already has four children and he knows he can't handle the scene of kids and bicycles and wives who have to stay at home. He's been through that. Most of all, he needs Maggie to share his life the way his ex-wife never could. The dominant side of Dan takes over in the relationship.

"That time I put my foot down," he says. "I said no. I said we can't have a baby. I already have four children. I know what it's like. I know I can't do it."

Maggie is stunned. To ask a woman not to bear a child? To deny a woman motherhood? Can Maggie, who is used to being dominant, make such a major sacrifice for the marriage? It's a heavy price for equalizing the balance of power between them, but they were getting close to Deadlock, with Maggie calling all the shots. It took a drastic action on Dan's part to even the score. For the next several years, Dan and Maggie go through a difficult time.

"It was tough, but I knew having a baby would be the finish of us. In the end, Maggie understood. It was hard on her and we went through some teary nights. It boiled down to how much we wanted each other, how much we wanted to stay together," he says.

In retrospect, the crisis over starting a family was essential to the success of the marriage. In his first marriage, Dan submitted completely to the dominance of his wife, and to survive he ran away. That's his special drama in relationships. He doesn't want to repeat the past with Maggie. In his second marriage, Dan submits to Maggie most of the time—because in a sense their motives are the same. But when Maggie initiates something he doesn't want or knows he can't handle, Dan is strong enough to stand up and takes the dominant role. That way, he keeps his self-respect and is able to bring Maggie and his marriage into the mainstream of his life.

"I think Maggie began to realize how much she means to me, how much I love her. She understood that I wasn't denying her or trying to hurt her. I just knew I couldn't have another family. I was over fifty and I knew my limits," he says.

Like many couples who stay together, Dan and Maggie successfully renegotiate their original contract. Maggie accepts Dan's decision and the Deadlock ghosts stop raging into the night. Dan and Maggie pick up their life on a new basis.

"We're closer now than ever before," says Dan. "We crossed a Rubicon of sorts. I can't imagine not being with Maggie. She's my life. She says I'm the only one who really knows her, who understands her. Certainly I'm the one who laughs at her jokes. She takes good care of me. She makes me eat carrots to prevent cancer. Sometimes she makes me feel like a rabbit, but I don't mind. I give Maggie a long leash. We both know we're always there for each other. That's what I need most in a woman. I'm a lucky man. Next June will be our fifteenth wedding anniversary."

Dan smiles. By bringing the marriage into the mainstream of his life, Dan has been able to preserve it. The marriage works the way the first one never did.

All couples go through a greening period. Often it's a matter of luck and timing how a relationship is going to work out. You soon discover that the psychological dynamics of a remarriage are not really different from the struggles in a first marriage. You are just more aware of them this time. You know how to handle your struggles. You learn to renegotiate your basic marriage contract again and again.

In fact, when it comes to recoupling, most people go through many marriages in a lifetime—often with the same person. Says a forty-year-old accountant in Kansas City: "I've had at least four marriages—all with my wife, but each one was very distinct. In the first marriage, my wife was just out of school and I had more experience sexually and in every other way. It took about three years before we were screaming at each other. In the second marriage, she zoomed up in her job as a social worker for the state government and we had a major crisis over having a baby. That brought us to our third marriage. In the end, we had the baby, she stopped working and I got assigned to a special project and was never home weekends. We started fighting again. That time, we went to a marriage counselor and now we're into our fourth marriage. My wife is working part time and my boss has promised me days off when I have to work weekends. Each 'marriage' has been very different and we'll probably have a few more before we're through. Officially, of course, we've only been married once."

All committed relationships—remarriages as well as first marriages—have to be tested by crisis. It's a psychological baptism by fire that severely strains the relationship but may be necessary to solidify the marriage.

As Carl G. Jung states: "Seldom, or perhaps never, does a marriage develop into an individual relationship smoothly and without crisis: there is no coming to consciousness without pain."

People who have been through a divorce have certain advantages in remarriage. You know about suffering and pain. You know how relationships don't work and you understand the fatal power plays that overtake many marriages. In many ways, you know more than people who remain in the original marriage. You know all about avoiding conflict and dying slowly in a marriage. You took the divorce route. There's something about going public with your marriage crisis that makes the significance of the confrontation stick with you.

It takes courage to stay married after you've been divorced. That's why people who are happily remarried are a special breed. Like a decorated war hero, you've been tested in the wars of both marriage and divorce. You've tasted loneliness and despair in and out of marriage. You lived through a number of crises now—with your own psyche, your children, the network, your boss, your current spouse, your new mother-in-law. Your sense of self is pretty strong by now or you wouldn't have gotten this far.

Most of all, you recognize the emotional value in sharing your life with someone else. You make the choice that being married is the way you want to live. The magic in a successful long-term marriage comes from bearing witness to one another. You both come from very different places having been married and divorced before. In time, the new marriage gets stronger as you get more involved with each other.

You also know that there are no guarantees for happiness.

The future is full of change and surprises. As Erich Fromm says: "Love . . . is a constant challenge; it is not a resting place, but a moving, growing, working together." But you decide to risk it and you enjoy each good day for what it's worth. After a while, you find that a good marriage can be very habit-forming.

EPILOGUE

How do you know when it's over?

How do you know you have gotten your emotional divorce?

In some ways, it's never completely over, especially if there are children.

But the trauma passes. You remember what it was like—the intense pain and anxiety of Crazy Time. You don't feel that way anymore. Often the end sneaks up on you. For the last six months, you realize, you haven't thought too much about your ex-spouse or your divorce at all. There was a time when everything revolved around the marriage breakup: getting the car fixed, paying for dental care, changing jobs, falling in love. Almost without your noticing it, your preoccupation with divorce gradually disappears.

Getting over a divorce takes time. Just how long varies with each person. As counselor Sharon Baker of the Los Angeles Divorce Warm Line says: "It depends on how intense the relationship was and how big a need it filled; how self-sufficient and mature a person is; and if you have the three good fairies of luck, money and health.

"Most of all, it's important to believe that life can get better," she says.

The majority of men and women who get divorced survive the trauma of the marriage breakup and go on to rebuild new and satisfying lives. You are forced to mature in order to meet the new demands placed on you, and many people blossom in this period of singlehood and rediscovery. You have a new chance at life. Your self-esteem improves and with it your sense of contentment.

"Divorce has the potential not only of freeing men and women from destructive and unsatisfactory relationships, but of allowing adults to develop and change in gratifying ways in the aftermath of divorce," concludes Joan Kelly. "The majority of men and women followed beyond the separation period reported that the divorce was a positive and necessary step which resulted in greater personal contentment, increased self-esteem and, for many, healthier levels of psychological functioning."

The basic issues of life don't go away. Loneliness is still a problem for divorced men and women. You have to learn how to live alone with yourself. At the same time, most people get involved in new relationships—love affairs, remarriages, or live-in arrangements. All over again, you feel the magic and anguish of trying to share a life with someone else. But whether you remain single or recouple after divorce, you still struggle with your essential aloneness and walk the fine line between dreams and experience.

You can't forget about the Flameouts in divorce, the people who don't rebuild their lives after the marriage breakup. Divorce isn't a solution to unhappiness and there are many casualties on the wasteland of marriage. But divorce is a passage that can teach you something. Most people who make it through see themselves as real survivors. You know something about life now. You can get more out of it. You know how to give more too.

* * *

You are also part of a social revolution that is much broader than changing patterns of marriage and divorce. As the twenty-first century approaches, the whole concept of family is evolving into a new code of kinship. No longer are biology and the law the only ways to make a family. Increasingly, family membership is based on choice and shared experiences. Who gathers together at your house for Thanksgiving? Whom do you call for support when a child is sick? When you have trouble at work? In an age of divorce, you choose your "relatives," who may include a friend or lover as well as a mother or brother. A *relative* is someone you have a *relationship* with; a person who is *relative* to your life. "Family life is getting much more complicated," says demographer Jeffrey Evans. "The family is developing a lot of extra dimensions. As a society we have to start sanctioning these extra places in the family structure."

The nuclear unit of a husband and wife in a first marriage raising their own children now represents a minority of families. It is not just separation or divorce that have created extra places in the family structure. The fact is that more men and women are living together and creating family units without getting married. A quarter of out-of-wedlock babies are born to cohabiting unmarried couples. These live-in relationships are quasi-marriages and often lead to marriage. Currently, about 50 percent of first marriages are preceded by the couple living together. In addition, many divorced men and women recouple and set up an unmarried family unit that includes children from previous marriages.

Getting married, it seems, has become less important as the entry point to some of the most basic benefits of family life—sex, companionship and parenting. Indeed, marriage and remarriage rates have been declining steadily, partly as a result of couples deciding to live together without a marriage certificate.

At the same time, men and women expect greater emotional satisfaction from marriage. Mutual happiness is the primary goal of many married couples. As Andrew Cherlin describes it, Americans are embarking on a "voluntary" marriage system that is geared to the needs of individuals over the traditional norms of society. This rise of individualism in family relationships reflects a major shift in values in the U.S. that coincides with a long period of general prosperity.

In past economic hard times, divorce rates went down, not because people were happier, but because they couldn't afford to get divorced. "In the Depression, no one ran around asking themselves if they were happy in their marriage," says Barbara Foley Wilson.

Today, however, happiness is a central question for many men and women—and one that is answered by divorce in a high percentage of cases. A generally rising standard of living since World War II and the fact that women hold jobs alongside men have rewritten the social contract of marriage and parenting. These trends, which started early in this century, show few signs of reversing themselves. In- and outside of marriage, equalizing the roles of men and women is at the core of the country's social revolution. Divorce is only one aspect of these changes in the family unit.

"The increasing opportunity to choose rewarding occupations and rewarding intimate relationships is not something many of us would wish to reverse," concludes Larry L. Bumpass of the University of Wisconsin in his 1990 address to the Population Association of America. "At the same time, we continue to care about the well-being of children, about those without adequate social and economic support, and about the human capital of the next generation."

The country is just beginning to come to grips with the consequences of this social revolution and make room for the "extra dimensions in the family structure," as Evans puts it. In the political arena, the debate centers on family leave policies, child care and job training programs. It involves new definitions of family relationships for purposes of health insurance and social services. It reflects the widening gap between the rich and the poor since

1980, with the poor more likely to be unmarried. It often puts the needs of the individual who gets a divorce at odds with the needs of a society that still depends on traditional nuclear families to raise children. For many Americans, the freedom to be unmarried is inherent in the pursuit of happiness; for many others, this freedom is a feature of poverty and despair. For some, divorce, instead of being a tumultous period of transition, becomes a permanent condition of turmoil.

In recent years, the debate over the family has become increasingly political. What is the obligation of society to support the family and all its extra dimensions? In matters of love, how does society strike a balance between promoting self-fulfillment and social welfare? These arguments go to the heart of the country's confusion about basic constitutional rights and equality. In an egalitarian society, the right to pursue happiness and success does not mean that every member of that society will be equally happy and successful. Under this system, however, two American ideals are pitted against each other: On the one hand, we believe that individual achievements should be compensated, and on the other we believe that all citizens, regardless of their level of success, should be protected from extreme misfortune.

In this debate, there is a lot of rhetoric about the demise of the American family. Divorce has become another D-word along with debt, drugs and deliquency. But the social unit of the family has not collapsed under the weight of divorce. Quite the opposite: What has ended are the rules that used to determine the roles of men and women at home and in the workplace. Just as the industrial revolution of the nineteenth century redefined the structure of middle-class families, so has the social revolution of the past thirty years.

When my marriage broke up, I did not see myself as part of these broad social changes. I saw myself simply as a failure—a personal failure as a woman in the most intimate adult relationship and a social failure as a parent and citizen. It took the hand of someone in another generation to put this sense of failure in perspective. My favorite great-aunt who lived in England wrote me as soon as she heard the news that my husband and I had separated. At the time, she was ninety-eight years old:

My dearest Abigail,

I feel such sympathy for what you are going through, and whatever happens, I wish for your happiness. . . . Please, please do not think of yourself as having failed, as these things happen all the time despite the best will in the world. . . . Try to think sensibly. I think it's always best to make decisions on the grounds of your own future.

You are very young and can start afresh.

It turned out that my great-aunt was right. I didn't believe her at the time. At thirty-five, I felt very old, finished with life. I could not imagine that divorce might be a beginning. Looking back, it was that long lonely stretch of single-hood that was the turning point. It was the time when the roof leaked, when the children had only a worm to bring to school for show-your-pet-and-tell, when the nights were cold and the paycheck never went far enough. But it was then that the divorce process took hold and my life started to change.

In time, I rebuilt my new family. Now it encompasses several generations and includes friends of my children, schoolmates of my mother, children of my cousins and spouses of my colleagues. It brings together memories of other marriages and expectations of new friendships that become part of the ever-widening circle of "relatives." These are people I'm *related* to and we form a network of kin that is as strong as any biologically extended family. Perhaps we are stronger because we have chosen these *relationships* and nurtured them over the years.

The launch window for divorce extends from about age thirty to sixty—the most vital years of your life. For a number of people, getting divorced is part of the midlife passage. With luck and perseverance, you can bring to this revolution in your personal life a tremendous amount of energy and talent. It can be a very dynamic period and in many ways divorce is the cultural phenomenon of middle age. You are too old for myths but too young to give up hope. With your divorce, you are echoing what my grandmother used to say: "The young have their dreams, the old their regrets. Only the middle-aged know how to live."

SELECTED BIBLIOGRAPHY

Beal, Edward W., and Hochman, Gloria. *Adult Children of Divorce: Breaking the Cycle and Finding Fulfillment in Love, Marriage, and Family.* New York: Delacorte Press, 1991.

Blumstein, Philip, and Schwartz, Pepper. *American Couples: Money, Work, Sex.* New York: Pocket Books/Simon & Schuster, 1983.

Bretall, Robert, ed. *A Kierkegaard Anthology.* Princeton, N.J.: Princeton University Press, 1946.

Bumpass, Larry L. "What's Happening to the Family? Interactions Between Demographic and Institutional Change." *Demography,* Vol. 27, No. 4, Population Association of America, 1990.

Cherlin, Andrew J. *Marriage, Divorce, Remarriage: Social Trends in the United States.* Cambridge, Mass., and London: Harvard University Press, 1981.

Corman, Avery. *Kramer vs. Kramer.* New York: Random House, 1977; Signet/New American Library, 1978.

Francke, Linda Bird. *Growing Up Divorced.* New York: Linden Press/Simon & Schuster, 1983.

Fromm, Erich. *The Art of Loving.* New York: Harper & Row, 1956.

Furstenberg, Jr., Frank F., and Cherlin, Andrew J. *Divided Families: What Happens to Children When Parents Part.* Cambridge, Mass., and London: Harvard University Press, 1991.

Hochschild, Arlie, with Machung, Anne. *The Second Shift: Working Parents and the Revolution at Home.* New York: Viking Penguin, 1989.

Jung, Karl J. *Contributions to Analytical Psychology.* New York: Harcourt Brace Jovanovich, 1928.

Kelly, Joan Berlin. "Divorce: The Adult Perspective." *Handbook of Developmental Psychology,* ed. B. Wolman and G. Stricker. Englewood Cliffs, N.J.: Prentice-Hall, 1982.

Kübler-Ross, Elisabeth. *On Death and Dying.* New York: Macmillan, 1969.

Laing, R. D. *The Politics of the Family.* New York: Vintage Books/Random House, 1972.

Levinson, Daniel J. *The Seasons of a Man's Life.* New York: Ballantine Books, 1978.

Lief, Harold I., ed. *Sexual Problems in Medical Practice.* Washington, D.C.: American Medical Association, 1981.

Napier, Augustus Y. *The Fragile Bond: In Search of an Equal, Intimate and Enduring Marriage.* New York: Harper & Row, 1988.

Rhys, Jean. *After Leaving Mr. Mackenzie.* New York: Vintage Books/Random House, 1974; Harper & Row, 1931.

Rofes, Eric, ed. *The Kids' Book of Divorce: By, For and About Kids.* Lexington, Mass.: Lewis Publishing Co., 1981.

Satir, Virginia. *Conjoint Family Therapy.* Palo Alto, Calif.: Science and Behavior Books, 1967.

Scarf, Maggie. *Intimate Partners: Patterns in Love and Marriage.* New York: Random House, 1987.

————. *Unfinished Business: Pressure Points in the Lives of Women.* New York: Doubleday, 1980.

Sheehy, Gail. *Passages: Predictable Crises of Adult Life*. New York: Dutton, 1976.

Simenon, Georges. *The Cat*. New York and London: A Helen and Kurt Wolff Book/Harcout Brace Jovanovich, 1967, 1976.

Strean, Herbert S. *The Extramarital Affair*. New York: The Free Press, 1980.

Tillich, Paul. *The Courage to Be*. New Haven and London: Yale University Press, 1952.

Updike, John. *Couples*. New York: Alfred A. Knopf, 1968.

Vaughn, Diane. *Uncoupling: Turning Points in Intimate Relationships*. New York and Oxford: Oxford University Press, 1986.

Volgy, Sandra S., ed. *Women and Divorce/Men and Divorce: Gender Differences in Separation, Divorce and Remarriage*. Binghamtom, N.Y., and London: The Haworth Press, 1991.

Wallerstein, Judith S., and Blakeslee, Sandra. *Second Chances: Men, Women, and Children a Decade After Divorce*. New York: Ticknor & Fields, 1989.

Wallerstein, Judith S., and Kelly, Joan Berlin. *Surviving the Breakup: How Children and Parents Cope with Divorce*. New York: Basic Books, 1980.

INDEX

Abandonment
  depression and, 140
  and disbelief, 82
  fear of, 242–52
Abortion, 122
Absent Father Syndrome, 163
Acceptance
  of divorce, 75–76, 93–97
    ambivalence and, 137
  of separation decision, 83, 111
  of the unacceptable, 159
Accidents, breakup of marriage and, 2
Achievement, from failure, 3
Active symbiotic union, 23
Addiction of spouse, 90
Adjustment to divorce, 11, 166
  gender differences, 163
Adolescence, and separation from spouse,
  72–73
Adult children of divorce, relationships of,
  164
Adversarial system in divorce law, 124
Aesthetic stage of human consciousness,
  156
Affairs, 55–58
  AIDS epidemic and, 188–89
  in Deadlock marriage, 25–28, 44–45,
    55–58

and divorce, 37, 41
and marriage breakup, 182
marriage-like, 240
as passive aggression, 103
After Leaving Mr. Mackenzie (Rhys), 16
Age
  and divorce, 270–71
  and remarriage, 224
  and success in marriage, 241
AIDS epidemic, 187–89
  and divorce, 4
  and sexual promiscuity, 157
Alcohol addiction of spouse, 90
Aloneness, acceptance of, 157
Ambiguity, feelings of, in Crazy Time, 72
Ambivalence, 72, 128–38
American Couples: Money, Work, Sex
  (Blumstein and Schwartz), 37
American ideals, conflicting, 268
Anger, 66, 87–88
  ambivalence of, 134
  Crazy Time, 112–27
  depression and, 140
  lack of, 125–27
  and legal settlement, 181
  in public divorce, 182–83
  repressed, sex with ex-spouse as expres-
    sion of, 133

Index

Angry blowup, necessity for, 117–19
Anxiety
  ambiguity and, 72
  ambivalence and, 127, 129
  of children, 164
  depression and, 141–42
  economic instability and, 162
Appropriate depression, 140
Art of Loving, The (Fromm), 22–23
Attachment to former spouse, 130
  ambivalence and, 135, 137
Autonomy in marriage, 21
Avoidance of depression, 140
Avoidance strategy
  coup de foudre as, 206
  sexual promiscuity as, 202

Bad behavior by ex-spouse, and ambiva-
    lence, 135–36
Bad sex experiences, 200–201
Baker, Sharon, 265–66
Balance of power in marriage, 19
  Deadlock relationships, 23
    extramarital affairs and, 28–29, 37
    working wife and, 44
  legal divorce and, 124–25
  Revisionists and, 255
  successful remarriage and, 242
  unequal, and sexual problems, 193–94
"Ballad of Redding Gaol, The" (Wilde),
    77
Bargains of marriage, 19
  broken, 20
Beal, Edward W., 164
Bearing witness, in remarriage, 263
Becoming nonexistent, in Deadlock mar-
    riage, 49
Beginning, divorce as, 2
Behavior
  disturbed, after divorce, 66–67
  of ex-spouse, and ambivalence, 135–36
Behavioral problems of children, 164
Best Friend, 171
  betrayal by, 184
Betrayal
  and anger, 113, 122
  by best friend, 184
  childhood feelings of, and sexual promis-
    cuity, 202
  by friends, in public divorce, 168
Bitterness, 157
  anger and, 120, 124
  separation and, 113
Blame for divorce, social network and,
    170–71
Bloom, B. L., *The Predicament of the Newly
    Separated*, 130
Blumstein, Philip, *American Couples:
    Money, Work, Sex*, 37

Breakup of marriage, 1–2, 5–9, 29, 34–35,
    50–51
  children and, 164–66
  confrontation scene, 1
  Deadlock contract and, 20
  and depression, 139–43
  economics of, 64
  pattern in, 27
  shock state, 99–111
  submissive person and, 79
  trauma of, 11
  and unresolved issues from childhood, 73
  and violence, 70–71
Buildup to divorce, 10
Bumpass, Larry L., 268
Burnout in marriage, 6

California Children of Divorce Project, 34,
    66–67
  and anger, 113
  and attachment to former spouse, 130–31
  and depression, 139, 141
  and extramarital sex, 191
  and relief at separation, 89
  and sexual deprivation, 193
Career change, 102–3
Carmichael, Douglass, 134
Caution about remarriage, 250
Change
  anxiety and, 129
  crisis and, 3
  divorce and, 266
  in ex-spouse, and ambivalence, 132
  in marriage relationships, 58–59
    in Deadlock marriage, 26–28, 34
    and renegotiation of wedlock contract,
      21
  personal, at midlife, 160
  psychological, in Crazy Time, 117
  remarriage and, 242
  in roles, and broken Deadlock, 102–3
Chaotic period after divorce, 66
Characteristics of divorced persons, 9–10
Chemistry
  of *coup de foudre*, 206
  in remarriage, 243
Cherlin, Andrew J., 5–6, 160, 267–68
  and children of divorce, 165
  and economics of marriage breakup, 161
  and remarriage, 250
Child abuse, 90
Child care programs, 268
Children
  and conflict, 5–6
  and confrontation, 48
  and depression in men, 142
  divorce and, 164–66
  and economics of divorce, 161–62
  passive role and, 107

and reconciliation, 130
and remarriage, 249–50
and traditional family roles, 161
Child support, 161–62
Chinese word for crisis, 14
Choices, Foundering Phase, 158–59
Chronic depression, 140
incidence of, 141
Chronic Passion Repeaters, 220–21
Chronic promiscuity, 202–4
Closeness, successful remarriage and, 243
Cohabiting unmarried couples, 267
Commitment, new, and separation, 54–58
Communication in marriage, 254
Community, and divorce, 167–86
Competition in marriage, 91
Condoms, 189, 204
Conflict
after divorce, 116–17
with ex-spouse, children and, 165
in marriage, children and, 164
period of, 60
separation and, 113
Conflicted marriage, extramarital affairs
and, 29
Conflicting emotions, 129–30, 134
in Crazy Time, 72
exploration of, 74
Conflicting ideals, 269
Conflict-ridden families, trust in, 249
Confrontation, incomplete, 54, 57–58
Confrontation scenes, 1, 17, 24, 29, 35,
36–49, 95–96
buildup to, 10
Constructive use of anger, 117–18, 120
Contempt for spouse, 53
Contradictory feelings, 129
acceptance of, 135
Control
battles for, 33, 238–39
intercourse as, 193–94
of emotional life, 74–75
language and, 116
of life, 162
Coping strategies, denial, 110–11
Counseling services for troubled relation-
ships, 80
Coup de foudre, 39, 65, 206
and remarriage, 251–52
Coupling, rules for, 6
Courage, 159
to be oneself, 155, 157
Courage to Live, The (Kierkegaard), 156–57
Court battles, 125, 168
Cowan, Carolyn and Philip, 161
Crazy Time, 65–80
ambivalence, 128–38
anger, 112–27
coup de foudre and, 212–17

depression, 139–51
economic instability and, 162
emotional growth levels, 157
and family routines, 165
Foundering Phase, 158–59
Hummingbird Phase, 157–58
public divorce and, 180–81
relief/disbelief phase, 81–98
remarriage and, 233, 238
sexual activity, 190, 194–95
promiscuous, 199
social network and, 167–68
Crazy Time (Trafford), first edition, 3
Creativity, from divorce, 11–12
Crime, and breakup of marriage, 90
Crisis
and change, 3
Chinese word for, 14
countdown to, 10
in Deadlock relationship, 23, 27–28, 35,
40, 42, 49
in life, deep shock and, 106–10
in marriage:
and change of structure, 36
and relationship imbalance, 22
origins of, 19
in remarriage, 243–46
testing of marriage by, 263
without divorce, 59
Cultural habits, and recovery from divorce,
160–61
Culture of divorce, 3
Curiosity, sex with ex-spouse and, 133–34
Custody agreements, anger and, 125

Danger signs in relationships, 10
Dating phase, after divorce, 10
Deadlock-breaking affairs, 78–79
Deadlock relationships, 20–35, 69–70,
85–87, 101–3, 107, 116, 175–76, 233
breaking of, 182
confrontation in, 36–49
extramarital affairs and, 37
injuries in, 90
loss of self and, 214
remarriage and, 225–27, 237–39
renegotiation of, 59–60
roles in, 37, 43–45, 51–52
change of, 102–3
and sex, 193
unrealistic expectations, 53–54
Deadlock Switch, 229–36
by Remarriage Reversalists, 254–55
Deadlock Wars, 76
Death
from AIDS, 188
divorce as, 66, 82, 113
of parent, children and, 165
of sister, deep shock and, 106–10

Deceivers, emotions after divorce, 66
Deception, in Deadlock marriage, 23–29,
	37–40, 44–45, 55–58, 182
	denial and, 95–96
	Divorce Seekers and, 179
Decision to separate, 51–52, 58
Denial, in Deadlock marriage, 23–29,
	32–33, 38, 45–46, 56, 70
	as coping strategy, 110–11
	and disbelief, 82–83, 93–97
	and public divorce, 180
	violence and, 75
Deniers, emotions after divorce, 66
Dependence
	economic, of women, 161
	on wife, 91–92
Dependent role, and remarriage, 233–34
Depersonalization of sexual promiscuity,
	202
Depression, 66, 139–51
	anger and, 118–19
	of children, 164
	and chronic promiscuity, 202
	economic, and divorce, 268
	guilt and, 148–49
	rage and, 120
	sadness and, 149–50
Despair, 179
	Foundering Phase, 158
	rage and, 120
Desperation, act of, divorce as, 42
Destruction of spouse, 76
Destructive anger, 120
Destructive relationships, 242
	breakup of, 90
	freedom from, 11
Development, divorce and, 266
Diedrick, Patricia, 163, 166
Dimsdale, Joel, 110
Disappointment in spouse, 53–54
Disbelief
	Crazy Time phase, 81–98
	depression and, 140
Disorganized behavior after divorce, 66
Disorientation
	after divorce, 64
	post-separation period, 72–73
Displaced homemakers, 161, 181
Disturbed behavior after divorce, 66–67
Dividing up of friends, 169
Divorce, 1–2, 14
	acceptance of, 75
	adjustment to, 11–12
	children and, 250
	common phases, 10
	courage in, 159
	culture of, 3
	emotional, 59, 78, 124, 134–35, 156, 162
		completion of, 265

public divorce and, 174
remarriage and, 232–33
unfinished, 183
emotions of, 65
experience of, 155–56
and insanity, 63–80
legal process:
	and ambivalence, 134
	and anger, 124–25
pain of, 81–82
prevalence of, 3–4, 7
process of, 36–37
psychological, 104–5, 233, 236
	anger stage, 112
	remarriage and, 225, 239–40
as psychological revolution, 117
public, 167–86
recovery from, 66
	emergence of self, 155–66
	falling in love and, 222–23
	gender differences in, 160–61
	sex and, 187–205
	stages of, 156
repeated, 224–44
sexual deprivation and, 193
social networks and, 171
successful, and remarriage, 242
wedlock contract and, 21
Divorce-connected depression, 140–51
Divorced persons
	fathers, 164
	social networks of, 171
Divorce Flameouts, 10–11, 76, 110–11, 120,
	129
	court battles, 125
	depression and, 143
	Foundering, 159
	public divorce and, 174–75
	remarriage and, 225, 240
	repeated falling in love and, 217
	sexual promiscuity and, 157, 202
Divorce Honeymoon, 92
Divorce Opposer. *See* Opposer of divorce
Divorce rate, U.S., 2–3, 5
Divorce relationship, 138
Divorce Seeker. *See* Seeker of divorce
Domestic abuse, 90
Dominant role in marriage, 19–21, 23–28
	and anger, 117
	and disbelief, 84
	Divorce Opposers and, 180
	of husband, 43–47, 69–71, 78–79, 85–87,
		175–77
		and disbelief, 93–97
		reversal of, 227–36
		and sexual promiscuity, 203–4
	and intimacy, 193–94
	and separation, 92
	sexual experimentation and, 194–96

of wife, 37–39, 51–53, 55–58, 91–92,
101–3, 131–32
and anger, 121–23
and remarriage, 251–53
Dominant-submissive imbalance, 22
Donne, John, 133
Doublefeel
ambivalence and, 129
psychological stalemate, 73–75
Dreams
divorce and, 113–14
of future, revision of, 82
Dropping out period, 99–101
Drug addiction of spouse, 90
Duet of separation, 50–53
Duration
of Crazy Time rage, 121–23
of denial period, 110
of depression, 140–41
of sexual experimentation phase, 202,
204

Earnings of women, 162
Ecclesiastes (Bible), 62
Economic independence of women, 160
Economics of marriage breakup, 64, 71–72,
161–63
Economy, and divorce rates, 268
Edge of sanity, divorce and, 63–80
Egalitarianism, ideology of, and reality, 161
Egalitarian relationships, 5
Eliot, T. S., "The Love Song of J. Alfred
Prufrock," 16
Emergence of self, 155–66
Emergency help, 90
Emotional balance, successful marriage and,
242
Emotional bonds, severing of, 155
Emotional divorce, 59, 78, 124, 134–35,
156, 162
completion of, 265
public divorce and, 174
remarriage and, 232–33
unfinished, 183
Emotional habits, breaking of, 226
Emotional independence, 72
Emotional inequality in marriage, 21
Emotional life, evolution of, 160
Emotional security, 251
Emotional separation, 136. *See also* Emo-
tional divorce
Emotional skill, sharing as, 242
Emotions
control of, 74–75
of divorce, 64–65
ambivalence, 72, 128–38
anger, 66, 87–88, 112–27
relief/disbelief, 81–98
Empathy in marriage, 54

Energy source, anger as, 118–19
Equality
between sexes, 5
in marriage, 21–22, 248, 254–55, 268
in successful remarriage, 242–43
E.T., 3
Ethical stage of human consciousness,
156–57
Etiquette of sex, AIDS epidemic and,
188–89
Euphoria of relief/disbelief phase, 83, 91
Evans, Jeffrey, 48, 165, 267
Expectations for marriage
unrealistic, 53–54
Experience of divorce, 155–56
Experimentation, sexual, 190, 194
Exposure of self
in confrontation, 49
in successful marriage, 248
Ex-spouse
change in, and ambivalence, 132
conflict with, children and, 165
relationship with, 78, 135
renegotiation of, 183
sex with, 133–34
Extended divorce family, 6
Extramarital Affair, The (Strean), 29
Extramarital affairs, 25–28, 44–45, 55–58,
95–96, 109. *See also* Sex; Sexual
promiscuity
AIDS epidemic and, 188
and ambivalence, 137
and breakup of marriage, 182
and divorce, 37, 41
as passive aggression, 103
public perception of, 176–78
in separation period, 192
Extramarital sex, gender differences, 191

Failure
acceptance of, 157, 159
divorce as, 3
feelings of, 269–70
and depression, 142–43
Fairness in marriage, 21
Falling in love, 18–19
after divorce, 206–23
Family
concept of, 267
and Crazy Time, 80
remarriage and, 249–50
Family home, sale of, 161–62
Family leave policies, at work, 268
Family-of-origin
psychological influences of, 248
psychological separation from, 166
Family roles, 160–61
division of, 163
Family routines, children and, 165

Index

Family therapy, 4
and Deadlock marriages, 27
Fantasy
in Deadlock marriage, 34
experience and, 214–16
of violent behavior, 76–77
Farewell to Arms, (Hemingway), 154
Fathers, divorce and, 163–64
Fear, in marriage, 23
Finances. *See* Economics of marriage
breakup
Financial responsibility, women and, 162
Finding oneself, 54
First marriages, and living together, 267
Flach, Frederic F., 140
Flameout, 68, 110–11, 138, 266
ambivalence and, 129
anger and, 120, 124, 127
court battles, 125
depression and, 143
disbelief period and, 93
Foundering, 159
public divorce and, 174–75, 178
remarriage and, 225, 240
repeated falling in love and, 217
sexual promiscuity and, 157, 202
and violence, 76
Flash Affairs, 198
Foundering Phase, 156–59
of public divorce, 168–69, 179
repeated passions and, 220
sexual promiscuity and, 197
Freedom from the past, 157
Friends
and Crazy Time, 80
and divorce, 167–86
need of, at breakup of marriage, 7–8
Friend Who Stands By You, 169
Fromm, Erich, 207–8, 243, 264
The Art of Loving, 22–23
Frontier life, 165
Future, 264
building for, 10
control of, 160
relationship with ex-spouse, 135

Gender differences
in adjustment to divorce, 163
in AIDS infection, 188
in depression, 141
in economics of divorce, 64, 161–63
in hostility after separation, 113
in post-separation sex activities, 190–91
in recovery from divorce, 160–61
in remarriage rates, 224
Generosity to others, divorce and, 11
Getting over divorce, 265–66
Gippius-Merezhkovskaya, Zinaida, 60
Goals

of marriage, 267
psychological, of relationships, 240
Good marriages, 241–68
Good public divorce, 180–81
Good times, memory of, 137
Grand Era of Divorce, 170
Greening period, 262
Grief, depression and, 140
Gross, Martha, 53–54, 248–49
Growing up, divorce and, 48
Growth
anxiety and, 129
emotional, 156
personal, divorce and, 3
unhappiness and, 3
Guilt
depression and, 148–49
Guilt feelings, 66, 92, 139
ambivalence of, 134
anger and, 118–19
behavior of ex-spouse and, 135
buried, sex with ex-spouse as expression
of, 133
depression and, 140
legal settlement and, 125
in public divorce, 179–83

Happiness
Americans and, 5
divorce and, media images of, 3
quest for, 268–69
Happy marriage, children and, 250
Haseltine, Florence P., 188–89
Health, breakup of marriage and, 2
Health insurance, 268
Hemingway, Ernest, *A Farewell to Arms,*
154
Heterosexual sex, and AIDS, 188–89
Hetherington, E. Mavis, 66
Hibernation, psychological, 99
Hodges, W. S., *The Predicament of the
Newly Separated,* 130
Homosexual person, marriage to, 89–90
Hostility, and chronic promiscuity, 202
Human consciousness, stages of, 156–57
Hummingbird Phase, 156–58
coup de foudre and, 217
parenting by fathers, 164
of public divorce, 168, 178
Remarriage Recidivists and, 232
repeated passions and, 220
sexual promiscuity and, 197, 202, 205

Ideal of marriage
divorce and, 113
and reality, 18–19
Ideals, American, conflicting, 269
Identity, anger and, 117
Illness

282

breakup of marriage and, 2
psychological, marital problems and, 233
Illusions, divorce and, 113
Impact of divorce, 66
on children, 164
Income, decline of, 5
Independence, 72, 162
economic, of women, 160
Individualism
American, and divorce, 5
in family relationships, 268
Individuality, sense of
and equality in marriage, 242
successful remarriage and, 243
Individuating, 157
Inequality in Deadlock relationship
emotional, 21
extramarital affairs and, 28–29
Initiation of breakup
and psychological problems, 67
of wife, 70
and relief/disbelief phase, 82
by submissive spouse, 79
Initiator of divorce, and legal settlement, 125
Intimacy
domination and, 193–94
marriage and, 240
Remarriage Recidivists and, 226
self-protection in, 249
"Intrapsychic Factors in Sexual Dysfunction," Levay, Weissberg and Woods, 193
Isolation, and symbiotic union, 22–23
"It Used to Be Her Town Too" (Taylor), 19

Jobs, for women, 162–63
Job training programs, 268
Jung, Carl G., 263
Justice, emotional, in public divorce, 181

Keller, Suzanne, 21, 142, 171
Kelly, Joan Berlin, 34, 66–67, 266
and anger, 113
and attachment to former spouse, 131
and depression, 139, 141
and friends of divorced persons, 171
and post-separation sex, 190
Kierkegaard, Sîren, *The Courage to Live*, 156–57, 160
Kinship
networks, 6
new code of, 267
Kirsch, Robert, 13, 59
and Crazy Time, 72
and relationship roles, 22–23, 28
and remarriage, 225
and success in marriage, 243
Knowledge of self, 248

and acceptance of divorce, 105
and success in marriage, 255

Lack of anger, 125–27
Lansdale, Lindsay Chase, 60
Lawyers, and litigation, 125
Leahy, Ann F., 58, 214
Learning
from divorce, 11–12
from trauma, 68
of independence, 72
Legal divorce
and ambivalence, 134
and anger, 124–25
Legal settlements, 181
Levay, Alexander N., "Intrapsychic Factors in Sexual Dysfunction, " 193–94
Life, control of, 160
Life expectancy, 6
Litigation, 125
Living alone, anxiety about, 141–42
Living together, and marriage, 267
Loneliness, divorce and, 266
Longevity, 6
Loss
from divorce, 66
of friends, 150–51, 168
of love, mourning for, 212–13
Love
after divorce, 206–23
challenge of, 264
Love-hate emotions, 73–74
"Love Song of J. Alfred Prufrock, The" (Eliot), 16
Low self-esteem, 21, 66, 139, 249
and depression, 140, 142–45

Madness, 63
Madonna, 4–5
Major depressive illness, divorce and, 139
Malfunction, period of, after divorce, 66
Manic quality, of relief/disbelief phase, 83
Manners of sex, AIDS epidemic and, 188–89
Marital instability, 165
Marriage, 267–68
assessment of, 18
breakup of, 29, 34–35
finances of, 64
change of, 58–59
emotional inequality in, 21
expectations for, 4
falling in love and, 214
good, 241–68
love and, 222–23
psychological separation in, 130
reasons for, 19
renegotiation of psychological contract, 36
roles in, 19

Marriage (cont.)
  separateness in, 214
  separation, 50–60
Marriage-breaking affairs, 37, 40–41
  and ambivalence, 137
Marriage-like affairs, 240
Marriage network of friends, division of, 169
Married lifestyle, AIDS epidemic and, 188
Mass murder, 67–68
Maturity, divorce and, 48, 266
Media, and divorce, 170
Membership in family, basis of, 267
Men
  adjustment to divorce, 163
  with AIDS, 188
  behavior after divorce, 66
  depressed, 139, 141–42
  economics of divorce, 64, 161
  extramarital affairs, 191
Men's movement, 163
Middle class, and divorce, 4–5
Midlife changes, 38, 160
Midlife passage, divorce as, 270–71
Minturn, B. Bradshaw, 156, 214
Moods, sharing of, 242
Moral judgments, in public divorce, 182
Moral stage of human consciousness, 156–57
Moral tone of public divorce, 171
Mothers of children, work outside home, 5
Mourning process
  anger and, 112
  Crazy Time and, 65–66
  depression and, 140
  for loss of love, 212–13
  for loss of marriage, 166
Mourning rituals, 165
Movies, image of divorced family in, 3
Murder, 63, 67–68, 74–76
  divorce and, 3
  fantasy of, 76–77
Mutual happiness, as goal of marriage, 267
Myths of marriage, 4

Napier, Augustus Y., 21, 161, 248
Nazi death camp survivors, 110
Negative image of divorce, 3–4
New commitment, and separation, 54–58
New life, establishment of, 155
New relationships, 10, 266, 270
  in old marriage, 36
  remarriage and, 6
Nonexistence, in Deadlock marriage, 49
Nostalgia, ambivalence and, 137
Not getting angry, 125–27
Nuclear family, 267
Numbing, depression and, 140
Numbness phase, after breakup, 81
  as coping strategy, 110–11
Nurturance, men and, 164

Older generation language, 116
Older women, economics of divorce, 162
Opposer of divorce, 27
  anger of, 125
  and depression, 140–41
  and disbelief, 82, 93
  psychological problems after breakup, 67
  and public divorce, 180
  role of, social network and, 149–50
  violent behavior, 75–76
Opposition to marriage, and beginning of
      separation, 84
Out-of-wedlock births, 267

Package Deal families, 249–50
Painless divorce, 81
Parenting
  and depression, 142
  men and, 163–64
Parents
  loss of, effect on children, 165
  relationships with, 166
Passion, reality and, 214–16
Passion Repeaters, 217–21
Passive aggression, extramarital affair as,
      103
Passive resistance, withholding of sex as,
      194
Passive role in marriage, 19
  AIDS epidemic and, 189
  and anger, 1, 117
  of husband, 51–53, 91–92
    and fantasy of murder, 76–77
  of wife, 69–71, 85–87, 175–77
Passive-submissive people as Passion
      Repeaters, 217–21
Passive symbiotic union, 22–23
Past
  freedom from, 136, 157
  memories of, 137
Perceptions
  divorce and, 167
  public:
    of divorce, 176–78
    of marriage breakup, 170
Perfect family, dream of, 45
Personal choices, 158–59
Personal contentment, divorce and, 266
Personal freedom, divorce and, 3
Personal growth, divorce and, 3
Personality, destruction of, sexual promiscu-
      ity and, 202
Phases of divorce
  ambivalence, 128–38
  anger, 112–27
  Crazy Time, 66–80
  depression, 139–51
  relief/disbelief, 81–98
  shock, 99–111

Phoenix Phase, 157, 159–60
  of public divorce, 169
  remarriage and, 240, 248
  sexual promiscuity and, 197–98
Physical dangers of promiscuity, 202
Politics
  of social revolution, 268–69
  of uncoupling, 60
Poor people, and divorce, 4
Popular music, and divorce, 4
Positive feelings for ex-spouse, 130
Post-separation depression, 141
Poverty, divorce and, 4
Power, psychological, in relationship, 21
Power balance in marriage, 5, 19, 23
  extramarital affairs and, 28–29, 37
  legal divorce and, 125
  Revisionists and, 255
  successful remarriage and, 242
  unequal, and sexual problems, 193–94
  working wife and, 44
Power play for control, 91
Practical problems of divorce, 82, 116, 130
  depression and, 142
  Hummingbird Phase and, 158
Predicament of the Newly Separated, The
  (Bloom and Hodges), 130
Premarital sex, gender differences, 191
Preparation for divorce, 67
Prevalence of divorce, 4, 7
Private divorce, 167–68
Problems in relationship, confrontation and,
  48
Promiscuity, sexual, 157, 195–205
  AIDS epidemic and, 187–89
  Passion Repeaters and, 217
Property settlements, anger and, 125
Protection of self, in intimate relationships,
  249
Protective emotion, disbelief as, 84
Protective strategy, deep shock as, 105–6
Psychic energy, relief phase and, 82
Psychological change, in Crazy Time, 117
Psychological contract of marriage, 19
  renegotiation of, 36
Psychological divorce, 104–5, 236
  anger stage, 112
  remarriage and, 225, 239–40
  successful, 233
Psychological drama, 251–52
  Remarriage Recidivists and, 225–36
  in second marriage, 245–46
Psychological dynamics of relationship, 19
  in Deadlock contract, 21, 23
  and remarriage, 262
Psychological functioning, divorce and, 266
Psychological growth, stages of, 156
Psychological illness, marital problems and,
  233

Psychological numbing, 110
  after breakup, 81
Psychological preparation for divorce, 67
Psychological problems of divorce, 82
Psychological revolution, divorce as, 117
Psychological separation, 50, 54, 134–36
  in divorce, 29
  from home, 166
  during marriage, 130
Psychological stalemate, 73–75
Psychological vacation, relief period as,
  90–91
Psychological warfare, anger and, 120
Public divorce, 167–86
Public figures, divorce of, 7
Public images of divorce, 3, 7
Punishment, anger and, 122–23

Quality of life, children and, 164

Rage. *See* Anger
Reactions to divorce decision, 36
Reagan, Ronald, 3
Reality
  of divorce, 114
    ambivalence and, 129
    economic, 162–63
    marital power relationships and, 23
    passion and, 214–16
  of separation, 92
  tolerance of, 157
Reasons for marriage, 19
Reconciliation, 130
Reconstruction of self, 166
Recoupling, 262
Recovery from divorce, 66
  emergence of self, 155–66
  falling in love and, 222–23
  gender differences in, 160–61
  sex and, 187–205
  stages of, 156
Redefinition of self, 156
Redivorce, 224–44
Reestablishment of self, 156
Reevaluation of marriage, confrontation
  and, 51
Re-examinations, 82
Rejection, feelings of, 142
  in childhood, and sexual promiscuity, 202
Relationships
  in adulthood, of children of divorce, 164
  after separation, 114–15
  death of, divorce as, 2
  emotional inequality in, 21
  equality in, 242
  with ex-spouse, after Crazy Time, 78
  imbalance in, 22
  intimate, self-protection in, 249
  new, 10, 270

Relationships (cont.)
  divorce and, 266
  in old marriage, 36
  remarriage and, 6
  with parents, divorce and, 166
  psychological goals of, 240
  renegotiation of, 156
  strength of, in second marriage, 244
Relatives, choice of, 267, 270
Relief, depression and, 140
Relief/disbelief phase of Crazy Time, 81–98
Religious stage of human consciousness, 157
Remarriage, 93, 224–44
  after divorce, 13–14
  children and, 249–50
  coup de foudre and, 206–8
  crisis in, 243–46
  to same spouse, 130
  social network and, 185–86
  success of, 241–68
Remarriage Recidivists, 225–44
Remarriage Renewers, 243–44
Remarriage Reversalists, 250–55
Remarriage Revisionists, 255–71
Renegotiation
  of marriage contract, 20–21, 58–59
  of psychological contract, confrontation
    scene and, 36
  of relationships, 156, 261–62
    with ex-spouse, 183
    with parents, 166
Renewal of remarriage contract, 243
Repressed anger, release of, 117–19
Rescue element in relationship, 252
Research on divorce, 3
  California Children of Divorce Project,
    34, 66–67, 89, 113, 130–31, 139, 141,
    191, 193
Resignation, Foundering Phase, 158–59
Respect in marriage, 21–22
  in successful marriage, 243
Responsibility
  for breakup
    recognition of, 105
    shared, 51
  new, anxiety about, 141–42
  for self, 72
    financial, 162
Revenge, anger and, 120
Reversals
  in remarriage, 250–55
  of roles in Deadlock, 229–36
Revisionist Remarriage, 255–62
Revolution, psychological, divorce as, 117
Rhys, Jean, *After Leaving Mr. Mackenzie*, 16
Rich people, and divorce, 4
Rigid morality, and anger, 122–24
Rip Van Winkle relationships, 240
Risk

in relationships, 242–43
  of remarriage, 240
  of sexual promiscuity, 202
Rituals
  for loss, 165
  of marriage, 18
Roles
  in Deadlock relationship, 23–28, 43–45,
    51–52, 55
  reversal of, 229–36
  in family, 160–61, 163
  in marriage, 19, 78–79
    change of, 20–21
    equality in, 22, 268
Romantic solution, search for, 65, 206, 212
Rules, social revolution and, 269

Sadness
  depression and, 149–50
Safe sex practices, 189, 204
Satisfactory marriages, 4–5
Satisfying life, expectation of, 5
Scarf, Maggie, 195
  and sexual promiscuity, 202
Schwartz, Pepper, *American Couples:
    Money, Work, Sex*, 37
Second marriages
  divorce in, 224–25
  success of, 241–42
Security, emotional, 251
Seduction, in Deadlock marriage, 25, 37,
    55–56
Seeker of divorce, 27
  and depression, 140
  and relief, 82, 93
  and social network, 171, 179–80
  stress period, 89
Self
  acceptance of, 157, 159
  demands on, 54
  emergence of, 155–66
    confrontation and, 49
    and successful remarriage, 242
  and emotional security, 251
  exposure of, in successful marriage, 248
  loss of, falling in love and, 214
  reconstruction of, 166
  redefinition of, 156
  rejection of, 50
  responsibility for, 72
    financial, 162
  sense of:
    promiscuity and, 202
    in remarriage, 263
  as source of rage, 123
Self-blame, and depression, 142
Self-confidence, *coup de foudre* and, 216
Self-destructive behavior, 76
Self-esteem

divorce and, 142–45, 266
growth of, in women, 163
low, 21, 66, 139, 249
depression and, 140, 142–45
in marriage, 214
Self-fulfilling prophecy, failure as, 143
Self-fulfillment, divorce and, 5
Self-image, divorce and, 3
Self-knowledge, 248
and acceptance of divorce, 105
and success in marriage, 255
Self-protection in intimate relationships, 249
Self-sufficiency, from divorce, 11
Separateness
in marriage, 214
in remarriage, 248
Separation, 50–60
adolescence and, 72–73
and anger, 113
depression before, 141
and emotional problems, 67
and extramarital sex, 192–93
psychological, 29, 134–36
and relief, 89
Severing of emotional bonds, 155
Sex
after breakup of marriage, 187–205
between ex-spouses, 132–34
equality in relationship and, 22
in remarriage, 243
Sexual promiscuity, 157, 195–205
AIDS epidemic and, 187–89
Passion Repeaters and, 217
Sexual revolution, 187
Shared responsibility for breakup, 51
Sharing
of life, value of, 263
in marriage, 248
successful, 255
in successful remarriage, 242–43
Sherman, Peter, 125
Shock state, 81, 99–111
Siamese-twin psychology, 117
Single motherhood, 162
Single parents, 5, 165
stresses of, 163
Social changes, and children, 48
Social contract of marriage, change of, 268
Social network
and divorce, 167–86
and sexuality of divorced woman, 191
Social revolution, 267
and equality in marriage, 268–69
Social services, 268
Society, and divorce, 170
Spite, anger and, 124
Spousal abuse, 90
Spouses
in Deadlock marriage, 23

swap of, 233–35
Stalemate, psychological, 73–75
Standard of living, and marriage, 268
Staples, Lawrence H., 3, 6
and Deadlock marriage, 49
and falling in love, 19
Stepparents, 250
Stories of divorce, 13
Strean, Herbert S., *The Extramarital Affair*, 29
Strengths
discovery in Crazy Time, 68
from marriage breakup, 11
Stress
anger and, 113
of children, remarriage and, 249–50
depression and, 140
for Divorce Seekers, 89
psychological numbing and, 110
women and, 163
Study of divorce, 34
Submissive role in marriage, 19–21, 23–28
and *coup de foudre*, 209–11
Divorce Seekers and, 179–80
of husband, 37–39, 55–58, 101–3, 182
Remarriage Revisionist and, 255–62
sexual experimentation and, 194
of wife, 43–45, 78–79, 115–16
and remarriage, 237–39
Successful remarriage, 225, 241–68
Sudden Male Friends, 172
Suicide, 63, 75
attempts, 68–71, 141
divorce and, 139
thoughts of, 64–65
threats of, 79
Sullivan, Harry Stack, 160, 242
Support, by social network, 170
Support groups, 80
Survival
breakup of marriage and, 42, 46, 49
Surviving the Breakup: How Children and Parents Cope with Divorce, (Wallerstein and Kelly), 34
Suspicious nature, 100–101
Symbiotic union, 22–23
Symptoms of Deadlock marriage, 23

Tasks of divorce, 155–56, 158
Taylor, James, "It Used to Be Her Town Too," 19
Television, and divorce, 3
Tenderness in relationship, 22
in successful marriage, 243
Testing of spouse, 54
Therapy, 59–60
after marriage breakup, 251
during Crazy Time, 80
for Deadlock marriage, 25–26, 39

Therapy (cont.)
  for remarriage, 246–48
Tillich, Paul, 155, 157, 181
Traditional family roles, children and, 161
Trafford, Abigail, *Crazy Time*, first edition,
  3
Transition
  divorce as, 224
  period of, 65
Transitional quality of marriage-breaking
  affairs, 37
Trauma
  of divorce, 265
    public, 169–70
  of marriage breakup, 11
Trial separation, 67
Troubled marriages, fathers in, 163–64
Troubled relationships, work on, 4
Trust, in conflict-ridden families, 249
Two-income families, 160
Twosome self, 117

Unconscious marriage bargains, 78–79,
  85–87, 91, 101–2
Uncontrolled behavior, 66, 75
Uncoupling, 48
  emotional tasks, 162–63
  politics of, 60
  process of, 36–37, 83
  without divorce, 58–59
Unequal marriage, sex life and, 243
Unfinished business, separation and, 73
Unhappiness, and growth, 11
United States, divorce rates, 2–3, 5
University of Colorado, study of separated
  adults, 89
Unmarried families, 267
Unobtainable Perfect Parent, search for, 202
Unrealistic expectations, 53–54
Unresolved divorce, 125–27
Unresolved issues from childhood, separa-
  tion and, 73

Values
  divorce and, 113–14
  family relationships and, 268
Victim of divorce, 159

passive, 178
Vindictiveness, anger and, 120, 123
Violent behavior, 66–68, 70–71, 75–77
  anger and, 120
  and breakup of marriage, 90
  disbelief period and, 93
Voluntary marriage system, 267–68

Wallerstein, Judith S., 34
  and depression, 141
Walpurgisnacht, 63
War
  court battles, 125
  divorce as, 66
Wedlock contracts, 19. *See also* Deadlock
  relationships
  broken, 20
  and divorce, 21
Weissberg, Josef H., "Intrapsychic Factors
  in Sexual Dysfunction, " 193–94
Wilde, Oscar, "The Ballad of Redding
  Gaol," 77
Wilson, Barbara Foley, 241, 268
Witnessing of anger, 119–20
Women
  adjustment to divorce, 163
  with AIDS, 188
  anger of, 113
  behavior after divorce, 66
  and condoms, 189
  depressed, 139, 141–42
  economics of divorce, 64, 161–63
  and post-separation sex, 191
  and social relationships, 171
  working, 44–47, 160, 162–63, 268
Women's movement, and earnings,
  162
Woods, Sherwyn M., "Intrapsychic
  Factors in Sexual Dysfunction,"
  193–94
Working women, 5, 160, 162–63, 268
  conditions for, 162
  and relationship change, 44–47
Workplace advances, and single motherhood, 162
Worry, chronic, 90–91
Wyman, Jane, 4